Journey of a Nation...

Journey of a Nation...

INDIAN NATIONAL CONGRESS
125
years
1885 - 2010

edited by **Anand Sharma**

published by **Academic Foundation, New Delhi**

Main title page photograph:
Jawaharlal Nehru addressing teeming crowds from the ramparts of the historic Red Fort, Delhi on 15 August 1947. Ever since, successive prime ministers have used the backdrop of this 17th century fort to deliver the Independence Day address to the nation.

First published in 2011
by

ACADEMIC FOUNDATION
4772-73 / 23 Bharat Ram Road, (23 Ansari Road),
Darya Ganj, New Delhi - 110 002 (India).
Phones : +91-11-23245001 / 02 / 03 / 04.
Fax : +91-11-23245005.
E-mail : books@academicfoundation.com
www. academicfoundation.com

Cataloging in Publication Data--DK
  Courtesy: D.K. Agencies (P) Ltd. <docinfo@dkagencies.com>

Journey of a nation- : Indian National Congress, 125 years / edited by Anand Sharma ; [editorial board, Rizwan Qaiser, Kiran Datar, Malini Sood].
    p.   cm.
    ISBN 9788171888405

    1. India--Politics and government--20th century--Pictorial works. 2. India--Politics and government--21st century--Pictorial works. 3. Indian National Congress--Pictorial works. I. Sharma, Anand. II. Qaiser, Rizwan. III. Datar, Kiran Kapur. IV. Sood, Malini.

DDC 320.95402   22

Designed and typeset by Italics India, New Delhi.
Printed and bound in India.

10 9 8 7 6 5 4 3 2 1

EDITOR

ANAND SHARMA

EDITORIAL BOARD

KIRAN DATAR

MALINI SOOD

SUPPORT TEAM

HARI SHANKER GUPTA

BHASHYAM KASTURI

Contents

ALL INDIA CONGRESS COMMITTEE
24, AKBAR ROAD, NEW DELHI - 110 011

Sonia Gandhi
President

FOREWORD

LEST WE FORGET

When the Indian National Congress was founded in 1885 and held its first modest session later that year, no one could possibly have foretold its future. No one could have imagined that it would become the breaker of the greatest empire of the age, the changer and maker of India's history, the champion of India's freedom, and the guardian of its future.

Few political organisations can match the record of the Indian National Congress. It is the largest political party the democratic world has ever seen. It is also one of the most long-lived. Its record of service to our country, before and after independence, remains unrivalled. Over the decades, it has attracted an array of outstanding talent, combining inspirational vision, idealism, creativity, dedication, and organisational skills. In the roll call of India's most illustrious men and women of the 20th century, the Congress figures crowd the landscape, towering over most others. There can be few political parties which have been so blessed for so long in their leadership, or which have attracted such loyalty and sacrifice from so many millions of people. On the 125th anniversary of the party's founding, there is therefore much to be thankful for, much to remember, and much to celebrate. This volume, with its rich archival pictures, is both a remembrance of things past and a commemoration of the long journey the party has travelled. It reminds us how closely the destinies of India and the Congress have been intertwined.

Beyond India, too, the Congress has had an enduring influence. As the standard bearer of emancipation in the world's largest and most populous colony, it brought revolutionary new ideas into the political domain and demonstrated their effectiveness on an unprecedented scale. Countries elsewhere in the developing world took lessons from the Congress's example and sought inspiration from its methods. The Mahatma's philosophy of *satyagraha,* with its related techniques of non-violent resistance, civil disobedience*,* and economic boycott, caught the world's imagination. These very methods have been adopted and used with success to empower the powerless in various struggles far beyond India's borders. In this sense, the imprint of the Congress is to be found in many parts of the world.

Its imprint is strongest, of course, in India itself. Much has been written about the miracle of India's post-independence survival as a stable democratic entity with an effective government. Many factors contributed to this miracle. Prominent among them was the Congress's ability to transform itself from the party of rebellion to the party of governance. Outside observers (and perhaps many within as well) thought that universal suffrage in a country as poor, diverse, and illiterate as India would be a daring leap of faith. Leap of faith it undoubtedly was, but the Congress contributed mightily to making it work. In this it was helped by its own inclusive character, with a membership from all classes, religions, regions, and shades of opinion. Its experience as a mass organisation with an effective presence in every part of the country, together with its highly developed skill in managing internal conflict, proved to be critical factors in the early decades of India's democratic life. It is with pride that the Congress can justifiably claim Indian democracy as its own most enduring monument.

The Congress could hardly have nurtured our democracy without an important internal attribute: its tradition of argument. It has never been a monolith, but a capacious umbrella of different views, perspectives, and interests competing with one another. The Congress's history is full of the contest of ideas and the clash of personalities, even sometimes resulting in splits. The first was in 1907. There have been others in our own lifetime. I believe these debates and differences have been a necessary part of the party's process of renewal, preventing stagnation in its thinking and keeping it relevant and responsive to changing circumstances.

From its very early years in the nineteenth century until today, the Congress has rightly been pre-occupied with the economic problems facing our country. If the degrading poverty and exploitation of India's millions was the dominant theme of the freedom movement, lifting them out of it has been the priority since independence. Our leaders shared a common vision for India: upholding our secular principles, ending poverty through the country's economic and social modernisation, creating a just and equitable economic order, and making full use of science and technology in pursuit of these goals. We have come some distance, but still have a long way to go. Liberalisation and globalisation have introduced a new dynamic with added pulls, pressures, and opportunities, but the party's commitment to marrying economic growth with social justice remains a core value from which it will not budge. Poverty and hunger still stalk our land. If the complete removal of poverty will take time, our endeavour is to protect the most vulnerable from its worst effects.

As is only to be expected, the Congress has had its ups and downs over its long history. It has experienced both glory and defeat. The rough and tumble of politics and the compromises inevitable in a democratic society have imposed their own limitations. Nevertheless, I believe that so long as the Congress remains true to its basic principles of secular democracy and economic and social transformation wedded to social equity, it will continue to be a vital factor in India's future. It must also remain the upholder and protagonist of pan-Indian consciousness. At this time of turmoil in our neighbourhood and political turbulence in our country, when narrower identities of caste, religion, and region are becoming more prominent, the Congress's broader and inclusive vision is more relevant and necessary than ever to take the country forward.

I am deeply conscious of the Congress's magnificent legacy. To be entrusted with its stewardship is a privilege, but also a deeply humbling experience. I draw strength and hope from the fact that the Congress's vision of politics has always been rooted in ethics. To lose this would be to lose all.

On this, the 125th anniversary of our Party, let us remember and cherish this unique heritage. Let us celebrate it by rededicating ourselves to the service of the people.

Introduction

ANAND SHARMA

On 28 December 1885, seventy-two eminent persons, representing the aspirations of a proud people in bondage, met at the Gokuldas Tejpal Sanskrit College in Bombay. This representative gathering was a microcosm of India, mirroring its intellect and diversity, embodying the richness of its culture and the pride of a civilisation.

Together, they articulated the collective resolve of their people, humiliated under the yoke of a repressive regime, giving expression to their shared urge for freedom. The birth of the Indian National Congress ushered in an era of struggle and sacrifice, marking the commencement of a momentous journey. The Congress mobilised the people of India to raise their voice against the British Raj, giving them the courage to fight for their inalienable right to human dignity and freedom. The message of the Congress spread across the length and breadth of the country, stirring the soul of the people ravaged by poverty, struggling in despair in sleepy villages and remote corners. It was truly the beginning of the biggest mass movement in human history.

Inspired by the *satyagraha* of Mahatma Gandhi, empowered by the tools of truth and non-violence, and led by men and women of extraordinary courage and commitment, the people of India emerged victorious. India won its long-cherished freedom at last. Upholding the values and ideals of the Congress, which had sustained the national movement, India declared itself a republic and a secular constitutional democracy. The task of nation building began in right earnest.

In the 125 years of this epoch journey, countless sacrifices were made and many milestones achieved. It is therefore a national imperative to recall and reconnect with this glorious past.

While it is difficult to give a comprehensive account of the historical events spread well over a century, an honest attempt has been made to document and share the same with the present and future generations. This book contains rare photographs and archival material, portraying the dreams and aspiration of our people through the pages of history. It provides a glimpse of the remarkable journey that began in 1885 and truly became the Journey of a Nation.

1885

The Formative Years

1920

The Formative Years

1885 - 1920

THE BEGINNING

The struggle for India's independence from British colonial rule, led by the Indian National Congress (INC), was a popular, broad-based movement that attracted support from all sections of society and from all parts of the country. After a long and difficult campaign, Indian nationalists succeeded in overthrowing the mightiest empire in the world, triggering a wave of decolonisation in Asia, Africa, and Latin America. The movement was truly national in character, galvanising people across the divides of class, caste, community, religion, gender, and age, towards a common objective. The Congress provided a platform for the representation of all shades of nationalist opinion, bringing together different streams of anti-colonial protest within its fold. Since its founding in December 1885 in Bombay, the Congress has retained this open, all-inclusive character, which has been a huge strength.

The aftermath of the events of 1857 had shaken the old order in India and weakened the credibility and position of the traditional political class of *rajas* (kings) and *zamindars* (landlords). The rising middle class, which emerged out of the spread of modern, Western-style education, comprised lawyers, teachers, and journalists. They aspired to enter the higher echelons of the civil service, although by 1880 only four had managed to join the elite Indian Civil Service (ICS). However, the new intelligentsia—with their commitment to liberal values and pride in Indian ethos and culture—was growing frustrated at being excluded from the higher offices of the civil service and being denied an opportunity to share in the governance of their own country.

Many factors contributed to the emergence of modern nationalism in India. Most important were India's colonial economic exploitation by Britain, imperial and racial arrogance, and exclusionist and discriminatory policies. The administrative and economic unification of the country under the British rule, the introduction of modern means of transport and communication, the spread of modern education, the rise of a new Indian middle class, and social reform movements of the nineteenth century created a national self-consciousness and a sense of common identity.

Raja Ram Mohan Roy, the founder of the Brahmo Samaj, which advocated monotheism and social reform (such as the abolition of *sati*), inspired many. The Prarthana Samaj, under the leadership of Mahadev Govind Ranade, in Maharashtra; the Arya Samaj, founded in 1875 by Swami Dayananda Saraswati; the Ramakrishna Mission, established by Swami Vivekananda; and the Theosophical Society, with its headquarters at Adyar, near Madras (1886), also prepared the ground for the birth of national self-consciousness.

In addition to these social reform campaigns, many organisations and regional movements articulated the growing nationalist spirit among urban, educated Indians. These included the British Indian Association and the Indian Association in Bengal; the Bombay Association, the Bombay Presidency Association, and the Poona Sarvajanik Sabha in Maharashtra; and the *Hindu* newspaper and the Madras Mahajana Sabha in Madras.

The Indian Association, founded in 1876 in Calcutta by Surendranath Banerjea, was one of the most important pre-Congress nationalist organisations. After graduating from Calcutta University in 1868, Banerjea went to England to appear in the ICS examinations. He passed, but was disqualified on flimsy grounds citing some discrepancy over his exact age. Banerjea felt strongly that he had suffered because he was an Indian, *'a member of a community that lay disorganised, had no public opinion and no voice.'* In 1883, he convened the All-India National Conference at Calcutta.

A.O. HUME (1829-1912)
Allan Octavian Hume, a civil servant in British India and a political reformer, was one of the key founders of the Indian National Congress. He served as General Secretary of the INC. Hume established a vernacular newspaper *Lokmitra* and is credited with introducing agricultural reforms in India. He also took up the cause of education and founded scholarships for higher education.

In the same year, Allan Octavian Hume, a retired English civil servant with a deep interest in Indian affairs, addressed an open letter to the graduates of Calcutta University, urging them to set up an association for the political regeneration of India, which, as he said, later might form *'the germ of a native parliament.'* In December 1884, some delegates of the annual convention of the Theosophical Society held a meeting in Madras at which they issued a circular convening a conference of the Indian National Union at Poona. Hume got in touch with prominent Indian leaders and, with their cooperation, took the initiative to convene the first meeting of this body. The meeting, however, could not take place at Poona due to the sudden outbreak of cholera and the venue was shifted to Bombay.

It was the Ilbert Bill of 1883, designed to remove distinctions between Indian and European judges, that prompted the emergence of an all-India political organisation. The bill aroused such strong racial feeling among the English community in Bengal that it was withdrawn. It outraged and angered many Indians.

On 28 December 1885, a group of 72 social reformers, journalists, and lawyers held the first session of the Indian National Union at Gokuldas Tejpal Sanskrit College, Bombay; the conference was renamed the Indian National Congress with the aim of securing self-govern-ment. Soon thereafter, Banerjea merged his own association with the Congress. The ground had been prepared by many public-spirited Indians and associations in different parts of the country. Nevertheless, Hume is credited with giving the idea a concrete and final shape.

The first president of the Indian National Congress was W. C. Bonnerjee, a legal luminary and one of the first four Indian barristers. The aims of the Congress, as stated by him, were that *'the basis of the government should be widened and the people should have their proper and legitimate share in it.'* Bonnerjee laid down the main objectives of the Congress, which were the promotion of friendship and the eradication of racial, communal, and provincial prejudice among all those working for the cause of national unity. This would be done by recording the mature opinion of the educated classes on the pressing social problems of the day, as well as by determining a line of action in the years to come.

The Indian Mirror of Calcutta declared that 28 December 1885 was a

red letter day . . . if we were asked what was the proudest day in our life we should unhesitatingly say it was the day on which we, for the first time, met all our brothers of Madras, Bombay, The North-West Provinces and the Punjab under the roof of the Gokuldas Tejpal Sanskrit College for the purpose of the National Congress.

W.C. BONNERJEE (1844-1906)
President, 1st Session, Bombay-1885 and
8th Session, Allahabad-1892.

Womesh Chandra Bonnerjee practised law in the
Calcutta High Court and was the first Indian to act
as a standing counsel. He founded the newspaper
Bengalee. Bonnerjee was the first to propose the
formation of standing committees of the Congress in
each province for the better coordination of the
party's work.

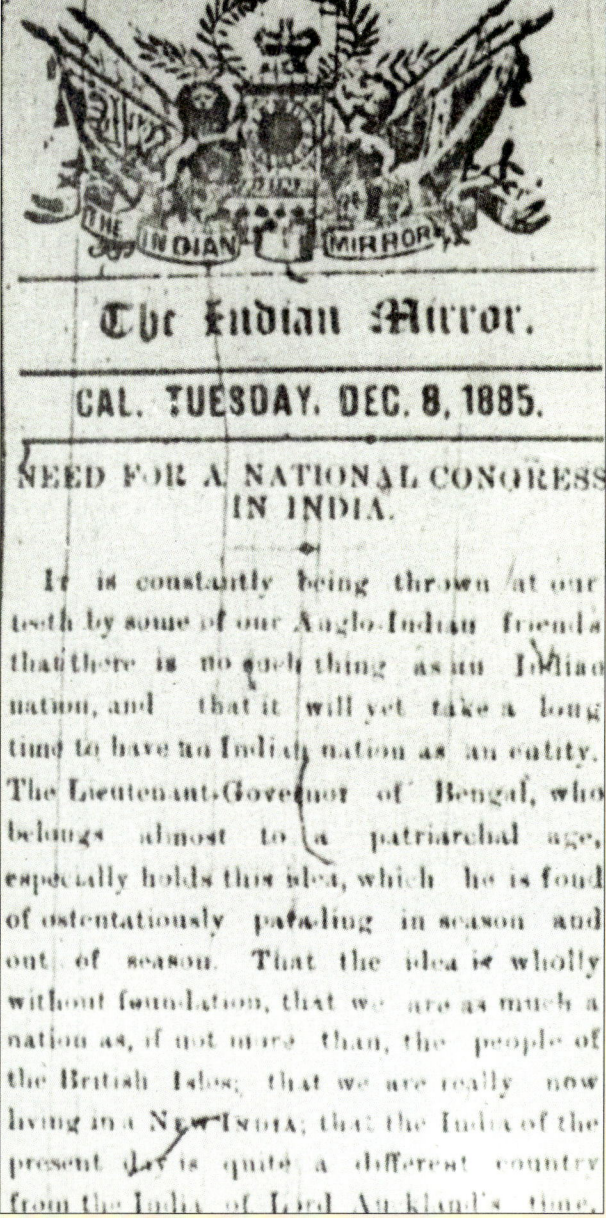

A clipping titled 'Need for a National Congress in
India' from *The Indian Mirror,* Calcutta, 8 December
1885.

FIRST INDIAN NATIONAL CONGRESS, BOMBAY, 1885.

Delegates to the first meeting of the Indian National Congress held at
the Gokuldas Tejpal Sanskrit College in Bombay, 28-31 December
1885. A.O. Hume is seated in the middle (third row from the front).
To his right is Dadabhai Naoroji; to his left, in sequence, are: S.N.
Banerjea, Pherozeshah Mehta, and Gopal Krishna Gokhale.

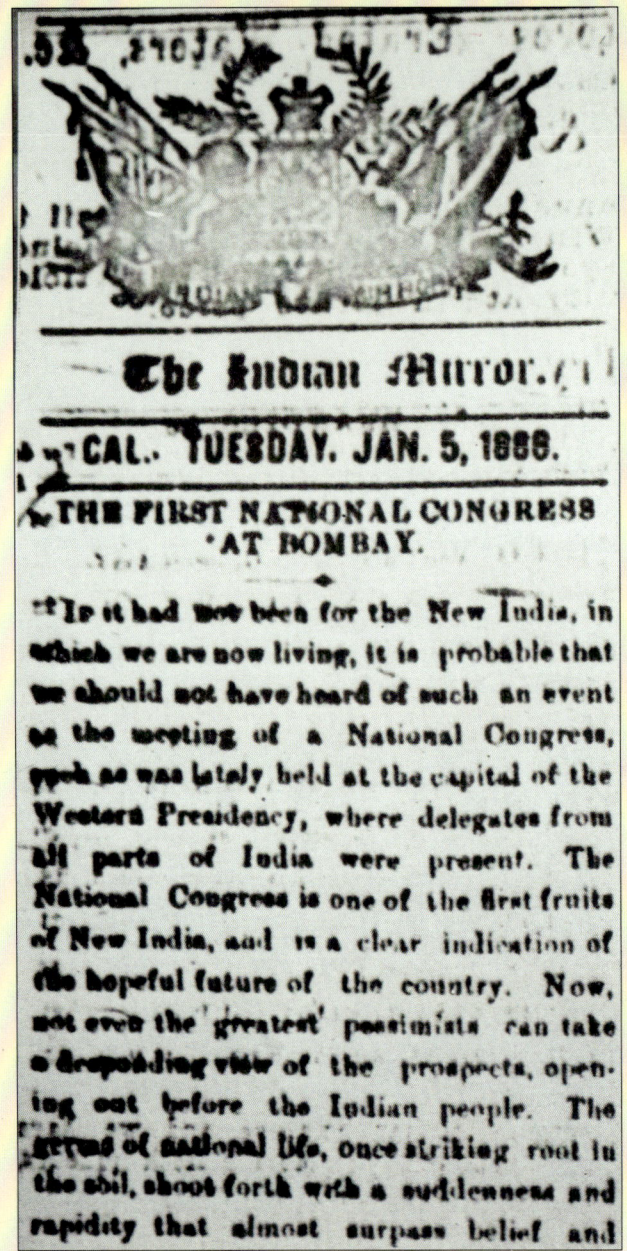

A clipping titled 'The First National Congress' from
The Indian Mirror, Calcutta, 5 January 1886.

SURENDRANATH BANERJEA (1848-1925)

President, 11th Session, Poona-1895 and
18th Session, Ahmedabad-1902.

S.N. Banerjea founded the Indian Association in 1876.
He framed the Calcutta Municipal Act of 1923.
Banerjea wrote *A Nation in the Making* and was editor
of the newspaper *Bengalee.* During the Congress split
at Surat in 1907, he sided with the radicals.

DADABHAI NAOROJI (1825-1917)

President, 2nd Session, Calcutta-1886; 9th Session, Lahore-1893; and 22nd Session, Calcutta-1906.

Dadabhai Naoroji founded the Rahnumae Mazdayasne Sabha. He put forward the theory of the 'Drain of Wealth' and wrote *Poverty and Un-British Rule in India* to highlight the extortionist policies of the British government towards India. He founded the newspapers *Voice of India* and *Rast Goftar,* and also established the East India Association. Naoroji was the first Indian to be a member of the Liberal Party in the House of Commons.

A clipping titled 'Political and Social Reform and the Present National Reawakening in India' from *The Indian Mirror,* Calcutta, 11 March 1886.

THE FIRST PHASE

In the first phase, the Congress sought the redressal of various grievances and focused attention on its demands through constitutional means, but subsequently it became a powerful exponent of the political ambitions of the Indian people.

The Congress aimed to rouse, through resolutions adopted at its annual meetings, the conscience of the British people about the inequities of British colonial rule and to ask for greater representation of Indians in the civil services, legislative councils, at the centre, and in the provinces. The early sessions of the Congress stressed issues such as the setting up of a royal commission to look into the working of the Indian administration with adequate representation for Indians; abolition of the Council of the Secretary of State for India; representation of elected members in the legislative councils along with increased powers; establishment of legislative councils for the North-West Frontier Province, Oudh, and Punjab; simultaneous holding of civil service examinations in England and India; reduction of military expenditure; and separation of upper Burma from the Viceroyalty of India.

Subsequently, more demands were made, articulating the grievances of Indians concerning the day-to-day administration of the country. These included extension of trial by jury; separation of judicial and executive functions; establishment of military colleges in India; amendment of the Arms Act and Rules, 1878; adoption of an active policy of technical education and industrial development; reform of the land revenue policy; constitution of an independent civil medical service in India; repeal of the cotton excise duty; abolition of forced labour; recruitment of members of the higher judiciary from the Bar; relief measures for agricultural indebtedness; grant of financial independence to the provinces; reorganisation of educational services; repeal of the Bengal, Madras and Bombay Regulations of 1818; and repeal of the notification of 1891 relating to the press in Indian states. A demand was also made for an inquiry into the economic condition of the people and for the holding of periodic parliamentary reviews of Indian affairs.

Learning to Walk

Pattabhi Sitaramayya, the first official historian of the Congress, observed: *'great institutions have always had small beginnings, even as the great rivers of the world start as their streams.'*

The first session of the Congress (1885) was contemptuously dismissed by the Viceroy, Lord Dufferin, as representing the views of a 'microscopic minority' of Indians. But so strong was the need for a nationalist platform that the

Congress attracted far greater numbers of participants the next year. The second session (1886) was attended by 436 delegates representing 69 associations. It was presided over by Dadabhai Naoroji, with Rajendra Lal Mitra as the chairman of the committee.

Thereafter, the Congress met every year in December in a different part of the country. The number of delegates continued to swell, including in its fold, lawyers, journalists, traders, industrialists, teachers, and landlords. In 1889, different bodies elected representatives to the Congress, and electoral divisions were created for these elections. In 1890, Kadambini Ganguly, the first woman graduate of Calcutta University, addressed the Congress session. By 1893, the Congress had enlisted the support not only of the Indian Parliamentary Committee but also of 154 members of the House of Commons. However, there was little response from the British government, leading Hume to remark that *'the National Congress had endeavoured to instruct the Government but the Government had refused to be instructed.'*

Through the 1880s and 1890s, India suffered from as many as 18 famines. But the government refused to lighten the burden of heavy duties and taxes, or to take ameliorative measures to reduce suffering. Excise duty on cotton and yarn evoked widespread resentment. The Congress raised many of these concerns vociferously. In 1901, it called the attention of the government to the deplorable condition of the poorest classes in India, 40 million of whom, according to a high-ranking official authority, *'drag out their miserable existence, on the verge of starvation.'* The many representations and issues that were agitated against in the early years of the national movement, however, were ignored by the government.

The Stalwarts

Gopal Krishna Gokhale, one of the most dynamic personalities of the time, joined the Congress in 1889 and became joint secretary in 1895, along with Tilak, another stalwart. In 1905, he founded the Servants of India Society with the objective of training youths to devote themselves to the service of India as national missionaries and to promote by all constitutional means the national interests of the Indian people.

Some of the great leaders of the Congress during its early years were Gopal Krishna Gokhale, Dadabhai Naoroji, Badruddin Tyabji, Pherozeshah Mehta, P. Ananda Charlu, Surendranath Banerjea, Romesh Chandra Dutt, Ananda Mohan Bose, Mahadev Govind Ranade, Bal Gangadhar Tilak, Rashbihari Ghosh, Madan Mohan Malaviya, C. Sankaran Nair, C. Vijayaraghavachariar, and Dinshaw E. Wacha. All of them deeply influenced many others who had joined the Congress.

GOPAL KRISHNA GOKHALE (1866-1915)
President, 21st Session, Benares-1905.

Gokhale played an instrumental role in the formation of the Morley-Minto Reforms of 1909. He emphasised western liberal education and fought for women's emancipation. The conflict between Gokhale's moderate views and the militant nationalist ideas of Bal Gangadhar Tilak led to a split in the Indian National Congress in 1907.

MADAN MOHAN MALAVIYA (1861-1946)
President, 24th Session, Lahore-1909 and 33rd Session, Delhi-1918.

Noted for his role in the espousal of Hindu nationalism, Pandit Madan Mohan Malaviya popularised the slogan 'Satyameva Jayathe'. He edited the weeklies *The Hindustan* and *The Indian Union* and founded the English daily, *Leader*. He was the founder of the Hindu Mahasabha.

Early Nationalists

The early nationalists pushed for civil and constitutional reform, which was to be achieved within the legal and administrative framework of British rule. The core of moderate thought was the culmination of a trend that can be traced to Raja Ram Mohan Roy, who stood for the rational and individualistic outlook of contemporary Europe. The moderates' demands for political reform shaped many of the policies and strategies of the Congress in the early years.

Constitutional Reform

The early leaders began with faith in British democracy, which had given to the world the model of free institutions and other liberal values. Many leaders of the early Congress sessions were chosen as judges and members of the executive council. Dadabhai Naoroji was the first Indian to be elected to the British House of Commons. Many of these early leaders believed, as Gokhale said, *'that the situation required not the policeman's baton, or the soldier's bayonet, but the statesman's insight, wisdom and courage.'*

The early nationalist leaders did pioneering work in exposing the true character of British imperialism in India. They were instrumental in bringing about a national awakening and in forging unity among people working for a common aim. One of their major achievements was training ordinary Indians to take up political work, a mission that was carried on by their successors.

Economic Issues

The early Congress leaders developed a sophisticated economic critique of imperialism known as the 'drain theory', propounded by Dadabhai Naoroji in his book, *Poverty and Un-British Rule in India* (1901). This clearly grasped that the subordination of the Indian economy, indeed its de-industrialisation, was vital to British economic growth, both as a supplier of raw materials and as a market for British manufacturers. Armed with this understanding, Indian nationalists focused attention on the problems of commerce, industry, and agriculture in the country. The resolutions passed by the Congress included those protesting the levy of excise duty on cotton goods manufactured in British India. At the Calcutta conference in 1906, Pandit Madan Mohan Malaviya, noting how raw materials were being taken out of the country and returned as manufactured goods to the detriment of Indian industry, observed, *'If we were free, we would adopt protection as all countries do when industries are nascent.'* This economic critique of imperialism engendered the *swadeshi* (indigeneous) spirit and led to the movement for the boycott of foreign goods.

BADRUDDIN TYABJI
(1844-1906)

President, 3rd Session, Madras-1887.

First Indian to be appointed as Chief Justice; founded the Bombay Presidency Association in 1885; a secular Muslim who supported the Age of Consent Bill of 1891, despite Hindu and Muslim opposition.

GEORGE YULE
(1829-1892)

President, 4th Session, Allahabad-1888.

First non-Indian president of INC, Yule was widely known in Indian circles for his breadth of outlook, liberal views, and marked sympathy for Indian aspirations; helped in strengthening the British Committee of the INC.

WILLIAM WEDDERBURN
(1838-1918)

President, 5th Session, Bombay-1889 and 25th Session, Allahabad-1910.

Sir William Wedderburn was instrumental in passing the Montagu-Chelmsford Reforms; published a series of articles, *A Call to Arms* (1903); campaigned for Hindu-Muslim unity.

PHEROZESHAH MEHTA
(1845-1915)

President, 6th Session, Calcutta-1890.

Sir Pherozeshah Mehta (knighted in 1904) started the newspaper *Bombay Chronicle*; co-founded the Bombay Presidency Association; was instrumental in setting-up the Central Bank of India in 1911.

P. ANANDA CHARLU
(1843-1908)

President, 7th Session, Nagpur-1891.

Co-founded the newspaper *The Hindu;* established the Madras Mahajana Sabha (1884); contributed articles to journals *Native Public Opinion* and *Madrasi*; established the Triplicane Literary Society.

ALFRED WEBB
(1834-1908)

President, 10th Session, Madras-1894.

A stalwart fighter for Irish independence, Webb started Britain's first anti-racism journal *Anti-Caste* (1888); supported the Society for the Furtherance of Human Brotherhood along with Dadabhai Naoroji.

RAHIMTULLA M. SAYANI
(1847-1902)

President, 12th Session, Calcutta-1896.

R.M. Sayani became President, Bombay Municipal Corporation in 1888. He was also the Sheriff of Bombay and acted as the secretary of Anjuman-i-Islam for a while.

C. SANKARAN NAIR
(1857-1934)

President, 13th Session, Amraoti-1897.

Nair (knighted in 1912) held the education portfolio in the Viceroy's Executive Council; was a judge at the Madras High Court; cooperated with the Simon Commission in 1928; wrote *Gandhi and Anarchy*.

ANANDA MOHAN BOSE
(1847-1906)

President, 14th Session, Madras-1898.

An ardent Brahmo, educationist and social reformer, Bose founded the Banga Mahila Vidyalaya; co-founded the New Sadharana Samaj (1878), and was Secretary, Indian Association. He participated in the Bengal partition agitations.

ROMESH CHANDER
DUTT (1848-1909)

President,15th Session, Lucknow-1899.

A moderate, Dutt was the first Indian economist to study and write on Indian agrarian problems; wrote his first book *Peasantry of Bengal* in 1875; was appointed Dewan of Baroda in 1904.

NARAYAN GANESH
CHANDAVARKAR
(1855-1923)

President, 16th Session, Lahore-1900.

Chandavarkar (knighted in 1910) was an ardent Brahmo, social reformer, and a moderate. He was editor, *Indu Prakash* and wrote *Minutes of Dissent* in the Despatches on Indian Constitutional Reforms.

DINSHAW EDULJI
WACHA (1844-1936)

President, 17th Session, Calcutta-1901.

Great nationalist, economic critic, financial wizard, and prolific writer, he was knighted in 1917; appointed Governor of the Imperial Bank of India; was a member of the Imperial Legislative Council.

LALMOHAN GHOSH
(1849-1909)

President, 19th Session, Madras-1903.

A prominent member of the British Indian Association, Ghosh took up cudgels against the Ilbert Bill of 1883. A powerful orator, he emphasised the importance of western education for the constitutional enlightenment of Indians.

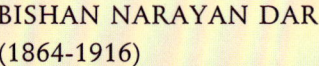

HENRY COTTON
(1845-1915)

President, 20th Session, Bombay-1904.

Started the newspaper *New India;* a leader of the Bengal partition agitation; genuinely interested in the welfare of India; shared the nationalist views of the likes of Tagore, and W.C. Bonnerjee; supported Indian Home Rule.

RASHBIHARI GHOSH
(1845-1921)

President, Surat Session-1907 (suspended) and 23rd Session, Madras-1908.

Top lawyer in the Calcutta High Court; first president of the National Council of Education (1906); played a prominent role in the Swadeshi movement.

BISHAN NARAYAN DAR
(1864-1916)

President, 26th Session, Calcutta-1911.

A prolific writer, Dar held very liberal views on religion and social reform; founded the Bishan Sabha; opposed special minority representation and limited franchise of Indians while favouring the Indianisation of the bureaucracy.

RAGHUNATH NARASINHA
MUDHOLKAR (1857-1921)

President, 27th Session, Bankipore-1912.

Started the newspaper *Vidarbha;* established the Berar Sarvajanik Sabha; championed industrialisation and technical education. A social reformer and a moderate, he vehemently opposed the regulation of separate electorates and unequal franchise.

NAWAB SYED MUHAMMAD
BAHADUR (1867-1919)

President, 28th Session, Karachi-1913.

A social reformer and educationist, Nawab Syed Muhammad helped the INC financially in its nascent stages. A nationalist in outlook, he propagated Hindu-Muslim unity.

BHUPENDRA NATH BOSE (1859-1924)

President, 29th Session, Madras-1914.

Joined anti-partition agitation and toured throughout Bengal, calling for *swadeshi;* represented Indian government at Labour Conference at Geneva (1922); favoured western educa-tion; a constitutionalist; fought the government from within.

SATYENDRA PRASANNA SINHA (1863-1928)

President, 30th Session, Bombay-1915.

First Indian Advocate-General of Bengal; knighted in 1914; first Indian member of the Governor General's Executive Council; piloted the Govern-ment of India Bill (1919); an ardent Brahmo.

AMBICA CHARAN MAZUMDAR (1850-1922)

President, 31st Session, Lucknow-1916.

Protested against the partition of Bengal; wrote *Indian National Evolution;* a moderate; advocated self-government; instrumental in bringing about the Congress-Muslim League union through the famous Lucknow Pact.

SYED HASAN IMAM (1871-1933)

President, Special Session, Bombay-1918.

Judge in the Calcutta High Court; instrumental in the framing of the Montagu-Chelmsford reforms; played a leading part in the Khilafat Movement; a strong advocate of social reform.

C. VIJAYARAGHAVA-CHARIAR (1852-1944)

President, 35th Session, Nagpur-1920.

Hailed as the 'Lion of South India', Vijayaraghavachariar was a close associate of A.O. Hume, who drew up the Swaraj Constitution for India; champion of the depressed classes.

HAKIM AJMAL KHAN (1863-1927)

President, 36th Session, Ahmedabad-1921.

Chief physician to the Nawab of Rampur; developed indigen-eous system of medicine, *Tibb-i-Yunani* and established the Tibbiya College of Delhi; instrumental in the founding of the Muslim League; received the title of *Masih-ul-Mulk.*

As time passed, the demands of the early nationalists became more comprehensive and well defined. By 1905, Gokhale was pointing to the evils of a bureaucratic government that could no longer be tolerated. He affirmed that the goal of the Congress was ensuring that India would be governed in the interest of the Indians themselves and that in course of time a form of government should be attained in India similar to the one that existed in the self-governing colonies of the British Empire. Constitutional agitation would be the means of achieving this end.

Militant Nationalists

The government's tardy and inadequate response to many of the demands put forward by the Congress led to frustration and impatience among some Congress leaders, who decided to adopt different means to achieve *swaraj* (self-rule). This shift in tactics can be traced to movements that emerged in the period after 1857. These leaders, guided by the nationalist ideas of *swadharama* and *swaraj,* drew inspiration from their own civilisation and culture, referring to Indian history and tradition to support their stance.

The militant nationalist movement had three major schools—the Maharashtra school headed by Bal Gangadhar Tilak; the Bengal school represented by Bipin Chandra Pal and Aurobindo Ghosh; and the Punjab school led by Lala Lajpat Rai, 'the Lion of Punjab'. In the history of the nationalist struggle, the trinity is known as Lal-Bal-Pal. The Bengal militant nationalists were deeply influenced by the ideas of Bankim Chandra, which later inspired other leaders also. Aurobindo—who was one of the most important militant nationalist leaders in the period 1905-1910 and who later turned to the study of religion, philosophy, and spiritualism—infused the movement with neo-vedantic mysticism and sanctified the nation as a deity worthy of 'mother worship'. As he said, *'I know my country as my mother. I adore her, I worship her.'*

Bal Gangadhar Tilak, popularly known as Lokmanya, was a dynamic leader of the early nationalists. In the 1880s, he helped found the New English School in Poona, which later became the Fergusson College. He also established two newspapers, the *Mahratta* (in English) and the *Kesari* (in Marathi). He used the traditional Ganapati festival and the example of Shivaji to arouse nationalist fervour among the youths to mobilise them for political action. In 1896-97, he launched a no-tax campaign and was sentenced to 18 months of rigorous imprisonment. In his long political career, he underwent many such punishments.

Tilak and other Congress leaders during this phase of the nationalist movement were deeply committed to the attainment of *swaraj.* The famous words of Tilak, *'Swaraj is my birthright*

LAL-BAL-PAL

Left to right: Lala Lajpat Rai, Bal Gangadhar Tilak, and Bipin Chandra Pal.

Lala Lajpat Rai (1865-1928), popularly known as Sher-i-Punjab, presided over a Special Session of the Indian National Congress, Calcutta-1920.

SRI AUROBINDO GHOSH (1872-1950)

Sri Aurobindo has been called a scholar, a literary critic, a philosopher, an aggressive Indian nationalist, a poet, and a yogi. He perceived the need for a mass-based movement; was at the forefront of the Bengal partition movement. He wrote a series of fiery articles under the title 'New Lamps for Old'; edited the English dailies *Bande Mataram* and *Karmayogin*, and started a Bengali weekly *Dharma*. Aurobindo established close contacts with Tilak and Sister Nivedita. In 1907, at the Surat Session where moderates and hardliners had a major showdown, he led the hardliners along with Tilak. In 1926, he founded an ashram in Pondicherry, with his close spiritual disciple, known as the Mother.

and I shall have it', resonated with the masses. These leaders were not willing to accept the slow and gradual pace of constitutional reforms under the 'benevolent' paternalism of the British government. Through their writings and speeches, they spread the message that Indians must author their own destiny to achieve their independence. They recognised the strength of mass action and used it effectively. The strategy of mass political mobilisation became a powerful force in the years to come.

Both moderates and militant nationalists unanimously condemned the adverse impact of British rule on the economic interests of the Indian people. The *Mahratta* of Tilak and the *Bengalee* of Banerjea both denounced the policy, as did R.C. Dutt and Gokhale. As Tilak wrote in *Kesari*, *'Surely India is treated as a vast pasture reserved solely for the Europeans to feed on.'* However, the moderates and the militant nationalists differed on the issue of *swadeshi* and boycott; the militant nationalists were not ready to work within the legal framework set up by the government.

FIRST ARRIVAL OF GANDHI ON THE NATIONAL SCENE

Mohandas Karamchand Gandhi, then a young London-educated lawyer, reached South Africa in 1893 because he *'wanted somehow to leave India to escape the petty politics of the country.'* Destiny had much bigger plans for this chosen one.

The experience and challenge of living under an oppressive colonial regime in South Africa had a transformational influence on Gandhi, moulding his thinking.

The humiliating experience at the Pietermaritzburg railway platform outraged and inspired him to challenge the might of the mightiest imperial regime ever. Gandhi gave a moving account of those defining moments:

I began to think of my duty. Should I fight for my rights or go back to India, or should I go on to Pretoria without minding the insults, and return to India after finishing the case? It would be cowardice to run back to India without fulfilling my obligation.

He worked tirelessly in South Africa, raising his voice against racial prejudice and unjust laws, and received an overwhelming response from the Indians there.

The Natal Indian Congress was born in May 1894 and Gandhi became its honorary secretary. After the Boer War, Gandhi set sail for Bombay as he felt that his work in South Africa was over and he had ensured the creation of a competent local leadership to carry on the struggle. He arrived in Bombay on 19 December 1901, just in time to attend the annual session of the Indian National Congress at Calcutta. It was here that Gandhi met stalwart Congress leaders, including Mehta, Tilak, and Gokhale. His visit provided him with insights into the deep divisions in Indian society and politics. His experience in South Africa had moulded his understanding, making him alive to the plight of the Indian people and the prevailing political situation in India. Gokhale was Gandhi's mentor in the early years. About Gandhi he said, *'He is without doubt made of the stuff of which heroes and martyrs are made. Nay, more. He has in him the marvelous spiritual power to turn ordinary men around him into heroes and martyrs.'* Gandhi stayed in India for barely five months, but his visit achieved the desired objective of garnering support for the struggle of Indians in South Africa. He rushed back to South Africa on receiving a cable from Dada Abdullah, one of his associates. History had greater things in store for him.

PARTITION OF BENGAL, 1905

By the early twentieth century, an articulate and assertive leadership had emerged in the Congress. However, the British government failed to respond with any meaningful gesture even to the limited aspirations of the Congress leaders. Indeed, the government sought to exercise greater control on all kinds of nationalist political activity than ever before. The Municipality Act of 1899 curbed the role of the elected commissioners of the Calcutta municipality. The Indian Official Secrets Act of 1904 restricted the freedom of the press, and regulations were passed under which anyone could be deported without trial. The Universities

Gandhi's Satyagraha in South Africa

On his return to South Africa, Gandhi continued to raise his voice tirelessly against oppression and injustice. On 22 August 1906, the Transvaal government published an ordinance enjoining all Indian 'coolies', Arabs, and Turks of eight years and above in age residing in the Transvaal to register their names and to carry a certificate of registration. Failure to comply would mean forfeiture of residence and a fine of £100 or imprisonment and deportation. Gandhi decided that the time had come for the Indian community to raise its voice firmly, believing that is was 'better to die than to submit to such a law.'

On 11 September 1906, a historic meeting was convened at the Empire Theatre in Johannesburg, attended by 3,000 delegates of all shades of opinion, religions, and communities in a surcharged atmosphere. Gandhi stirred the emotions of the Indian community, saying, *'If ever a crisis in community affairs warranted a vow, now was the time. Caution had its place but also its limits. The government has taken leave of all sense of decency. We will be revealing our unworthiness and cowardice if we cannot stake our all in the face of the conflagration that envelops us.'* So determined was he that he boldly declared, *'There is only one course open to me, namely, to die, but not to submit to the law, even if everyone else were to hold back, leaving me alone. I am confident that I should never violate my pledge. So long as there is even a handful of men true to their pledge, there can be only one end to the struggle and that is victory.'* History was made that day and the spark that gave birth to the philosophy of Satyagraha—the soul force—giving a moral basis to the struggle against injustice and oppression.

Gandhi's message resonated across the Indian Ocean and captured the imagination of millions of Indians and attracted the respectful attention of the Congress leaders. Satyagraha later became an effective tool for the mass mobilisation for India's freedom movement.

On 16 August 1908, outside the Hamidia Mosque in Johannesburg, thousands gathered in response to Gandhi's call and publicly burnt their registration certificates, protesting against the 'Black Act'.

Act of 1904 sought to curtail nationalist trends by placing universities under more effective imperial control.

The partition of Bengal, on 20 July 1905, proved to be the most provocative act by the government, leading outraged Indians to undertake mass mobilisation in protest against the division of the province. Lord Curzon, Viceroy of India, issued an order dividing Bengal, with Eastern Bengal and Assam constituting a separate province. The ostensible reason for partitioning Bengal was administrative convenience because the province, with a population of over 85 million, was difficult to govern. However, Bengal was divided along communal lines; Eastern Bengal (predominantly Muslim) and Assam were made into one province, with its capital at Dacca, while Western Bengal (predominantly Hindu) along with Bihar and Orissa formed another province, with Calcutta as its capital. Clearly, the government's objective was to stem the rising tide of nationalism by creating dissension and division. This act of Lord Curzon went against the wishes of the people and triggered nationwide protests and agitations. It also sowed the seeds of communalism in the freedom struggle and provided the impetus for the birth of the Muslim League in 1906.

The anti-partition movement was initiated on 7 August 1905 with a massive demonstration in Calcutta, followed by major *hartals* and *bandhs.* The day of the partition, 16 October 1905, was observed as a day of national mourning.

SWADESHI AND BOYCOTT

The partition of Bengal engendered a new wave of anti-government feeling, seen in calls for imbibing self-reliance *(swadeshi)* and for rejecting British goods. At mass meetings, Indians, full of nationalist fervour, pledged to boycott foreign goods. They burnt foreign clothes publicly in huge bonfires, and demonstrators picketed shops selling it. Indians set up many indigeneous enterprises such as textile mills, factories, national banks, and insurance companies. Acharya P.C. Ray organised his famous Bengal Chemical Swadeshi Stores, and even Rabindranath Tagore helped set up a *swadeshi* store. Indians also established many national educational institutions. In 1906, in Calcutta, a national council of education was set up, and a national college began operating with Aurobindo Ghosh as principal.

The partition also led to a great flowering of cultural activities and inspired an outpouring of poetry by eminent authors like Rabindranath Tagore and Mukunda Das. Tagore composed his famous poem, 'Amar Sonar Bangla', which was later adopted as the national anthem of Bangladesh in 1971.

RISE OF MILITANCY

The repressive policies of the government aimed at crushing the anti-partition movement led to a spurt in militancy. Many students were awarded corporal punishment, and freedom of the press was suppressed. As a result, newspapers like *Yugantar, Sandhya,* and *Bande Matram* faced severe persecution. In 1907, Lala Lajpat Rai and Ajit Singh were deported following riots in the canal colonies of Punjab. In 1908, nine Bengal leaders were deported, including Krishna Kumar Mitra and Ashwini Kumar Datta. In 1908, Tilak was arrested and given six years' imprisonment.

The militant nationalists called for armed resistance in addition to *swadeshi* and boycott. Those who felt that *'force must be stopped by force'* also called for action. In 1907, an attempt was made on the life of the Lieutenant Governor of Bengal. In April 1908, Khudiram Bose and Prafulla Chaki threw a bomb at a carriage believed to be occupied by Judge Kingsford of Muzaffarpur. Chaki shot himself dead to escape arrest, and Bose was tried and hanged. An attempt was also made on the life of the Viceroy, Lord Hardinge.

In addition, the militant nationalists established centres of activity abroad. In London, the lead was taken by Lala Hardayal and Shyamji Krishna Varma. In Europe,

MADAME BHIKAJI CAMA (1861-1936)

Madame Cama devoted her life to philanthropic and social activities and in spreading awareness about India's cause in other parts of the world. In 1907, while attending the International Socialist Conference in Stuttgart, Germany, she boldly unfurled what she called 'the Flag of Indian Independence', as she appealed in her address for human rights, equality, and autonomy from Great Britain. In London, as private secretary, she assisted Dadabhai Naoroji who was then president of the British Committee of the Indian National Congress.

Madame Cama and Ajit Singh spearheaded the nationalist movement.

SURAT SESSION, 1907

People across the country were deeply distressed by the partition of Bengal, and all sections of the Congress united in opposing the measure. The Congress raised the demand for *swaraj* at a meeting in 1906. Gokhale and the moderates, however, envisioned responsible government within the British Empire, a position that was untenable for Tilak and his supporters, who wished to move beyond the goal of limited constitutional reform. Differences were also emerging with militants like Bipin Chandra Pal and Aurobindo Ghosh, who tried, albeit unsuccessfully, to get Tilak elected as president of the Congress in 1906. The two groups also had differences of opinion on the effectiveness of *swadeshi* and boycott. The moderates wanted to confine the boycott movement to Bengal and to limit it to the rejection of foreign goods, but this was not acceptable to the militants.

In 1907, at the Surat session, a major showdown took place between the two groups, leading to a split, with the militants walking out. Tilak now espoused more aggressive methods of political agitation against the British. The government reacted with even greater repressive measures to control what it regarded as terrorism, and Tilak was arrested. The government played the game of divide and rule by suppressing the militant nationalists, on the one hand, and by announcing limited constitutional concessions to satisfy the moderates, on the other hand.

MORLEY-MINTO REFORMS, 1909

In response to increasing nationalist demands, the British government passed the Morley-Minto Reforms in 1909, seeking to accommodate a part of the moderate demand for political representation. This concession was made against the backdrop of limited representation granted to the legislative councils thus far. Under the Indian Councils Act of 1861, three Indians were appointed to the Advisory Legislative Council at the centre as non-official members. In 1892, this number was increased, with the holding of direct and indirect elections. The 1909 reforms now expanded the scope of the legislative councils, increased Indian representation, introduced direct election of non-official members under limited property franchise, and in the provinces provided for non-official majorities. The recommendations of the legislative councils, however, could be disregarded at the discretion of the Viceroy or of the provincial governor. Thus, the councils were representative to a degree, but lacked sufficient administrative authority. Moreover, the Morley-Minto

Reforms accepted the demand of some Muslims for separate electorates, thus introducing the principle of communal representation in the country.

The Congress reached out to Muslims and appealed for a combined show of strength against foreign rule. Many nationalist Muslims responded to the call and joined the Congress, including Maulana Abul Kalam Azad, Saifuddin Kitchlew, A.K. Fazlul Huq, and Abdul Rahman. However, some other Muslims felt that without separate electorates the Muslim minority would be swamped by the Hindu majority. In 1906, the Aga Khan, the Nawab of Dacca, and Nawab Mohsin-ul-Mulk organised the Muslim League. Its leadership was primarily middle class and its objective was to seek more jobs and educational opportunities for Muslims.

At this time, Mohammed Ali Jinnah, a young lawyer from Bombay, entered the political arena. In the early years, he was an admirer and follower of Congress stalwarts such as Gokhale, and he attended the Congress session in 1904. It was not until much later that he joined the Muslim League, becoming its president in 1916.

Congress Response

The Congress attacked the award of separate electorates to Muslims as an attempt to weaken national unity and divide Indians. The Congress at its special session in Delhi (1918) condemned the Morley-Minto Reforms of 1909 as 'inadequate, unsatisfactory and disappointing.' The Congress resolution recorded displeasure over:

The excessive and unfair preponderant share of representation given to followers of a particular religion, the unjust, invidious and humiliating distinctions made between the Muslim and the non-Muslim subjects of His Majesty in the matter of electorates, franchise and qualification of candidates, the arbitrary and unreasonable disqualifications and restrictions for candidates seeking election to the councils, the general distrust of the educated classes running through the regulations and the unsatisfactory composition of the non-official majorities in the provincial councils, rendering them ineffective and unreal.

However, the government as usual chose to ignore the growing clamour for change.

In 1911, King George V was crowned Emperor of India at the Delhi Durbar, and the British government used this opportunity to annul the partition of Bengal. At the same time, the seat of government was transferred from Calcutta to New Delhi. The Viceroy, Lord Hardinge, in his despatch of 26 August 1911, stated that the basis of future reforms in India would have to acknowledge the claims of provincial autonomy in any scheme of national reconstruction.

FIRST WORLD WAR

In June 1914, the First World War broke out in Europe, and many nationalist leaders, including Tilak, decided to support Britain's war effort in the hope that the government would respond by taking steps towards the realisation of self-government for India. This did not materialise and militant nationalists became active in many parts of Bengal, Maharashtra, and northern India.

In 1913, Indian revolutionaries in the USA and Canada established the Ghadar Party, led by Lala Hardayal, Mohammed Barkatullah, and Bhai Bhagwan Singh. They planned an armed revolt in Punjab in February 1915, but the authorities were forewarned and ruthlessly suppressed them. Forty-two Ghadar leaders were arrested and many more were deported and sentenced to long-term imprisonment. Inspired by their example, nearly 1,000 men of the Fifth Native Light Infantry at Singapore revolted, but were crushed after a fierce battle.

HOME RULE

The support extended by many Congress leaders to the war effort gradually waned, with mounting frustration and resentment. They felt that Indians were being asked to make sacrifices for an alien rule and that Indian soldiers were being recruited to fight an imperialists' war, but the government was reluctant to give anything in return. This was in sharp contrast to the statements of other world leaders like Woodrow Wilson, the President of the United States, who asserted the right of all nations to self-determination. In India, the Congress revived the demand for self-government. At the Madras session in 1914, Annie Besant asked for Home Rule, renewing the call for *swadeshi,* national education, and the boycott of foreign goods.

Annie Besant was foremost among the many Westerners sympathetic to the cause of Indian nationalists and joined them in their struggle. Besant, who hailed from a distinguished Irish-English family, had been deeply influenced by Madame H.P. Blavatsky and by the teachings of the Theosophical Society. She came to India in 1893 and became an ardent supporter of the cause for independence. One of her first acts was to found the Central Hindu College in Benaras, which later became the Benaras Hindu University under the guidance of Madan Mohan Malaviya. In 1914, she purchased the *Madras Standard* and renamed it *New India.* This became an organ not only of nationalist opinion but also the voice of her Home Rule movement. She launched her Home Rule League on 1 September 1916. Tilak, who had been released from jail, had established his Home Rule League in April 1916. Later, the two leagues were merged. In 1917, Annie Besant presided over the Calcutta session of the Congress, the first woman to do so.

LUCKNOW PACT, 1916

Divisions in the ranks of the Congress, which had led to a split in 1907, were injuring the wider nationalist cause, and unity was the need of the hour. The Lucknow session in 1916 was significant because it demonstrated the growing nationalist feeling in the country. The session was attended by Tilak, G.S. Khaparde, Rashbihari Ghosh, Motilal Nehru, Surendranath Banerjea, Annie Besant, Mazharul Haque, Mohammed Rasul, Ajmal Khan, and M.A. Ansari. The Lucknow session was also attended by Gandhi, an event of great significance. He traversed the length and breadth of the country, preparing the people for mass mobilisation.

Divergent shades of opinion, both moderate and militant, were expressed and debated. The Congress and the Muslim League came together in support of the demand for self-government at an early date, and a joint scheme of political reforms was envisioned based on separate electorates. This Congress-League scheme of reforms came to be known as the Lucknow Pact of 1916.

As the demand for *swaraj* intensified under the Home Rule movement, Edwin Montagu, the new Secretary of State for India, announced the government policy of increasing the participation of Indians in every branch of the administration and of undertaking the gradual development of self-governing institutions for a

ANNIE BESANT (1847-1933)
President, 32nd Session, Calcutta-1917.

A prominent Theosophist, social reformer, political leader, women's rights activist, writer and orator, and supporter of Irish and Indian self-rule, Annie Besant was the first woman president of the Indian National Congress. She was a leading speaker for the Fabian Society and the (Marxist) Social Democratic Federation. Besant first visited India in 1893 and later settled here, becoming involved in the Indian nationalist movement and establishing the Home Rule League. She founded the weekly newspaper *Commonweal* and edited *New India*.

HOME RULE LEAGUE - ANNIE BESANT.

Group photograph: Annie Besant, Oman Sobani, Mohammed Ali Jinnah, and others, Bombay, 1918.

HOME RULE LEAGUE - B.G. TILAK.

Group photograph: Gangadharrao Deshpande, Kelkar, Karandikar, Belvi, Tilak, Khaparde, Dr Munje, Udhoji, Velkar, Dr Sathaye, and others.

progressive realisation of a responsible government in India as an integral part of the British Empire.

MONTAGU-CHELMSFORD REFORMS, 1919

In 1918, Edwin Montagu and the Viceroy, Lord Chelmsford, announced the Montagu-Chelmsford Reforms, which led to the Government of India Act of 1919. Under this Act, authority was decentralised, with division of functions between the centre and the provincial governments. At the centre, there was little change. Bicameralism was introduced, with an elected non-official majority in the lower house, but the Governor-General, who was responsible to the British government in London, retained overriding powers. In the provinces, the act introduced diarchy or dual government under which the governor retained authority over some 'reserved subjects'. The principle of separate electorates was extended both at the centre and in the provinces.

Congress leaders were not satisfied with the Montagu-Chelmsford Reforms of 1918-19, which were considered grossly inadequate. In 1918, the special session of the Congress in Bombay declared that nothing less than self-government would satisfy the legitimate aspirations of the Indian people. At the Delhi session presided over by Pandit Madan Mohan Malaviya, there was a split on the issue of provincial autonomy.

The months following the Delhi session witnessed no peace. Congress leaders were unhappy with many features of the 1919 act. Anger was also mounting across the country at the detention of the Ali brothers, Maulana Azad, Hakim Ajmal Khan, and Maulana Hasrat Mohani for having participated in the Khilafat movement.

JALLIANWALA BAGH, 1919

Tension was increasing in Punjab where the forthcoming Congress session in Amritsar in 1919 was being planned. In an effort to stall the event, the government introduced a series of repressive measures. Dr Kitchlew and Dr Satyapal, who were organising the Amritsar session, were suddenly spirited away by the district magistrate to an unknown place. A large crowd gathered to enquire about their whereabouts and was fired upon. This angered the people, who set the National Bank building ablaze, killing its European manager. The military took control of the situation, but sporadic violence continued. Gandhi was prevented from entering Punjab and was sent away by a special train to Bombay.

In this volatile atmosphere, the government introduced the brutally repressive Rowlatt Acts of 1919. These acts extended certain emergency powers that had been assumed during the war, permitting trial without jury and internment of suspects without trial in certain political cases. These repressive measures further fuelled resentment and anger among Indians. Demonstrations and strikes broke out all over the country, and passions ran particularly high in Punjab when the two Congress leaders were

arrested. The government declared martial law and banned public meetings.

On 13 April 1919, a large, peaceful, and unarmed crowd gathered at Jallianwala Bagh in Amritsar. General Dyer ordered 150 troops to open fire at the defenceless men, women, and children. The innocent people, victims of premeditated brutality, could not escape the assault since Jallianwala Bagh had only one entrance, which was blocked by the troops. Around 400 men, women, and children were killed and many more wounded. General Dyer's justification for the action was that the crowd had defied the curfew that was then in effect in the city. Unrepentant, he declared that he intended *'to teach the natives a lesson.'*

The Jallianwala Bagh massacre was followed by severe repression in Punjab, which was placed under martial law. Public hangings and whippings were held. The infamous 'crawling order' forced all Indians to crawl through a street where a British lady doctor had been attacked while cycling. Hundreds of people were convicted by the martial law commissioners.

In September 1919, the Viceroy appointed the Hunter Commission to enquire into the Punjab disorders, followed by the passage of an Indemnity Bill that sought to indemnify the actions taken by British officers in 'good faith' during the period of martial law.

A view of the Crawling Lane, Amritsar.

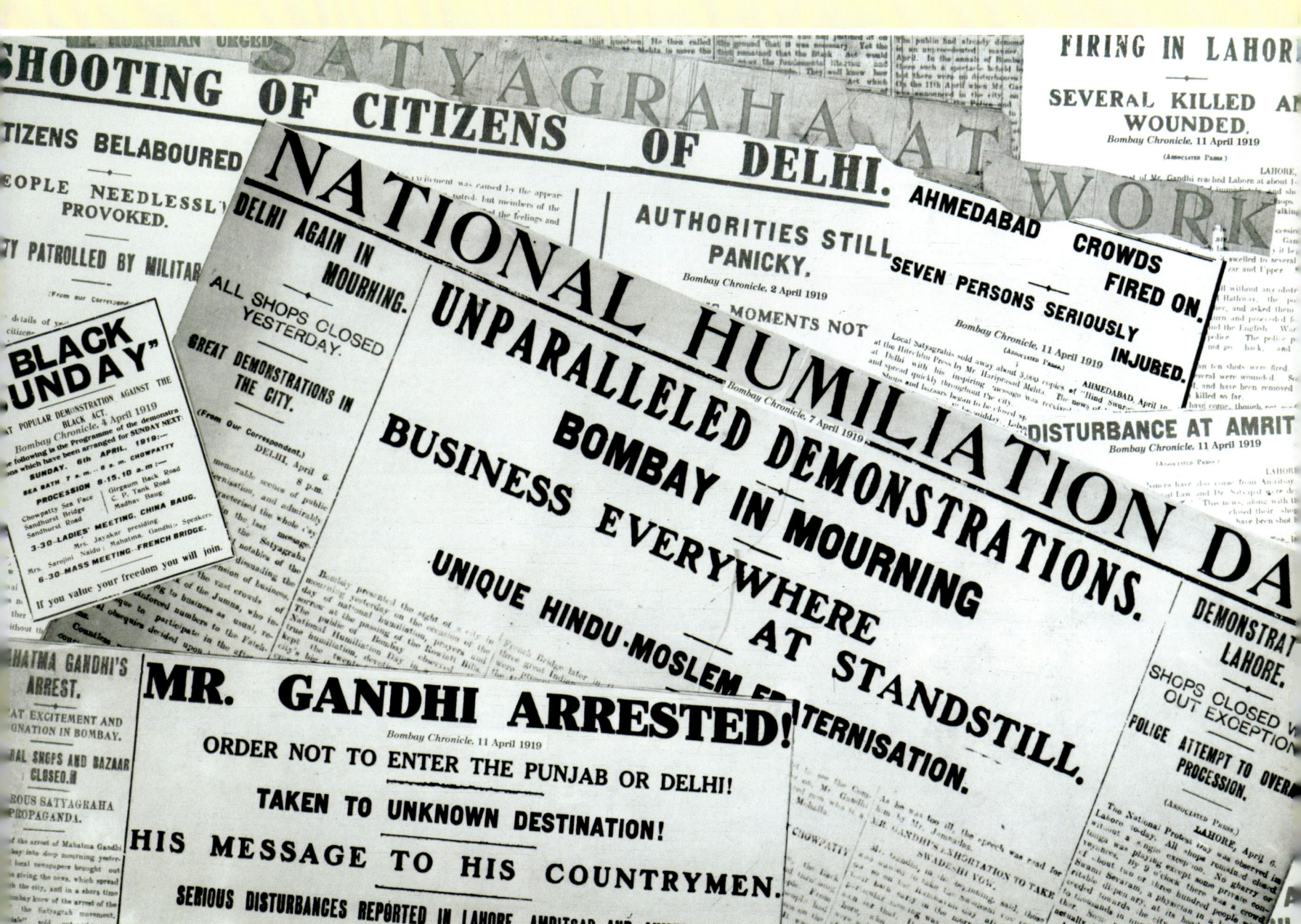

A glimpse of newspaper headlines, April 1919.

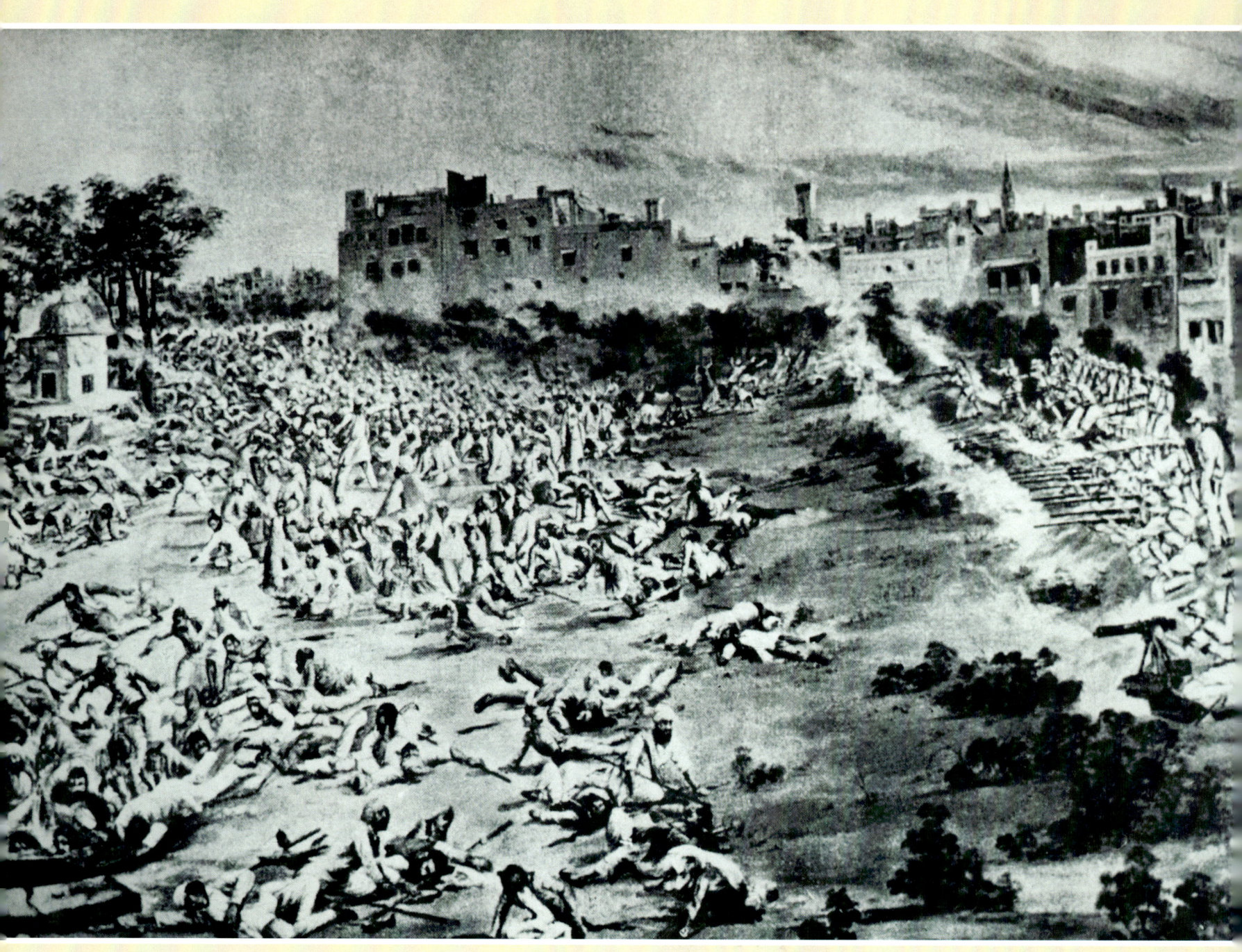

Massacre at Jallianwala Bagh. A painting by Gurdit Singh.

The Congress set up a separate enquiry under a subcommittee consisting of Gandhi, Motilal Nehru, C.R. Das, A.K. Fazlul Huq, and Abbas Tyabji, with K. Santhanam as the secretary. The enquiry revealed that General Dyer's action was nothing but a cold-blooded and calculated massacre of innocent and unarmed people. In 1920, the House of Lords voted its appreciation of General Dyer for his services, leading Gandhi to proclaim that *'cooperation in any shape or form with this satanic Government is sinful.'* Tagore was so distressed that he renounced his knighthood in protest against the Jallianwala Bagh massacre.

The events of 1919-20 set the stage for the next phase of the national movement led by the Congress.

Group photo taken at the time of Amritsar Congress of 1919. Motilal Nehru seated in the centre. Others seated on chairs include Madan Mohan Malaviya, Annie Besant, Swami Shradhanand and Bal Gangadhar Tilak. Jawaharlal Nehru is also seen sitting amongst others on the ground.

Motilal Nehru

Pandit Motilal Nehru, one of the topmost advocates of the Allahabad High Court, was the first member of the Nehru family to enter politics. After the Congress session of 1905, he decided to lend his support to the Moderate party. His first major public appearance was in 1907 when he presided over a UP Provincial Political Conference held in Allahabad.

1920

The Gandhian Era

1935

The Gandhian Era

1920 - 1935

MOHANDAS KARAMCHAND GANDHI

Pandit Jawaharlal Nehru observed that the Gandhian era in Congress politics began with the special session of the Congress at Calcutta in 1920. In *The Discovery of India,* he described it thus:

And then Gandhi came. He was like a powerful current of fresh air that made us stretch ourselves and take deep breaths; like a beam of light that pierced the darkness and removed the scales from our eyes; like a whirlwind that upset many things, but most of all the working of people's minds . . . The essence of his teaching was fearlessness and truth, and action allied to these, always keeping the welfare of the masses in view. The greatest gift for an individual or a nation, so we had been told in our ancient books, was abhaya (fearlessness), not merely bodily courage but the absence of fear from the mind . . . It was against this all-pervading fear that Gandhi's quiet and determined voice was raised: 'Be not afraid.'

Mohandas Karamchand Gandhi was born on 2 October 1869 at Porbandar in Gujarat. After completing his university studies in Bombay, he read law at the Inner Temple, London. He returned to India in 1891, but not for long. He left for South Africa in 1893 to handle the legal matters of a Kathiawadi merchant, Dada Abdullah.

Durban, then a booming town in the grip of gold fever, attracted a steady stream of Europeans and Americans. Indians, too, had started arriving in large numbers since 1860. Some were wealthy merchants, but most were poor indentured labourers working on sugar plantations and in coal mines, earning meagre sums. They formed the backbone of the domestic economy, but all Indians, both rich and poor, faced severe discrimination.

Gandhi experienced this racial prejudice first hand when he travelled by train to Pretoria on a first-class ticket, but was ordered to go to the van compartment reserved for blacks and Indians. When he refused, he was thrown off the train at Pietermaritzburg.

It was during this struggle that Gandhi began his experiments with *satyagraha,* non-violent resistance, based on the firmness of the force of truth, which crafted his approach to a lifelong struggle based on non-violence. This formed the basis of individual and collective social relations. Gandhi believed that *satyagraha* would inspire a change of heart in exploiters and oppressors.

Above:
Maulana Azad's 'Al-Hilal'
dated Calcutta, 3 December 1913,
backs Gandhi's struggle in South Africa.

Right:
Gandhi and Kasturba with G.A. Natesan
in Madras, 1915.

So effective was his strategy that as he was leaving South Africa for India, General Smuts remarked, *'The saint has left our shores, I sincerely hope for ever.'*

In 1915, Gandhi returned to India, but silently observed the political scene for a while, following the advice of his political mentor, Gokhale, to keep *'his ears open and his mouth shut.'* On 20 May 1915, he founded the Satyagraha Ashram near Ahmedabad.

His work in South Africa had convinced him that *satyagraha* was particularly relevant in tackling the problems confronting India in the early decades of the twentieth century. He kept himself aloof from the Home Rule movement, but used the time to travel across the country extensively to acquaint himself with various challenges confronting India. One such issue was the condition of tenant farmers in Champaran district in Bihar.

SATYAGRAHA AND THE MOBILISATION OF PEASANTS

Champaran

The tenant farmers of Champaran district, in Bihar, were forced to cultivate indigo even though it was an unprofitable proposition. Their protests were suppressed with a heavy hand by the planters, mostly European. In 1917, Gandhi, went to Champaran, accompanied by Babu

Arrival of Gandhi, 1915.

GANDHI'S SATYAGRAHA ON INDIAN SOIL

Satyagraha at Viramgam

It was through Bhai Motilal that Gandhi (1915) first became interested in the Viramgam question regarding customs and the hardships suffered by railway passengers on account of it. He met Lord Chelmsford and within a few days of this interview, the customs cordon was removed. Gandhi was of the strong opinion that the imminent possibility of passive resistance was the chief factor in obtaining the desired redress.

Anti–Indenture Struggle

The anti-indenture struggle (1917) prevented indentured Indian labour from being recruited for the British colonies. Although there was considerable public agitation, here, too, like Viramgam, success came merely through preparedness for satyagraha.

Champaran Satyagraha

The Champaran Satyagraha (April 1917) was undertaken to remedy the evils connected with indigo plantations. Here *satyagraha* was actually offered. The Champaran episode was a turning point in Gandhi's life. 'What I did,' he explained, 'was a very ordinary thing.

This is the beauty of Satyagraha. It comes up to us; we have not to go out in search for it. There is a virtue inherent in the principle itself. A *dharmayudha* (war of righteousness) in which there are no secrets to be guarded, no scope for cunning, and no place for untruth, comes unsought; and a man of religion is ever ready for it. A struggle which has to be previously planned is not a righteous struggle. In a righteous struggle God Himself plans the campaigns and conducts the battles. A war of righteousness can be waged only in the name of God; and it is only when the Satyagrahi feels quite helpless, when he is apparently on his last legs, and finds utter darkness all around him, that God comes to the rescue. God helps us when we feel ourselves humbler than the very dust under our feet. Only to the weak and helpless is divine succour vouchsafed.

—M.K. Gandhi

I declared that the British could not order me about in my own country.'

Mill Workers Satyagraha
The fourth struggle was that of the mill-hands of Ahmedabad against the mill-owners (1918). Gandhi succeeded in getting the mill owners to accept the principle of arbitration.

Kheda Satyagraha
The Kheda struggle (1917-18) concerned the over-assessment of land revenue by the government in a time of scarcity. A compromise was reached between the peasantry and the government without a fresh inquiry. It is noticeable, however, that the Joint Parliamentary Committee on Indian Reform in 1919 reported that there was a flaw in the land-revenue system of India, and asserted that a constitutional method for revising of these land-revenue assessments was badly needed. The result was that Gandhi was obliged to lead **Satyagraha in Bardoli** in 1928, in order to obtain a revision of the land assessment in that district. The Bardoli struggle was also carried out through non-violence, and it ended in a revision being granted.

Nationwide Hartal in Protest against Rowlatt Act
The sixth struggle was in connection with the Rowlatt Act involving persons who might be innocent being kept in prison without an open trial. The Rowlatt Act was finally repealed.

Non-Cooperation Movement
The non-cooperation movement was formally launched in 1921 to right the Khilafat and the Punjab wrongs and to win Swaraj. It received a very wide response all over the country, betokening a general mass awakening, the extent and intensity of which was a revelation, both to the people and to the government.

Vykom Satyagraha
In March 1925, a *satyagraha* campaign was launched at Vykom, in the erstwhile state of Travancore, to uphold the right of so-called untouchables to pass through the common roads to which access was denied to them.

Civil Disobedience Movement (or Salt Satyagraha)
Mahatma Gandhi launched the Civil Disobedience Movement as he marched on 12 March 1930 from Sabarmati Ashram to the seashore at Dandi to offer disobedience to the government by breaking the Salt Law by making salt himself.

Individual Satyagraha
The Second World War began in 1939 and the British government without consulting Congress leaders or the Indian Legislative Assembly declared India to be at war on 3 September 1939, the day England declared war on the German Reich. India was ready to consider giving help to the British government provided it made a firm commitment that independence would be granted to India. The British government was not ready to concede and this was what provoked Gandhi to launch individual *satyagraha* on 15 October 1940 to openly pursue the anti-war propaganda, with Vinoba Bhave being the first *satyagrahi*.

Quit India Movement
On 8 August 1942, under the leadership of Gandhi at the AICC meeting in Bombay, it was resolved *'to sanction for the vindication of India's inalienable right to freedom and independence, the starting of a mass struggle on non-violent lines on the non-violent strength....'* And to his countrymen and women Gandhi gave the mantra of *'Do or Die'*. The mass awakening and mass revolt witnessed during the Quit India Movement eventually led India from slavery to freedom on 15 August 1947.

Rajendra Prasad, Mazharul Haque, J.B. Kripalani, Narahari Parikh, and Mahadev Desai, in order to study the situation and to help the peasants. The authorities, seeing this as a threat, ordered him to leave. He refused and courted arrest. His willingness to face trial and imprisonment forced the authorities to appoint an inquiry committee on which Gandhi served as a member. This led to the amelioration of some of the conditions faced by the peasants in Champaran and the redressal of their grievances. The success of *satyagraha* as a method of peaceful agitation and protest, as well as of mass peasant mobilisation, encouraged its adoption elsewhere in the country.

Kheda

In 1918, Kheda district in Gujarat became the next arena for the implementation of *satyagraha.* Here, this revolutionary new strategy of mass action was used to get revenue collection waived in times of acute famine. Before Gandhi's arrival on the scene, the peasants had never imagined that they could dare question the right of the government to collect taxes or demand remission of assessment in years of famine when the crops failed. They used to only petition for waivers, but their pleas always went unheard.

The Kheda *satyagraha* also saw the entry of Vallabhbhai Patel into public life. Sardar Patel, as he came to be known later, was elected municipal councillor and the secretary of the Gujarat Sabha in Ahmedabad. From 1924 to 1928, he was chairman of the Municipal Committee. He joined the Kheda campaign and became a follower of Gandhi, working with him to educate the peasants on their right to question the government authorities to tax them. He urged them to shed their fear of officials, encouraging them to meet coercion with civility, force with restraint.

Under the leadership of Gandhi and Sardar Patel, the peasants of Kheda courted arrest after removing crops from the lands that had been wrongfully attached by the authorities. Their efforts forced the government to suspend revenue assessment in the case of poor peasants.

Ahmedabad

In 1918, Gandhi intervened in a dispute between weavers and mill owners in Ahmedabad, Gujarat. He succeeded in getting the mill owners to accept the principle of arbitration. However, negotiations broke down and there was a lockout. Gandhi advised the workers not to resume work until their demands were met. He himself undertook a fast unto death.

Eventually, a compromise was reached through the good offices of Sarladevi and Anasuyabai, the wife and the sister respectively of Ambalal Sarabhai, one of the principal mill owners. This laid the foundation of a strong union between Congress leaders and workers and led to the establishment of the Textile Labour Association.

KHILAFAT MOVEMENT

Gandhi gradually began to make his presence felt in the national movement and eventually came to deeply influence the leadership of the Congress. Initially, he had been open to cooperation with the government, but the events in Punjab in 1919 and the Khilafat movement, in which he supported the protest of the Muslims, changed his thinking, and altered the course of the national movement as well.

The Khilafat movement rose in protest against the British government's refusal to return to Turkey the lands taken from it. Indian ministries reacted strongly, as the British prime minister, Lloyd George, went back on his promise to do so, and Khilafat movement was launched. The All India Khilafat Conference held in Delhi in November 1919 decided to withdraw all cooperation from the government if their demands were not met. Many Congress leaders, led by Gandhi and Tilak, supported the movement. The protesters observed 19 March 1920 as a day of national mourning, marked by

The accused in the famous Karachi Trial in 1921: Shaukat Ali, Shankaracharya, Muhammad Ali, and Dr Kitchlew.

hartals, fasting, and prayers. Given the government's indifference to their demands, an all-party conference convened at Allahabad in June 1920 approved a programme of boycott of schools, colleges, and law courts.

NON-COOPERATION

The Congress formally adopted Gandhi's plan of non-cooperation at a special session in Calcutta in 1920. The resolution stated:

THE CIVIL RESISTANCE PART OF SATYAGRAHA

OR

TEMPORARY SUSPENSION TO CONTINUE.

MR. GANDHI'S LETTER TO THE PRESS.

The Government of India have given me, through His Excellency the Governor of Bombay, a grave warning that resumption of Civil Disobedience is likely to be attended with serious consequences to the public security. This warning has been enforced by His Excellency the Governor himself at interviews to which I was summoned In response to this warning and to the urgent desire, publicly expressed by Dewan Bahadur Govinda Raghava Iyer, Sir Narayan Chandavarkar and several editors, I have, after deep consideration, decided not to resume Civil Resistance for the time being. I may add that several prominent friends belonging to what is called the Extremist Party have given me the same advice on the sole ground of their fear of recrudescence of violence on the part of those who might not have understood the doctrine of Civil Resistance. When in common with most other Satyagrahis, I came to the conclusion that time was ripe for the resumption of the Civil Resistance part of Satyagraha, I sent a respectful letter to His Excellency the Viceroy advising him of my intention so to do and urging that Rowlatt Legislation should be withdrawn, that an early declaration be made as to the appointment of a strong and impartial committee to investigate the ... disturbances with power to revise the sentences passed, and that Babu Kalinath Roy who was, as could be proved from the record of the case, unjustly convicted should be released. The Government of India deserve thanks for the decision in Mr Roy's case. Though it does not do full justice to Mr. Roy, the very material reduction in the sentence is a substantial measure of justice. I have been assured that the Committee of Inquiry, such as I have urged for, is in the process of being appointed. With these indications of goodwill it would be unwise on my part not to listen to the warning given by the Government. Indeed it is a further demonstration of the true nature of Civil Resistance. A Civil Resister never seeks to embarrass Government.

He often co-operates and does not hesitate civilly to resist where resistance becomes a duty to resist where the goal by creating goodwill. He attains the goal that unfailing exercise believing as he does that unjust acts of goodwill even in the face of unjust acts of a Government can only result in good will being ultimately returned by the Government. Further suspension of Civil Resistance is, therefore, nothing but a practical application of Satyagraha.

Yet it is no small matter for me to suspend Civil Resistance even for a day while ment Civil Legislation continues to disfigure Rowlatt Legislation continues to disfigure our statute book. The Lahore and Amritsar judgments make suspension still more difficult. Those judgments, read by me with an unbiassed mind, have left an indelible impression that most of the Punjab leaders have been convicted without sufficient proof and that the punishments inflicted on them are inhuman and outrageous. The judgments go to show that they have been convicted for no other reason than that they were connected with stubborn agitation against Rowlatt Legislation. I would, if I had my way, have therefore preferred to court imprisonment to resuming the restricted liberty vouchsafed to me by the Government of India. But a Satyagrahi has to swallow many a bitter pill and the suspension is one such. I feel that I shall better serve the country and the ... Government and those Punjab leaders who, in my opinion, have been so unjustly convicted and so cruelly sentenced by suspension of Civil Resistance for the time being.

But this suspension while it lightens my responsibility by reason of the feared outbreak of violence, makes it incumbent upon the Government and the eminent public men who have advised suspension to see that the Rowlatt Legislation is removed without delay.

I have been accused of throwing lighted matches. If my occasional Civil Resistance is a lighted match, Rowlatt Legislation and persistence in retaining it on the statute book is a thousand matches scattered throughout India, and the only way to avoid Civil Resistance altogether is to withdraw that legislation. Nothing that the Government have published in justification of that legislation has moved the Indian public from the attitude of opposition to it.

I have thus suspended Civil Resistance. But hasten the end of that legislation by Satyagrahis will pay for its removal by their lives if it cannot be removed by their lives. The period of suspension is lesser remain. The period of suspension is for Satyagrahis an opportunity for further discipline in an enlightened and willing

obedience to the laws of the State. The right of Civil Resistance is derived from the duty of obedience ... voluntarily performed ... And Satyagraha consists not merely, or even chiefly, in civilly resisting laws, but mainly in promoting national welfare by strict adherence to Truth. I would respectfully advise fellow Satyagrahis and seek the co-operation of all great and small in the propagation of pure Swadeshi and promotion of Hindu Moslem unity. Swadeshi is, I hold, a necessity of national existence. No Englishman or Indian can view with equanimity the huge enforced waste of the labour of twenty crore peasants during half the year. That labour can be quickly and immediately utilised only by restoring to the women their spinning wheels and to the men their handlooms. This means the elimination of the Japanese and Lancashire interest and the unnatural connection and makes the partition of the unnatural connection and makes the elimination of the city possible. The elimination of the Japanese menace will avert a national and Imperial disaster. Extension of Japan's Imperial commerce can hold upon India through her commerce can end only in India's degradation or a bloody war.

The Hindu Moslem unity is equally a national and Imperial necessity. A voluntary League between Hindus, Mahomedans and Englishmen is a league in my conception infinitely superior to, and purer than the League of Nations just formed. Permanent union between Hindus and Mahomedans is the preliminary to such a Triple Union. That unity can be materially advanced by the Hindus whole heartedly associating themselves with the Mahomedans in their very just aspirations regarding the Caliphate, the holy Mecca and the other holy places of Islam.

The Swadeshi propaganda and work for Hindu Moslem unity require powers of organisation, honesty of purpose, integrity in trade, and immense self sacrifice and self restraint. It is, therefore, easy enough to perceive that Swadeshi propaganda on the purest lines and promotion of Hindu Moslem unity cannot but have an indirect, though none the less effective, bearing on the movement for securing withdrawal of Rowlatt Legislation for which the Government can claim no justification little as they can claim even now when we give an unexampled demonstration of the qualities named above.

Laburnum Road,   M. K. Gandhi
July 21, 1919.

YOUNG INDIA, Wednesday, July 23, 1919.

'The Civil Resistance Part of Satyagraha'

Temporary Suspension to Continue

Mr. Gandhi's Letter to the Press

The Government of India have given me, through His Excellency the Governor of Bombay, a grave warning that resumption of Civil Disobedience is likely to be attended with serious consequences to the public security. This warning has been enforced by His Excellency the Governor himself at interviews to which I was summoned. In response to this warning and to the urgent desire, publicly expressed by Dewan Bahadur Govinda Raghava Iyer, Sir Narayan Chandavarkar and several editors, I have, after deep consideration, decided not to resume Civil Resistance for time being. I may add that several prominent friends belonging to what is called the Extremist Party have given me the same advice on the sole ground of their fear of recrudescence of violence on the part of those who might not have understood the doctrine of Civil Resistance. When, in common with most other Satyagrahis, I came to the conclusion that time was ripe for the resumption of the Civil Resistance part of Satyagraha, I sent a respectful letter to His Excellency the Viceroy advising him of my intention so to do and urging that Rowlatt Legislation should be withdrawn, that an early declaration be made as to the appointment of a strong and impartial committee to investigate the Punjab disturbances with power to revise the sentences passed, and that Babu Kalinath Roy who was, as could be proved from the record of the case, unjustly convicted, should be released. The Government of India deserve thanks for the decision in Mr. Roy's case. Though it does not do full justice to Mr. Roy, the very material reduction in the sentence is a substantial measure of justice. I have been assured that the Committee of Inquiry, such as I have urged for, is in the process of being appointed. With these indications of goodwill it would be unwise on my part not to listen to the warning given by the Government. Indeed my acceptance of the Government's advice is a further demonstration of the true nature of Civil Resistance. A Civil Resister never seeks to embarrass Government. He often co-operates and does not hesitate civilly to resist where resistance becomes a duty. He attains the goal by creating goodwill, believing as he does that unfailing exercise of goodwill even in the face of unjust acts of a Government can only result in goodwill being ultimately returned by the Governments. Further suspension of Civil Resistance is, therefore, nothing but a practical application of Satyagraha.

Yet it is no small matter for me to suspend Civil Resistance even for a day while Rowlatt Legislation continues to disfigure our statute book. The Lahore and Amritsar judgments make suspension still more difficult. Those judgments, read by me with an unbiased mind, have left an indelible impression that most of the Punjab leaders have been convicted without sufficient proof and that the punishment inflicted on them are inhuman and outrageous. The judgments go to show that they have been convicted for no other reason than that they were connected with stubborn agitation against Rowlatt Legislation. I would, if I had my way, have therefore preferred to court imprisonment to retaining the restricted liberty vouchsafed to me by the Government of India. But a Satyagrahi has to follow many a bitter pill and the present suspension is one such. I feel that we shall better serve the country and the Government and those Punjabi leaders who, in my opinion, have been so unjustly convicted and so cruelly sentenced, by suspension of Civil Resistance for the time being.

… I have been accused of throwing lighted matches. If my occasional Civil Resistance be a lighted match, Rowlatt Legislation and persistence in retaining it on the statute book is a thousand matches scattered throughout India, and the only way to avoid Civil Resistance altogether is to withdraw that legislation…

… Satyagraha consists not merely, or even chiefly, in civilly resisting laws, but mainly in promoting national welfare by strict adherence to Truth. I would respectfully advise fellow Satyagrahis and seek the co-operation of all great and small in the propagation of pure Swadeshi and promotion of Hindu-Moslem unity. Swadeshi is, I hold, a necessity of national existence…

The Hindu-Moslem unity is equally a national and Imperial necessity…. The Swadeshi propaganda and work for Hindu-Moslem unity require powers of organisation, honesty of purpose, integrity in trade, and immense self-sacrifice and self-restraint. It is, therefore, easy enough to perceive that Swadeshi propaganda on the purest lines and promotion of Hindu-Moslem unity cannot but have an indirect, though none the less effective, bearing on the movement for securing withdrawal of Rowlatt Legislation for which the Government can claim no justification—little as they can claim even now—when we give an unexampled demonstration of the qualities named above.

M.K. GANDHI

Laburnum Road

This Congress is further of the opinion that there is no course left open for the people of India but to approve of and adopt the policy of progressive non-violent, non-cooperation inaugurated by Mahatma Gandhi until the said wrongs are righted and Swarajya is established.

In pursuance of this, the Congress advised the following actions:

- Surrender of titles and honorary offices, and resignation from nominated seats in local bodies.

- Refusal to attend government levees, *durbars,* and other official and semi-official functions held by government officials, or those held in their honour.

- Gradual withdrawal of children from schools and colleges owned, aided or controlled by the government, and in place of such schools and colleges, the establishment of national schools and colleges in the various provinces.

- Gradual boycott of British courts by lawyers and litigants, and the establishment of private arbitration courts for the settlement of disputes.

- Refusal on the part of the military and the clerical and labouring classes to offer themselves as recruits for service in Mesopotamia.

- Withdrawal by candidates of their candidature for election to the reformed councils, and refusal on the part of the voters to vote for any candidate who may, despite the Congress advice, offer himself for election.

- Boycott of foreign goods.

The Congress also advised the adoption of *swadeshi* and encouraged hand spinning and hand weaving for the production of *khadi*.

Response to the Call

More than 30,000 Congressmen, including Motilal and Jawaharlal Nehru, courted arrest in defiance of 'lawless laws'. Gandhi had opened up a new path for mass participation of ordinary people in the national movement, bringing within its fold peasants, industrial workers, and tribal communities who could identify with him and his philosophy. People from all over the country responded to his call—Hindus and Muslims, the mercantile and professional classes, as well as workers and peasants. This further legitimised the struggle led by the Congress by imparting it a moral and ethical dimension.

The resolution on non-cooperation was reaffirmed at the Nagpur session in December 1920. It evoked a tremendous response throughout the country. In 1921, the Congress Working Committee (CWC) took up the task of collecting 10 million rupees for the Tilak Swarajya Fund, the enlistment of 10 million Congress members, and the introduction of

Mahatma Gandhi, with shaved head, donned a loincloth in the last week of September 1921 in Madura. Thereafter, he began promoting handspun *khadi* and its adoption by one and all, as he appealed publicly to workers and businessmen alike to reject foreign cloth.

Right: A news story from *Ananda Bazar Patrika,* 8 July 1921.

Business in Foreign Cloth to be Totally Stopped

MAHATMA GANDHI'S INJUNCTION

BOMBAY MERCHANTS GIVEN TWO MONTHS' TIME TO CLEAR STOCKS

SUPREME DUTY OF INDIAN MILL-OWNE...

(Associated Press of India.)

Bombay, July 6.

Anxiety is felt among the wholesale piece goods merchants of Bombay over Mr. Gandhi's latest injunction that business in foreign cloth should be stopped within the next two months and that all should ... nothing but homespun coarse cloth, ... ing the Indian mill-made cloth to be ... amed by the poor country folks. Mr. ... hi asserts that the problem of the ... poverty of India can only be solv-... the revival of handspinning and that ... for foreign article has so vitally in-... jured, the country as foreign cloth by tak-... ing away annually sixty crores of rupees out of India.

An informal Conference was recently held between Mr. Gandhi and dealers in piece-goods when it is stated that the former gave them two months' time to clear their present stocks and cancel their orders. He warned them that their shops would be picquetted if they did not within these two months refrain from dealing in imported piecegoods. As a result some dealers have already signed a pledge promising to re-frain from importing foreign cloths and others regard the future with anxiety since at the present moment about seventy five thousand packages of foreign piece-goods worth nearly fifteen crores of rupees are lying in Bombay ... beside goods in their own ...

owing to the last year's unsatisfactory mon-soons.

One of the leading piecegoods merchants interviewed to-day by a representative of the "Associated Press" expressed the opi-nion that Mr. Gandhi's new movement is bound to affect the trade materially at least for a time and further accentuate the present depression in the import trade, though for economic reasons it might not be possible to shut out imports altogether. Since December last the im-port of piecegoods had practically stopped. Their anxiety was for the disposal of the stocks in hand as re-exports were Practi-cally nil, Persia, Arabia, East Africa and Afghanistan being at present out of the Indian Market.

Other dealers are inclined to think that the effect on the market will be only tem-porary, as the public cannot totally do without some special lines of imported goods and the up country demand should increase with the progress of the monsoon and the future depended upon that factor. The prices of Lancashire goods are nominally steady.

All merchants are however agreed on the point that Mr. Gandhi's movement will give a big impetus to local mill made goods the prices of which are hardening. Mr. Gandhi has addressed an open letter to the mill-owners urging them to help the country by not raising the prices of their goods, when

200,000 *charkhas*. The Nagpur session also made some changes in the Congress constitution, including the linguistic reorganisation of Provincial Congress Committees (PCCs), establishment of the 15-member Congress Committee, and reduction of membership fee to four *annas* for broad-basing the party membership. In this session, the Congress for the first time enunciated its policy regarding the people's movement in the princely states, asking the provinces to grant full government facility and protection to the people living within their borders.

In a move aimed at weakening the growing momentum of the national movement, the British government announced a visit by the Prince of Wales to India in 1921. However, as a result of the non-cooperation movement, the event faced boycott and massive demonstrations. When the Prince landed in Bombay on 17 November 1921, Gandhi was addressing a large group of 60,000 in the heart of the city. In contrast, so few turned up to welcome the Prince that he remarked wryly after a visit to the university that empty stands and seats had been sought to be filled with high school boys, scouts, and Europeans.

CIVIL DISOBEDIENCE

The Ahmedabad session of the Congress in 1921 reaffirmed the party's determination to continue with non-cooperation with greater vigour with the objective of attaining *swaraj*. The session resolved that civil disobedience was the only civilised and effective substitute for armed rebellion. In response, thousands of students left government schools and colleges and joined national schools and colleges. Jamia Millia Islamia, Bihar Vidyapith, Kashi Vidyapith, and Gujarat Vidyapith were established during this period.

Thousands of peasants in the United Provinces, Bengal, Punjab, Assam, Andhra Pradesh (Guntur district), and along the Malabar coast responded to the call. The Congress-led movement was now transformed into a nationwide mass movement. Hundreds of lawyers like Motilal Nehru, Rajendra Prasad, and Sardar Patel gave up their lucrative practices. Women donated their jewellery for the nationalist cause. Huge bonfires of foreign clothes were organised publicly. *Khadi* became the symbol of the freedom struggle. The Congress now took the movement to a higher level, encouraging the Provincial Congress Committees to begin civil disobedience of British laws, including non-payment of taxes.

The government met this move with severe repression. By the end of 1921, most of the important Congress leaders, except Gandhi, were in jail. However, some Congress members, who favoured a truce between the Congress and the government, advocated the more traditional modes of agitation. During this time, Mohammed

Left: A successful drive for the collection of one crore rupees for the Tilak Swarajya Fund. Mahatma Gandhi portrayed as 'India's Miracle-Worker', as reported in the Special Supplement of the *Bombay Chronicle*, 1 July 1921.

Centre: 'Perhaps My Last Words', Mahatma Gandhi's moving appeal, published in the *Bombay Chronicle*, 18 November 1921, relates to his distress over the Bombay riots.

Right: 'Complete Hartal in Calcutta', a news story from *Ananda Bazar Patrika*, 18 Novemver 1921.

Ali Jinnah, G.S. Khaparde, Bipin Chandra Pal, and Annie Besant broke away from the Congress. .

A representative meeting of all parties, held in Bombay in January 1922, proposed the postponement of civil disobedience and called for an early convening of a Round Table Conference in London with authority to settle the questions of Khilafat, Punjab, and *swaraj*. However, the British government did not respond favourably.

As a result, mass civil disobedience—a no-tax campaign—was planned in the Bardoli *taluka* of Gujarat under Gandhi's direct supervision. The Bardoli Satyagraha of 1928 was one of the most important civil disobedience campaigns. Vallabhbhai Patel, who played a major role in ensuring its success, was given the title of 'Sardar' by Gandhi.

Similar campaigns were also planned in four districts of Andhra Pradesh.

Chauri Chaura

In February 1922, the civil disobedience movement received a setback when a Congress procession of about 3,000 peasants in Chauri Chaura, in Gorakhpur district in the United Provinces, was fired upon by the police. The angry protesters surrounded the police *thana,* in which about 20 policemen were trapped, and burnt it. This so anguished Gandhi that he

Bonfire of foreign clothes: public notice and the public in action.

called off the movement. Many Congress leaders were upset by this decision as they felt that it had slowed down a movement that was gaining momentum. The younger nationalists saw this as a retreat.

On 12 February 1922, the Congress Working Committee, at its meeting in Bardoli, endorsed the decision to suspend civil disobedience for the time being and urged Congressmen to take up constructive programmes.

Arrest of Gandhi

On 10 March 1922, Gandhi was arrested on charges of sedition and sentenced to six years' imprisonment.

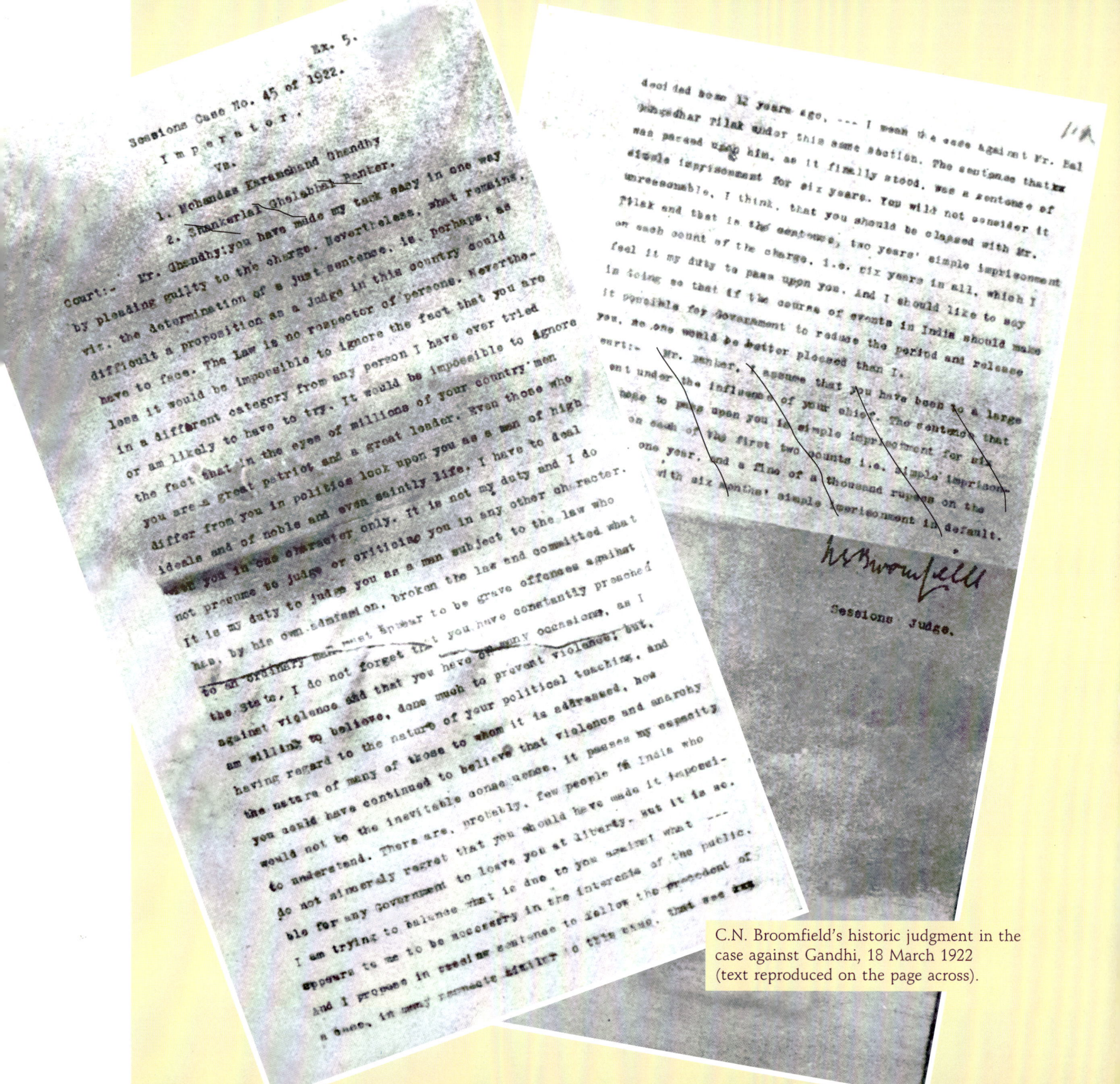

C.N. Broomfield's historic judgment in the case against Gandhi, 18 March 1922 (text reproduced on the page across).

Session Case No. 45 of 1922
Imperator v/s Mohandas Karamchand Ghendhy

Court:- Mr. Ghendhy: you have made my task easy in one way by pleading guilty to the charge. Nevertheless, what remains viz. the determination of a just sentence, is perhaps, as difficult a proposition as a Judge in this country could have to face. The Law is no respector of persons. Nevertheless it would be impossible to ignore the fact that you are in a different category from any person I have ever tried or am likely to have to try. It would be impossible to ignore the fact that in the eyes of millions of your countrymen you are a great patriot and a great leader. Even those who differ from you in politics look upon you as a man of high ideals and of noble and even saintly life. I have to deal with you in one character only. It is not my duty and I do not presume to judge or criticise you in any other character. It is my duty to judge you as a man subject to the law who has by his own admission, broken the law and committed what to an ordinary man must appear to be grave offences against the State. I do not forget that you have constantly preached against violence and that you have on many occasions, as I am willing to believe, done much to prevent violence: but, having regard to the nature of your political teaching, and the nature of many of those to whom it is addressed, how you could have continued to believe that violence and anarchy would not be the inevitable consequence, it passes my capacity to understand. There are, practically, few people in India who do not sincerely regret that you should have made it impossible for any Government to leave you at liberty. But it is so. I am trying to balance what is due to you against what appears to me to be necessary in the interests of the public. And I propose in passing sentence to follow the precedent of a case, in many respects similar to this case, that was decided some 12 years ago—I mean a case against Mr. Bal Gangadhar Tilak under this same action. The sentence that was passed upon him, as it finally stood, was a sentence of simple imprisonment for six years. You would not consider it unreasonable, I think, that you should be classed with Mr. Tilak and that in the sentence, two years' simple imprisonment on each count of the charge, i.e. six years in all, which I feel it is my duty to pass upon you. And I should like to say in doing so that if the course of events in India should make it possible for Government to reduce the period and release you, no one would be better pleased than I.

18/3/1922

C.N. Broomfield
(Sessions Judge)

Above: Gandhi's cell in Sabarmati Prison, 1922.

SWARAJISTS

Meanwhile, a major debate emerged within the Congress on the question of Congressmen contesting elections to legislative councils. Some members like Dr M.A. Ansari, C. Rajagopalachari, and S. Srinivasa Iyengar were in favour of boycotting the councils. Others like Motilal Nehru and Hakim Ajmal Khan recommended the entry of Congress members to the councils in order to oppose the government from within. Many Congressmen felt that it was important to move into positions from where they could influence the achievement of *swaraj*. At the Gaya session of the Congress in 1922, sharp differences emerged on this issue.

While Gandhi was in prison, some members like C.R. Das and Motilal Nehru left the Congress in December 1922 to form the Congress-Khilafat Swarajya Party to contest the next council elections with the aim of focusing attention on their demands from within by means of *'uniform, consistent and continuous obstruction.'* Many Swarajists increasingly favoured a position of 'responsive cooperation' with the government for the achievement of *swaraj*. They, however, continued to function as a group within the Congress.

At the special session of the Congress at Delhi in September 1923, presided over by Maulana Abul Kalam Azad, the pro-council section had its way.

MOTILAL NEHRU (1861-1931)

President, 34th Session, Amritsar-1919 and 43rd Session, Calcutta-1928.

Pandit Motilal Nehru was a brilliant lawyer, an eloquent speaker, a great parliamentarian, and an able organiser. In 1928, he drafted the first constitution for India, known as the Nehru Report. He also founded the newspaper *Independence*.

CHITTARANJAN DAS (1870-1925)

President, 37th Session, Gaya-1922.

C.R. Das, fondly called Deshbandhu, was known for his handling of both civil and criminal law. He formed the All India Swarajya Party along with Motilal Nehru. Deshbandhu stressed the need for constructive work in villages and called for 'swaraj for the masses, not for the classes.'

MAULANA ABUL KALAM AZAD (1888-1958)

President, Special Session, Delhi-1923 and 53rd Session, Ramgarh-1940.

Maulana Abul Kalam Azad was a scholar and poet par excellence. He founded two weekly journals, *Al-Hilal* and *Al-Balagh*. He was one of the most prominent Muslim leaders to support Hindu-Muslim unity, opposing the partition of India on communal lines. After independence, he became the first Minister of Education in the Indian government.

MAULANA MOHAMMAD ALI (1878-1931)

President, 38th Session, Cocanada-1923.

Maulana Mohammad Ali, a journalist by profession, wrote on contemporary political issues and was among the leading figures of the Khilafat movement. He established an English weekly, *Comrade,* and an Urdu daily, *Hamdard.* He was one of the founders of the Jamia Millia Islamia in Delhi.

S. SRINIVASA IYENGAR (1874-1941)

President, 41st Session, Gauhati-1926.

Srinivasa Iyengar, a prominent Indian lawyer, freedom fighter, and political leader, published the Swaraj Constitution. He also organised the Independence League along with Nehru and Bose. A believer in 'linked leadership', Iyengar is credited with bringing the Madras region into the Congress fold.

MUKHTAR AHMAD ANSARI (1880-1936)

President, 42nd Session, Madras-1927.

Dr M.A. Ansari, a well-known physician and a respected nationalist leader, played an important role in the negotiations leading to the 1916 Lucknow Pact. A Gandhian, he was against the separatist stance of the Muslim League. He was one of the founders of the Jamia Millia Islamia in Delhi.

DIFFERENT VOICES

In 1924, Gandhi was released from jail prematurely for an appendicitis operation. He did not support the issue of council entry as he felt that this was inconsistent with the principle of non-cooperation. Hence, after his release from prison, Gandhi moved to the Sabarmati Ashram to work for the Harijans (Children of God) and continued with his *swadeshi* campaign for popularising the use of *khadi*. The *charkha* (spinning wheel) and *khadi* became the symbols of Gandhi's aim of achieving a *'self-reliant society attuned to the needs of the weak and the peasants.'* Gandhi's own simple loincloth represented his identification with the common people.

On 1 May 1923, a procession carrying the national flag in Nagpur was attacked and many people were arrested, among them Jamnalal Bajaj, and the Nagpur Satyagraha soon developed into an all-India movement.

During this phase of the national movement, there were many occasions when Gandhi's views were at variance with those of other leaders. There were times when, depending on the circumstances, he recommended a different course of action, which has sometimes been interpreted as vacillation and indecision. However, it should be viewed as evidence of the vibrancy of the movement, which encouraged debate and dissent. This

MOHANDAS KARAMCHAND GANDHI (1869-1948)

President, 39th Session, Belgaum-1924.

Mahatma Gandhi pioneered *satyagraha*—the firmness of the force truth—in South Africa in the fight against apartheid in 1906. A philosophy firmly founded upon *ahimsa,* or total non-violence, *satyagraha* helped India gain independence, and inspired movements for civil rights and freedom across the world. The advent of Mahatma Gandhi on the scene transformed the Indian freedom struggle into a mass movement. He launched the Non-cooperation and Civil Disobedience campaigns throughout the country. He gave the 'do or die' slogan, which galvanised his countrymen to action. He dedicated his life to alleviating poverty, liberating women, and ending caste discrimination, with the ultimate objective being self-rule for India. Gandhi promoted the *charkha* (spinning wheel) as a symbol of people's empowerment and *khadi* as a symbol of self-sufficiency. He wrote *Hind Swaraj* and *My Experiments with Truth* and edited the journals *Young India* and *Harijan.* Revered as the Father of the Nation, his birthday, 2 October, is commemorated as Gandhi Jayanti, a national holiday in India, and worldwide as the International Day of Non-violence.

73

encouraged people to express conflicting views and thoughts, without losing sight of the eventual goal—India's independence.

It is a mark of Gandhi's sagacity that as president of the Belgaum session of the Congress in 1924, he reached an agreement with Motilal Nehru and C.R. Das, emphasising that *'the Swaraj party represents, if not a majority, at least a strong and growing minority in the Congress.'* He also stated significantly, *'It is easy for me to get out of the Congress . . . but it was not, so I thought, and still think, in the interest of the country for me to take that step.'*

Gandhi delivering the presidential address at the opening session of the Belgaum Congress, 1924.

A caricature that appeared in a British journal, 1928.

Emergence of Jawaharlal Nehru

A new leader—young, dynamic, inspirational, fiery—emerged on the horizon, Jawaharlal Nehru. He soon came to dominate the national stage with his intellect, charisma, and towering personality.

Jawaharlal, son of Pandit Motilal Nehru, was born into a distinguished family from Allahabad, and was educated at Harrow and Cambridge. In England, he was exposed to Fabian socialism. He attended the Conference on Colonial Oppression and Imperialism at Brussels as a representative of the Congress in 1927. His visit to Russia greatly influenced his thinking. He presided over the first All Bengal Conference of Students in August 1928.

He firmly believed that the objective of the Congress was to free the poor and the oppressed from exploitation. He also saw the national movement in India as part of a wider struggle between the capitalist societies of Europe and the subject societies of Asia and Africa, pointing to the organic relationship between the capitalist mode of production and imperialism. Strongly convinced that complete independence was the only worthy goal for the country, he joined the Congress.

Broadening of the Movement

Throughout the 1920s, the national movement gained momentum and the Congress

JAWAHARLAL NEHRU (1889-1964)

President 44th Session, Lahore-1929; 49th Session, Lucknow-1936; 50th Session, Faizpur-1937; 57th Session, New Delhi-1951; 58th Session, Hyderabad-1953; and 59th Session, Kalyani-1954.

Pandit Nehru, one of the most important figures of the Indian independence movement, was a charismatic and radical leader. He was the first prime minister of India (1947-1964); was awarded the Bharat Ratna in 1955; and authored *The Discovery of India*. Nehru was an advocate of Fabian socialism. He believed that the public sector was an effective means for addressing the long-standing challenges of economic development in poorer nations. As a co-founder of the Non-aligned Movement, he was also an important figure in the international politics of the post-war era.

Jawaharlal Nehru being taken out in a procession in
Calcutta in 1928.

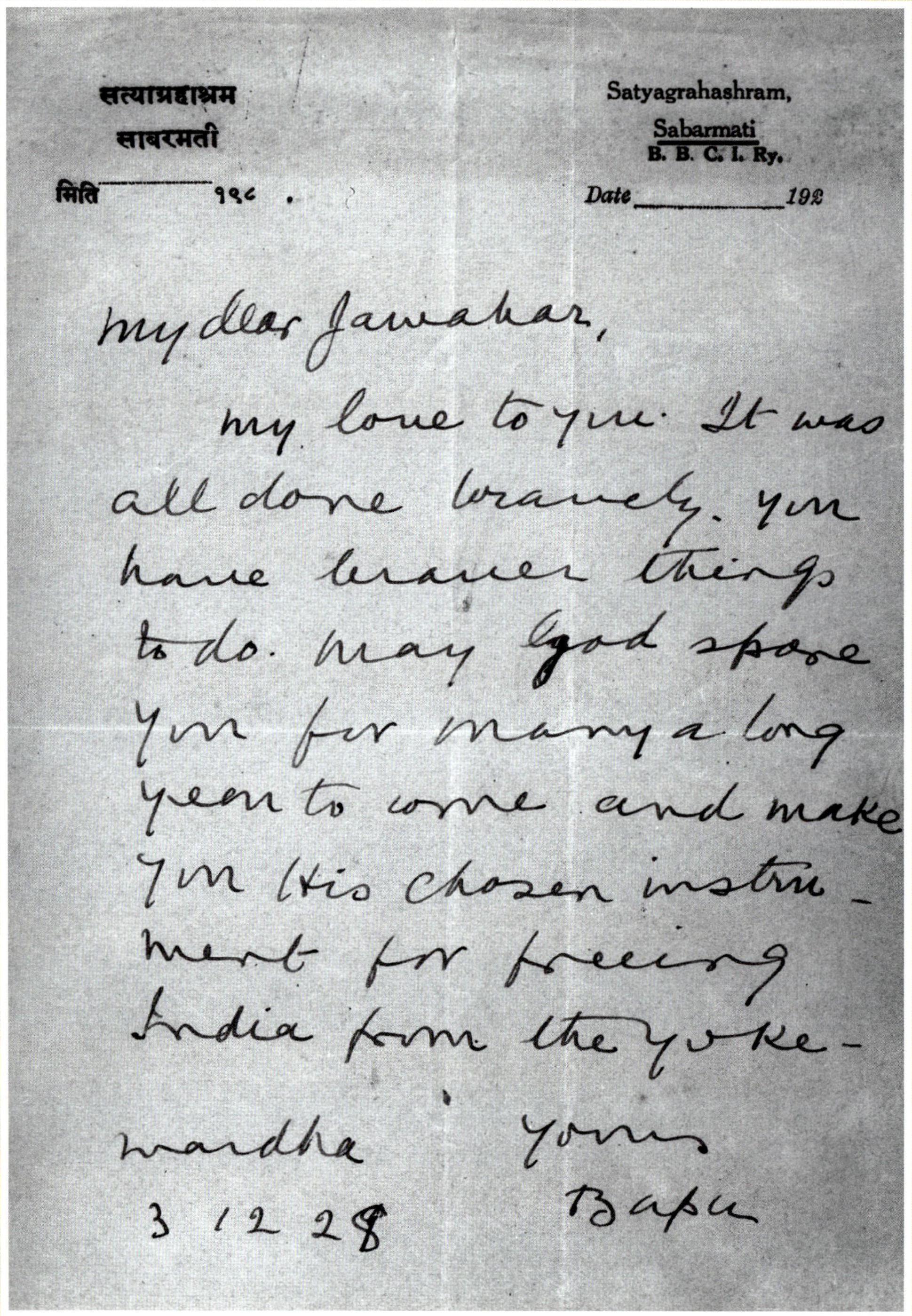

सत्याग्रहाश्रम
साबरमती

मिति _____ १९८ . ?

Satyagrahashram,
Sabarmati
B. B. C. I. Ry.

Date _____ 192

my dear Jawahar,

my love to you. It was all done bravely. you have braver things to do. may God spare you for many a long year to come and make you His chosen instru-ment for freeing India from the yoke-

wardha
3 12 28

yours
Bapu

Gandhi's letter to Jawaharlal Nehru dated 3 December 1928. Nehru had earlier led a demonstration in Lucknow during which he had faced *lathi* blows by mounted police.

Gandhi with the workers of
Kheda district, Gujarat, 1929.

attracted people from different regions, social groups, and classes. Youth leagues and *kisan sabhas* were established in many parts of the country under the Congress umbrella, and strong regional groups associated themselves with the party. The people of the princely states, numbering about 562 and covering roughly two-fifths of the area of India, were also drawn into the movement for *swaraj*. *Praja mandals* were organised in the princely states.

AKALI MOVEMENT

In Punjab, the Akali movement, which began as a movement for gurudwara reform, gained strength. Its links with the Congress grew stronger when it joined the movement for independence. After the Jallianwala Bagh massacre in Amritsar, the Akalis began to move closer to the nationalist cause. Many Akali leaders under a new leadership joined the non-cooperation movement launched by Gandhi, and the Akali Dal offered 5,000 *kar sevaks* (volunteers). The Central Sikh League supported him in opposing communal representation in Punjab. Inspired by Gandhi, leaders like Master Tara Singh, Swaran Singh, Partap Singh Kairon, and Giani Kartar Singh joined the nationalist movement.

WOMEN IN THE NATIONAL MOVEMENT

By the late 1920s, women were found increasingly in the public arena. Many women, inspired by their association with great leaders, joined them in the freedom struggle, such as Swarup Rani, Kasturba Gandhi, and Kamala Nehru. Madame Bhikaji Cama, influenced by her association with Dadabhai Naoroji as his secretary, had unfurled the first national flag at the International Socialist Conference in Stuttgart, Germany, in 1907.

Women responded in large numbers to Gandhi's call for *satyagraha,* facing police *lathi* charges and going to prison *en masse.* They participated in *dharnas* and public bonfires of foreign clothes in the mill areas even at night. By 1930, all-night, exclusively women-led *dharnas* were organised. Thousands of rural women, along with their children, challenged oppressive laws in forests and villages. They provided sanctuary to *satyagrahis,* and as *satyagrahis* themselves went to prison. They picked up the baton from *satyagrahis* during the salt campaign, facing brutal police action undaunted. They picketed toddy shops, even pursuing *'the drunkards to their dens with courage in their hearts.'*

Women also organised themselves, seeking a more prominent role in the freedom struggle. Starting as small local clubs, women's auxilia-

Kamala Nehru (sitting, extreme left) and Kasturba Gandhi
among other women activists participating in a meeting.

ries of the Indian National Congress and the Indian National Social Conference (1887) were formed as forums for the discussion of social issues. Between 1917 and 1927, three major women's organisations were established—the Women's India Association, the National Council of Women in India, and the All India Women's Conference.

Gandhi—with his personality, moral force, and stature—inspired women in large numbers to join the national movement. This was particularly true of the civil disobedience movement in which women played a significant role. The impact and contribution of women leaders such as Sarojini Naidu and her daughter Padmaja Naidu, Sarla Devi Chaudhrani, Muthulakshmi Reddy, Rajkumari Amrit Kaur, Lilawati Munshi, Lotika Ghosh, Lado Rani Zutshi and her daughter Manmohini, Sucheta Kripalani, Sister Nivedita, Madeline Slade, and Vijaylakshmi Pandit are part of historical folklore.

Sarojini Naidu presided over the Congress session at Cawnpore (Kanpur) in 1925. Nellie Sengupta presided over the Congress session in Calcutta in 1933 when Madan Mohan Malaviya, president of the session, was arrested and most Congress leaders were in jail.

Many unsung, unknown women left the comfort and safety of their homes to perform the ordinary tasks that the movement demanded. In Bengal, women such as Binodini Sen, Manorama Gupta, Kalpana Dutta, and Kalyani Das supported the militant nationalists at great personal risk. Many women, convinced of the rightness of the cause, went to jail, leaving behind children to be looked after by others. Women also began demanding civil and political rights. On 15 December 1917, Sarojini Naidu led an all-India delegation to meet Montagu and Chelmsford, demanding equal rights for women.

The national movement led by the Congress was rapidly becoming a mass movement, a rushing river joined by many other streams.

Swarup Rani

Kasturba Gandhi

Kamala Nehru

Vijaylakshmi Pandit

Sister Nivedita

Rajkumari Amrit Kaur

Muthulakshmi Reddy

Sucheta Kripalani

Aruna Asaf Ali

SAROJINI NAIDU (1879-1949)

President, 40th Session, Cawnpore-1925.

Sarojini Naidu was the first Indian woman to preside over a Congress session. A distinguished poet, a renowned freedom fighter, and one of the great orators of her time, she is famously known as the Nightingale of India (*Bharatiya Kokila*). Naidu played a leading role during the Civil Disobedience and Quit India movements. After India gained independence, she became the governor of Uttar Pradesh.

NELLIE SENGUPTA (1886-1973)

President, 47th (banned) Session, Calcutta-1933. An Englishwoman, earnestly serving the cause of Indians and their freedom; worked extensively for the upliftment of Chittagong during the Non-cooperation Movement; promoted *khadi*.

SIMON COMMISSION, 1927–28

In 1927, the British government appointed the Indian Statutory Commission, led by Lord Simon, to enquire into the question of further constitutional reforms for India. This was in accordance with the provisions of the Montagu-Chelmsford Reforms calling for a parliamentary review after 10 years. The Congress considered the Simon Commission's all-British membership as incompatible with the principle of self-determination and an insult to Indians, and resolved to boycott its proceedings. At the Madras session in 1927, which was presided over by Dr M.A. Ansari, the Congress decided to boycott the forthcoming visit of the Simon Commission.

In 1928, the Congress, the Muslim League, and the Liberal Federation came together at an all-parties convention to frame an alternative constitution for an independent India. The report, drafted by Motilal Nehru, called for responsible government and dominion status. However, the resolution was opposed by those who wanted complete independence, including Jawaharlal Nehru and Subhas Chandra Bose.

Subhas Chandra Bose had emerged on the national political scene by organising the boycott of the Prince of Wales when he had visited Calcutta in 1921. He was imprisoned in Mandalay, and after three years of deten-tion without trial, was released in 1927. Bose joined Jawaharlal in moving an amendment seeking complete independence. However, their amendment was not carried. Non-Congress leaders, such as the Aga Khan and Jinnah, also opposed the proposed scheme of dominion self-government.

SIMON GO BACK

The Simon Commission during its tour of the country met with great opposition and widespread demonstrations, resulting in clashes between the public and the police. When the Simon Commission arrived in Bombay on 3 February 1928, it was confronted by *hartals* and black-flag demon-strations. In Madras, the police opened fire, and clashed with students and demonstrators.

Wherever the British went, they were greeted with cries of 'Simon go back!' It was during one such clash that Lala Lajpat Rai was severely beaten by the police and died soon thereafter. Outraged by this, angry youths took radical action and a wave of militancy followed. On 17 December 1928, Bhagat Singh, Chandra Shekhar Azad, and Rajguru assassinated an official named Saunders, wrongly assuming him to be the police chief, Scott, who had led the *lathi* charge against Lala Lajpat Rai.

On 8 April 1929, Bhagat Singh and B.K. Dutt threw a bomb in the Central Legislative Assembly in New Delhi *'to make the deaf hear.'* In April 1930, Surya Sen led a well-planned and large-scale armed raid on the government armoury at Chittagong, in Bengal. He was arrested and hanged in 1934. Many trade union leaders who were active during this time were arrested. In 1932, after a long trial known as the Meerut Conspiracy Case, they were sentenced to long terms of imprisonment.

Chandra Shekhar Azad was killed in a police encounter in February 1931, and on 23 March 1931, Bhagat Singh, Sukh Dev, and Rajguru were executed.

In response to increasingly strident demands by the nationalists for concrete and meaningful action, and given the volatile situation in the country, the Governor-General, Lord Irwin, announced the British government's intention to grant dominion status to India and to convene a Round Table Conference in London to discuss the recommendations of the Simon Commission.

'POORNA SWARAJ'

The Congress met at Lahore in December 1929, with Jawaharlal Nehru presiding. Interestingly, the son succeeded the father, as Motilal Nehru had been the previous Congress president. The Lahore Congress declared that the time for the acceptance of dominion status had lapsed and called upon Congress members in the central and provincial legislatures to resign. It authorised the AICC to launch a programme of civil disobedience, including non-payment of taxes.

At midnight on 31 December 1929, the Congress adopted *poorna swaraj,* complete independence, as its goal and unfurled the tri-colour flag of India's independence on the banks of the river Ravi amidst impassioned cries of *'Bande Mataram'* and *'Inquilab Zindabad'.* **Jawaharlal Nehru called for 26 January 1930 to be celebrated as the day of independence,** with the pledge: *'We hold it to be a crime against man and God to submit any longer to a rule that has caused this fourfold disaster to our country and ruined India economically, politically, culturally and socially.'*

DANDI MARCH AND THE SALT SATYAGRAHA, 1930

Gandhi planned to renew the civil disobedience movement with the salt satyagraha in 1930. This single campaign captured the hearts and minds of not only Indians but also of people all over the world, and became a major turning point in the national movement. Salt became a universal symbol of popular suffering, representing the burden of the oppressive salt tax imposed by an unjust regime.

THE PLEDGE OF INDEPENDENCE

(As taken by the People of India on Purna Swaraj Day, January 26, 1930)

We believe that it is the inalienable right of the Indian people, as of any other people, to have freedom and to enjoy the fruits of their toil and have the necessities of life, so that they may have full opportunities of growth. We believe also that if any government deprives a people of these rights and oppresses them, the people have a further right to alter it or to abolish it. The British Government in India has not only deprived the Indian people of their freedom but has based itself on the exploitation of the masses, and has ruined India economically, politically, culturally and spiritually. We believe therefore that India must sever the British connection and attain Purna Swaraj or complete independence.

India has been ruined economically. The revenue derived from our people is out of all proportion to our income. Our average income is seven pice per day, and of the heavy taxes we pay 20% are raised from the land revenue derived from the peasantry and 3% from the salt tax, which falls most heavily on the poor.

Village industries, such as hand spinning, have been destroyed, leaving the peasantry idle for at least four months in the year, and dulling their intellect for want of handicrafts, and nothing has been substituted, as in other countries, for the crafts thus destroyed.

Customs and currency have been so manipulated as to heap further burdens on the peasantry. British manufactured goods constitute the bulk of our imports. Customs duties betray clear partiality for British manufacturers, and revenue from them is used not to lessen the burden on the masses but for sustaining a highly extravagant administration. Still more arbitrary has been the manipulation of the exchange ratio which has resulted in millions being drained away from the country.

Politically, India's status has never been so reduced as under the British regime. No reforms have given real political power to the people. The tallest of us have to bend before foreign authority. The rights of free expression of opinion and free association have been denied to us and many of our countrymen are compelled to live in exile abroad and cannot return to their homes. All administrative talent is killed and the masses have to be satisfied with petty village offices and clerkships.

Culturally, the system of education has torn us from our moorings and our training has made us bug the very chains that bind us.

Spiritually, compulsory disarmament has made us unmanly and the presence of an alien army of occupation, employed with deadly effect to crush in us the spirit of resistance, has made us think that we cannot look after ourselves or put up a defence against foreign aggression, or even defend our homes and families from the attacks of thieves, robbers and miscreants.

We hold it to be a crime against man and God to submit any longer to a rule that has caused this fourfold disaster to our country. We recognise, however, that the most effective way of gaining our freedom is not through violence. We will therefore prepare ourselves by withdrawing, so far as we can, all voluntary association from the British Government, and will prepare for civil disobedience, including non-payment of taxes. We are convinced that if we can but withdrew our voluntary help and stop payment of taxes without doing violence, even under provocation, the end of this inhuman rule is assured. We therefore hereby solemnly resolve to carry out the Congress instructions issued from time to time for the purpose of establishing Purna Swaraj.

Gandhi calling for the breach of the salt law,
Surat district, Gujarat, April 1930.

On 12 March 1930, Gandhi began his momentous Dandi March from Sabarmati Ashram, by saying *'this is a sacred pilgrimage...'* Gandhi, then 61 years old, was accompanied by 78 *satyagrahis,* including Hindus, Muslims, Christians, untouchables, scholars, newspaper editors, and weavers. The *satyagrahis* slept in the open and ate the simplest food.

Jawaharlal Nehru remarked, *'Today the pilgrim marches onward on his long trek . . . the fire of a great resolve is in him and the unsurpassing love of his miserable countrymen.'* He appealed to young people, saying, *'Will you be mere onlookers in this glorious struggle? Who lives if India dies? Who dies if India lives?'*

On the day of the march, Gandhi rose at 4.00 a.m., as was his custom, and performed his daily work of spinning and writing for *Navajivan* and *Young India.* He then set off, walking so fast that others found it difficult to keep pace. They drew large crowds wherever they went—20,000 in Nadiad, 10,000 in Anand, 15,000 in Broach, and 30,000 in Surat.

Gandhi reached Dandi on 5 April 1930. The next morning, he bathed and then broke the salt law by picking up a lump of natural salt on the seashore. This seemingly simple gesture symbolised the refusal of Indians to accept British-made laws. Louis Fischer called it *'an insurrection without arms.'* All over the

Gandhi leading the Dandi March.

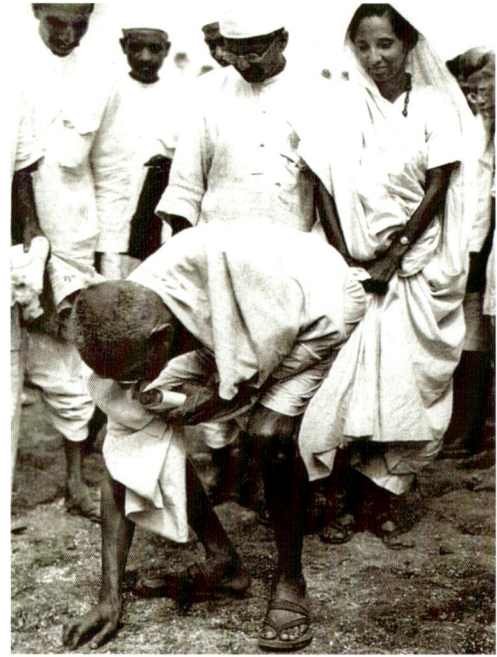

Gandhi breaking the salt law by picking up a lump of natural salt at 8.30 a.m., 6 April 1930.

Dear Motilal,

So Jawahar is to have six months' rest. He has worked like a Trojan. He needed this rest. If things continue to move with the present velocity he won't have even six months—

2

rest. The Jamnalal you saw the other day is different today. Whole villages have turned out. I never expected this phenomenal response. In many villages Government servants can get no service

3

The removal of some four picked men has only stiffened the up resistance of the people. But enough of this optimism. He will be a brave man who can say what will happen tomorrow. Accounts arriving

4

from Bombay too are most encouraging. I take it you are following the pages of Young India. How are you keeping?
Dandi   Yours
14.4.   M K Gandhi
30

Left: Gandhi's letter to Motilal Nehru from Dandi, 14 April 1930.

Above: Scenes of police atrocities during the struggle, 1930-31.

country, people responded with passionate conviction by performing similar acts. On 13 April, Pandit Madan Mohan Malaviya launched a campaign for the boycott of foreign cloth in Punjab.

Repression

As nationalist fervour swept the land and people began to mobilise on a mass scale, the government became more repressive. On 14 April, Jawaharlal was arrested for violating the salt law in Allahabad and was sentenced to six months' imprisonment. The Indian Press Act of 1910 was revived, large-scale arrests were made, and more than 60,000 Indians were jailed. On 5 May, Gandhi was arrested and taken to Yeravada jail, near Poona. Abbas Tyabji took Gandhi's place in continuing the movement. *Satyagrahis* organised a series of raids on salt depots, most notably the Dharasana (Surat) raid on 21 May and the Wadala raids in May and June, in which almost 15,000 *satyagrahis* participated.

People's Response

Peasants and workers, the middle classes and business groups, men and women, town dwellers and villagers—all joined the civil disobedience movement.

Throughout the 1930s, the peasant movement acquired a national character. The civil disobedience movement took up many of the issues confronting farmers in the form of no-tax and no-rent campaigns in many parts of the country, most prominently in the United Provinces and Andhra. The Congress at its Karachi session in 1931 included many of their demands in its list of Fundamental Rights and Economic Programme. Support for this step came from Assam, Orissa, Bihar, the United Provinces, and Punjab.

In the NWFP, Khan Abdul Ghaffar Khan and his older brother, Khan Sahib, organised the civil disobedience movement. Abdul Ghaffar, popularly known as the Frontier Gandhi and Badshah Khan, led his corps of volunteers, the Khudai Khidmatgars (Servants of God), also known as the Red Shirts *(Surkh Posh),* in supporting Gandhi's call to action. He was arrested on 23 April 1930, leading to massive unrest in Peshawar. This Pashtun leader, known for his pacifism and non-violent opposition to the British Raj, was a devout Muslim who nevertheless strongly opposed the Muslim League's demand for the partition of India.

In the central zone, people engaged in massive violations of forest laws. In Buldhana district in Berar, labourers and peasants formed a peasant union and launched a no-tax campaign. In the west, in Gujarat and Maharashtra, too, there was widespread support for the campaign. In the south, the movement was led by

KHAN ABDUL GHAFFAR KHAN (1890-1988)

Khan Abdul Ghaffar Khan, a Pashtun political and spiritual leader, was widely respected for his non-violent resistance to British rule in India and was a devoted follower of Mahatma Gandhi. He organised the Pathans as the Khudai Khidmatgars—Servants of God. He refused the office of the Congress president when it was offered to him in 1931, but remained a member of the Congress Working Committee for a very long time. He attended the Congress centenary session in Bombay in 1985. Popularly known as Badshah Khan (King of Chiefs) and Gandhi-e-Sarhad (Frontier Gandhi), he was the recipient of the Nehru World Peace Award (1967) and the Bharat Ratna (1987).

Gandhi with Khan Abdul Ghaffar Khan and the Khudai Khidmatgars.

Left: A view of the Karachi session in 1931 showing Gandhi with Jawaharlal Nehru, Sardar Patel, and Madan Mohan Malaviya. Sardar Patel was the president of the Congress at the time.

Across: Gandhi at the microphone at the Karachi session, 1931.

Below: The Congress Working Committee meeting at Swaraj Bhawan, Allahabad, February 1931.

C. Rajagopalachari. In Karnataka, it took the form of a forest *satyagraha*. In the east, the Manipuris played an impressive role. In Nagaland, Rani Gaidilieu, at the young age of 13, raised the banner of rebellion. She was arrested in 1932 and was released only in 1947 when India became free.

Across the length and breadth of the country, Indians of all backgrounds rallied to the nationalist cause in large numbers, demonstrating mass support for the civil disobedience movement.

GANDHI-IRWIN PACT, 1931

On 26 January 1931, Gandhi and the members of the Congress Working Committee were released. The Viceroy, Lord Irwin, and Gandhi began a dialogue in an attempt to resolve the political situation. The outcome was the Gandhi-Irwin Pact, under which the British government agreed to release imprisoned activists and to annul the ordinances under which the Congress and its sister organisations had been declared unlawful bodies. The Congress agreed to suspend the civil disobedience movement and to participate in the Second Round Table Conference in London in 1931. This issue, however, was deadlocked when no consensus could be reached on the question of separate electorates for Muslims and Harijans. Dr B.R.

Ambedkar, the leader of the depressed classes, had pressed for this provision for Harijans. Gandhi was criticised for returning 'empty-handed' to India. With the renewal of government repression, the Congress relaunched the civil disobedience campaign.

In January 1932, the Congress and its allied bodies were banned. Many leaders were arrested, amongst them Gandhi, Jawaharlal Nehru, and Khan Sahib. Meanwhile, the government announced its decision to provide separate electorates for the depressed classes. In jail, Gandhi went on a fast unto death as he strongly opposed this measure, believing that untouchables were an integral part of Indian society and that untouchability should not be perpetuated through this provision. On the fifth day of the fast, in what came to be known as the Poona Pact, Dr Ambedkar reached an understanding with the government on the demand for separate electorates, and Gandhi called off his fast.

Gandhi's Crusade against Untouchability

For the next two years, 1933-34, Gandhi devoted all his energies to fighting untouchability. He took up the cause of the *daridra narayana,* the marginalised, the downtrodden, and the oppressed whom he called Harijan. He undertook his famous Harijan tour, traversing 20,000 km to collect funds for the Harijan

Mahatma Gandhi at the Federal Structure Sub-committee meeting, presided over by Lord Sankey, in London during the Second Round Table Conference meeting, 1931. Madan Mohan Malaviya is seen sitting next to Gandhi.

Sewak Sangh and campaigned against untouchability. Gandhi connected with common people across the country, giving a voice to the voiceless.

The Third Round Table Conference ended in 1932, with neither the Congress nor the Labour Party attending it.

In 1933, the government published a white paper outlining the British proposal for constitutional reforms. In October 1934, the Congress, under the presidentship of Rajendra Prasad, rejected the white paper, stating that the only acceptable solution would be a constitution drawn up by a constituent assembly.

The Government of India Act was passed by the British Parliament in July 1935 and received royal assent. However, the proposals were too little, too late. The country, led by the Congress, had already proceeded far beyond limited goals such as the attainment of dominion status. Now the demand was for *poorna swaraj,* complete independence.

1935

Towards Independence

1947

Towards Independence

1935 - 1947

3

GOVERNMENT OF INDIA ACT, 1935

In 1935, the Indian National Congress completed half a century both as a party and as a national movement. On this occasion, Jawaharlal Nehru observed:

Fifty years are not much in the life of a nation, a mere flash in the millennia of India's long past . . . Fifty years are a long period in a human life and within their span can be crowded a world of endeavour and achievement.

As the Congress celebrated its golden jubilee, it was clear that it was moving slowly but surely towards its goal. The Government of India Act, 1935 paved the way for its final struggle. This followed Gandhi's civil disobedience movement, which galvanised thousands to join the Congress in the struggle for independence.

The Act of 1935, the product of long and difficult deliberations, satisfied nobody. Complete independence had been the Congress demand since December 1929, and Gandhi had made it known to the British at the Round Table Conference that a constitution not based on this basic principle would be unacceptable to India. He had declared on 1 January 1932:

Nothing short of complete independence, carrying full control over the defence, external affairs and finance, with such safeguards as may be demonstratively necessary in the interest of the nation, can be regarded by the Congress as satisfactory.

The Act of 1935 provided for the establishment of an all India federation and a new pattern of government. It abolished diarchy and provided for provincial autonomy with responsible government, accountable to an expanded electorate. However, the franchise continued to carry a property qualification. The federal arrangement, which was never actually brought into operation, provided for the integration of the princely states into British India. The All India Federation, which provided the model for the federal structure of independent India, was to consist of governor's provinces, chief commissioner's provinces, and the acceding princely states. Representation in the federal legislature was heavily weighted in favour of the princes.

At the centre, the Governor-General, who was responsible only to the British Parliament, was invested with a number of discretionary powers and given reserved powers over such departments as defence and external affairs.

In spite of great criticism, the bill was passed on 2 August 1935. Under the act, only about 10 per cent of the Indian population got the right to vote. In addition, the electorate was to be divided on communal lines. Even before the bill was passed, the Congress observed 7 February 1935 as the All India Protest Day against the report on the proposed constitutional reforms. During 1935 and the early months of 1936, while the Congress fiercely debated the merits and demerits of this legislation, Gandhi devoted his time to village reconstruction programmes.

LUCKNOW SESSION, 1936

Nehru was in prison when the Constitution of 1935 was being finalised and passed. He was arrested in February 1935 and was released later that year, in September, because his wife, Kamala, was gravely ill. He returned to India from Europe after the sad demise of Kamala in February 1936 in Switzerland. Nehru presided over the Lucknow session of the Congress in April 1936, which was attended by several former Congress presidents, including Gandhi.

At the Lucknow session, the Congress faced the important issue of deciding whether to contest the elections to the provincial legislatures under the provisions of the new act. As Nehru stated:

I think that, under the circumstances, we have no choice but to contest the election to the new provincial legislatures, in the event of their taking place. We should seek election on the basis of a detailed political and economic programme, with a demand for a constituent assembly in the forefront. I am convinced that the only solution to our political and communal problems will come through such an assembly, provided it is elected on an adult franchise and a mass base.

Gandhi, Jawaharlal Nehru, and Maulana Azad, Wardha, August 1935.

He went on to explain his position on the communal question:

I am not concerned so much with what it gives to this group or that but more so with the basic idea behind it. It seeks to divide India into numerous separate compartments, chiefly on a religious basis and this makes the development of democracy and economic policy very difficult.

At the same time when the Lucknow session of the Congress was in progress, the All India Muslim League met in Bombay, with Jinnah presiding. The League condemned the federal scheme of the 1935 Act, but decided to accept the provincial government scheme. It also decided to form its central and provincial parliamentary board to prepare for the coming election.

ELECTION OF 1937

At a meeting in Wardha, in Maharashtra, towards the end of April 1936, the CWC formed a Parliamentary Committee, with Rajendra Prasad, Vallabhbhai Patel, Abul Kalam Azad, Bhulabhai Desai, Narendra Dev, Govind Ballabh Pant, and Khan Sahib from the North-West Frontier Province (NWFP) as members, to look after the organisation of the 1937 election.

The electorate of 37 million went to the polls in the opening months of 1937. The election afforded an opportunity to politically educate the masses as the Congress penetrated all parts of the country to spread its message. The election results were an outstanding success for the party. Congress ministries were formed in seven out of 11 provinces. Later the Congress formed coalition governments in two other provinces as well. It captured 711 out of the total of 808 general seats. In contrast, the Muslim League did not do so well. The results showed that it did not have a base in the Muslim-majority provinces of Punjab, Bengal, Sind, and the NWFP. It did well in the United Provinces, Bombay, and Madras. Overall, the League failed to obtain even 25 per cent of the Muslim seats and could not present itself as the real representative of Indian Muslims.

At this stage, Mohammed Ali Jinnah approached the Congress with an offer of joining them in forming coalition ministries. However, the Congress refused to recognise the League as the sole representative of Indian Muslims. In the words of Nehru, *'There are only two forces in India today, British imperialism and Indian nationalism as represented by the Congress.'* On 26 July 1937, a bitter Jinnah claimed that the Congress had deliberately decided to ignore and non-cooperate with the Muslim League parties in the various provincial legislatures. As he put it, *'No, there is a third party—the Musalmans.'*

A view of the procession taken out at the time of the Congress session at Lucknow, 1936. Jawaharlal Nehru is standing in an open car.

CONGRESS MINISTRIES IN OFFICE

The Congress Working Committee (CWC) met at Wardha and adopted a resolution permitting Congressmen to accept office. During their term in office, the Congress ministries demonstrated considerable administrative ability and produced a distinguished record of achievements in social reform. In a message to Congressmen asking them to introduce simplicity in the administration of their provinces, Gandhi said, *'Its representatives dare not live in a style and manner out of all correspondence with their electorate.'* However, the ministries faced some difficulties in implementing policies because the governors often hampered free decision making, and at times confrontation became inevitable, leading to a constitutional crisis. When the Congress ministries decided to release political prisoners in Bihar and the United Provinces, the Governor-General instructed the governors not to implement these decisions, leading the ministries to resign in protest. Subsequently, the Governor-General agreed to the gradual release of prisoners and the ministries withdrew their resignations.

HARIPURA SESSION, 1938

The Congress held its 51st session at Haripura, in Gujarat, in February 1938 under the presidentship of Subhas Chandra Bose, who had been released after detention and exile lasting more than five years. This session was the first one attended by ministers in-charge of provinces who participated as All India Congress Committee (AICC) delegates or members. Delegations from South Africa and Ceylon also attended. The event attracted so many participants that it came to be described as the biggest session in the history of the Congress. Subhas Chandra Bose appealed to the delegates to work as one supreme organ of mass struggle to fight the imperialist forces.

To counteract the growing hostility of Jinnah and the Muslim League towards the Congress, Nehru moved a resolution on 20 February 1938 stating that:

The Congress regards it as its primary duty and fundamental policy to protect the religious, linguistic, cultural and other rights of the minorities in India and will give widest scope for their development and their participation in the fullest measure in the political, economic and cultural life of the nation.

TENSIONS WITHIN THE PARTY

The post-Haripura months were eventful. The annual Congress session at Tripuri in March 1939 was held amidst increasing tensions, both internationally and domestically, as war clouds gathered in Europe. Within the Congress a problem arose because Subhas

Right: Gandhi and Subhas Chandra Bose at the Haripura session, 1938.

Below: Subhas Chandra Bose receiving the salute as the president at the Haripura session of the Congress, 1938. Seen next to him is Sardar Patel. Among those standing below on the deck are Sarojini Naidu, Jawaharlal Nehru, and J.B. Kripalani.

SUBHAS CHANDRA BOSE (1897-1945)

President, 51st Session, Haripura-1938 and 52nd Session, Tripuri-1939.

Subhas Chandra Bose, popularly known as Netaji, was one of the iconic leaders of the Indian independence movement. He devoted much of his time and energy to the organisation of the youth and to the trade union movement. In 1928, the Motilal Nehru Committee appointed by the Congress declared in favour of dominion status, but Subhas Chandra Bose along with Jawaharlal Nehru opposed it. Finally, at the historic Lahore Congress session, the Congress adopted *Poorna Swaraj* (complete independence) as its motto. Bose created the Azad Hind Fauj and gave the famous call 'Give me blood and I will give you freedom.'

Chandra Bose, popularly called Netaji (respected leader), was in the race for a second term as president. Gandhi, who had earlier supported his candidature for the Haripura session, was now supporting Dr Pattabhi Sitaramayya. However, Dr Sitaramayya withdrew his nomination and eventually Bose became the president. Several members of the CWC resigned, leaving Bose in a weakened position. The situation worsened further when Govind Ballabh Pant moved a resolution calling upon the president to nominate members to the CWC in accordance with Gandhi's wishes. These issues and other ideological differences surfacing amongst the leaders led Bose to resign as Congress president in April 1939 at the meeting of the AICC in Calcutta. He was stripped of the presidentship of the Bengal Provincial Congress Committee and was disqualified from being on any elective Congress committee for three years. Bose left to form the All India Forward Bloc. In 1941, he campaigned in Germany and Japan in support of the government of a free India, later moving to Singapore to organise the Indian National Army (INA) and setting up a government of India in exile. Bose, who was imprisoned by the British 11 times, continued to call for the full and immediate independence of India from British rule, inspiring many Indians with his motto, *'Give me blood and I will give you freedom.'*

PATTABHI SITARAMAYYA (1880-1959)

President, 55th Session, Jaipur-1948-49.

Dr Sitaramayya is considered the historian of the Indian National Congress. He was the Governor of Madhya Pradesh from 1952 to 1957. Though a popular Congress leader and held in high esteem by Gandhi, he did not hanker after office and did not take part in elections to the provincial assemblies or to the central legislature. He took pleasure in working for the party and in writing and publishing books.

PRINCELY STATES

A major issue facing the Congress was the integration of people of the Indian princely states in the nationalist movement. Queen Victoria's proclamation of 1858 had assured the princes of their continuation as rulers with the right of hereditary succession. The British government had also committed to honouring all *sanads,* treaties, and agreements that had been entered into with the princes. As the independence movement gained momentum, many organisations, *praja mandals,* were established in the princely states. In 1920, the Congress enunciated its policy towards people's movements in the states. It recognised that although people in the states could enrol themselves as members of the Congress, they could not initiate political activity in the states in the name of the Congress. At the Lahore session in 1929, Jawaharlal Nehru in his presidential address observed, *'The Indian states cannot live apart from the rest of India . . . The only people who have a right to determine the future of the states must be the people of those states.'* This position was reiterated at the Lucknow session in 1936 as well as at the Haripura session in 1938, which stated that *poorna swaraj* was the objective for the whole of India, including the princely states. This proved to be a contentious issue and a source of tension when India became independent.

SECOND WORLD WAR

On the international front, the world was heading towards a crisis. Adolf Hitler, who had captured power in Germany, annexed Austria and Czechoslovakia, and eventually Poland in September 1939. France and Britain declared war on Germany on 3 September 1939. On the same day, the Viceroy of India unilaterally announced to the world that India was at war with Germany.

The CWC met at an urgent session in Wardha during 8–15 September 1939 to decide its policy with regard to the war. The session was attended by Gandhi, Jawaharlal Nehru, Subhas Chandra Bose, Narendra Dev, and Jaiprakash Narayan. The Congress passed a resolution:

The issue of war and peace for India must be decided by the Indian people, and no outside authority can impose this decision upon them, nor can the Indian people permit their resources to be exploited for imperialist needs . . . India cannot associate herself in a war said to be for democratic freedom when that very freedom is denied to her and such limited freedom as she possesses taken away from her.

The Congress leaders made it clear that only a free and democratic India could associate herself with other free nations for mutual defence against aggression. The reaction of the

British government, however, was along expected lines. As Gandhi observed, *'The Congress asked for bread and it has got a stone.'*

DIFFERENCES WITH THE MUSLIM LEAGUE

The Congress decided to ask its ministers in all the major provinces to resign. However, the non-Congress ministers in Bengal, Punjab, and Sind continued to function as before, and in Assam a coalition ministry was formed under Mohammed Saadullah. The Muslim League did not reject the British position. Instead, it expressed satisfaction that the government had recognised the League as the true representative of the Muslims. On 2 December 1939, from Bombay, Jinnah called upon his followers to celebrate the fall of the Congress ministries, which had resigned, stating, *'I wish the Musalmans all over India to observe Friday, December 22 as the day of deliverance and thanksgiving as the mark of relief that the Congress regime has at last ceased to function.'*

RAMGARH SESSION, 1940

The situation was grim when the Congress met at its 53rd session at Ramgarh in March 1940, with Maulana Abul Kalam Azad presiding. In an impassioned address, Maulana Azad pointed to the long history of the country when the *'Muslims had lived as children of the soil,*

enjoyed brotherhood with the Hindus in developing a common nationality.' He went on to say that there could be absolutely no reason why the Muslims should feel oppressed just by virtue of being a minority.

Moving the final resolution of the Congress on the war crisis, Nehru pointed out that since the policy of Britain was to fight the war for imperialist needs and for the preservation of her empire, *'The Congress cannot in any way, directly or indirectly, be party to the war.'* Declaring that its goal was nothing short of complete independence, the Congress now also asked for the formation of a constituent assembly to be elected on the basis of adult suffrage.

Differences with the Muslim League were deepening, with the party insisting that no constitutional changes should be announced for India without its consent and approval. The League met at Lahore in March 1940 and demanded the creation of Pakistan by resolving:

It is the considered view of this session of the All India Muslim League that no constitutional plan would be workable in this country or acceptable to the Muslims unless it is designed on the following basic principle viz., that geographically contiguous units, demarcated in two regions, which should be so constituted with such territorial adjustment as may be necessary, that the areas in which Muslims are numerically in a majority as in the North western and East zones of India, should be grouped to constitute independent states in which the constituent units shall be autonomous and sovereign.

This was in accordance with the two-nation theory, which the League had been advocating since the 1930s.

AUGUST OFFER, 1940

The Viceroy, Lord Linlithgow, caught between the intractable attitude of the British prime minister, Winston Churchill, on the one hand, and the intransigent position of the Muslim League, on the other, announced a scheme in August 1940, which came to be known as the August Offer. This scheme proposed an expansion of the Executive Council and the establishment of a War Advisory Council, and suggested that after the war a body representing the principal elements of India's national life be established to frame a constitution. This was not acceptable to the Congress, but Gandhi felt that at this time of crisis for Britain, he *'would not be guilty of embarrassing the British people or the British government when their very existence hung in the balance.'*

In September 1940, Gandhi met the Viceroy at Shimla, but again with no sign of a changed attitude on the part of the government, he launched his plan for individual *satyagraha*.

Mahatma Gandhi and Mohammed Ali Jinnah.

Gandhi chose Vinoba Bhave, an advocate of non-violence and compassion, to lead the individual *satyagraha* movement. Vinoba Bhave, often called Acharya (teacher), was seen as Gandhi's spiritual successor. He led the *bhoodan* (land gift) movement, walking across India and asking people with land to regard him as a son and to give him a one-seventh share of their land, which he then distributed to the landless poor. He also later participated in the Quit India movement.

The government arrested Vinoba Bhave and also Pandit Nehru on 31 October 1940, and sentenced the latter to four years of imprisonment. Soon many leaders, among them Sardar Patel and Maulana Azad, were also arrested. Undaunted, other leaders joined the individual *satyagraha* movement in large numbers.

Eventually, in December 1941, the government released the *satyagrahis,* including Nehru and Maulana Azad. The Congress, however, was not happy because it did not see this step as a reflection of change of policy on the part of the government. During this time, about 25,000 Congressmen were imprisoned and many more paid exorbitant fines. Nehru stated that with no resolution of the issue in sight, *'It is not good to come out of the narrow confines of a jail into the larger prison that is India today.'*

CRIPPS MISSION, 1942

The AICC met at Wardha in January 1942 to review the contemporary political scene. In March 1942, the British government sent the Cripps Mission to India to meet a cross-section of Indian leaders. It met the leaders of various political parties and announced that all steps would be taken after the end of the war to set up in India an elected body to frame a new constitution. The CWC rejected the proposal, considering this a dangerous move since it also accepted the principle that any province of British India that was not prepared to accept the constitution would have the right to retain its present constitutional position and structure.

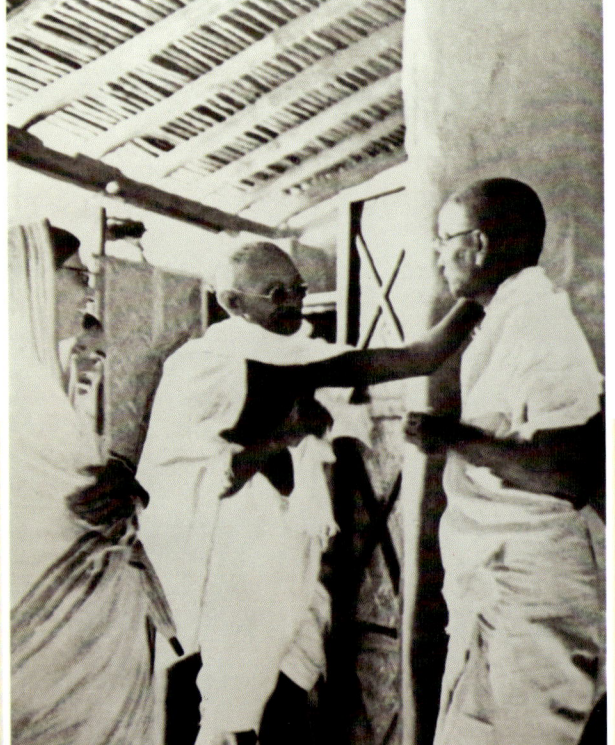

Left: Gandhi instructs Vinoba Bhave on the eve of the launching of the individual *satyagraha* movement, Sevagram, October 1940.

Across: Sir Stafford Cripps with Maulana Azad and Jawaharlal Nehru, New Delhi, 1942.

QUIT INDIA MOVEMENT, 1942

The situation on the international front was becoming increasingly threatening. In February 1942, Singapore—and soon after Rangoon—fell to Japanese forces. Within the Congress, the feeling now was, as Gandhi said, that the British must leave India. In these critical circumstances, the AICC met at Bombay in August 1942. Pandit Nehru moved the resolution for Quit India. In his address, Gandhi said:

The members of the All India Congress Committee are like members of Parliament representing the whole of India. The Congress from its inception has not been of any particular group or any particular caste or of any particular province. It has claimed ever since its birth to represent the whole nation and on your behalf I have made the claim that you represent not only the registered members of the Congress but the entire nation.

The Congress decided to launch a mass struggle to demand the withdrawal of the British from India. Gandhi called upon the people to *'Do or Die'*. His message was:

Everyone is free to go the fullest length under ahimsa . . . Satyagrahis must go out to die, not to live. They must seek and face death.

The British government reacted with severity. It declared the Congress illegal and arrested many Congress leaders, including Gandhi. The news of the arrests triggered massive demonstrations in

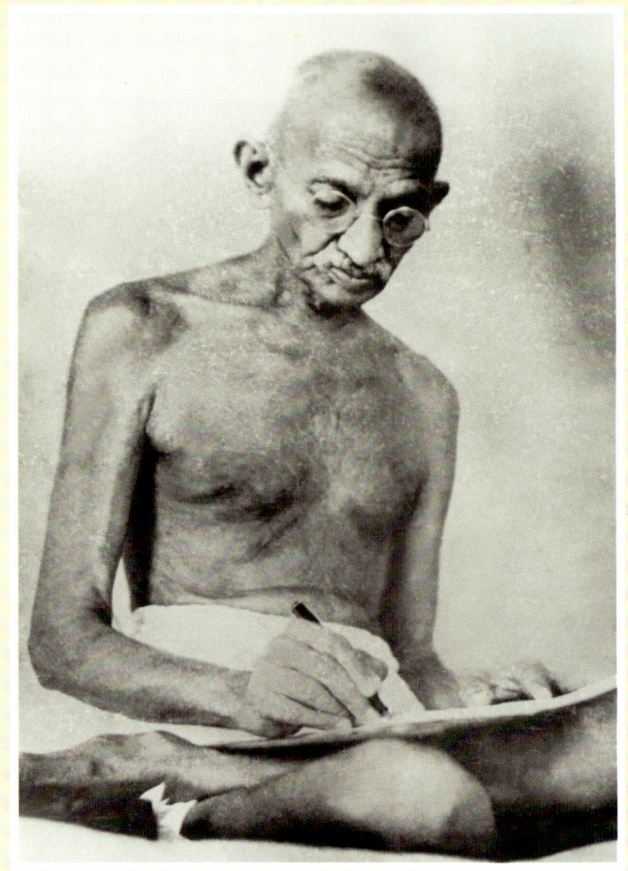

Above: Gandhi drafts the Quit India resolution, 1942.

Below: Gandhi addressing the historic session of the AICC, Bombay, August 1942.

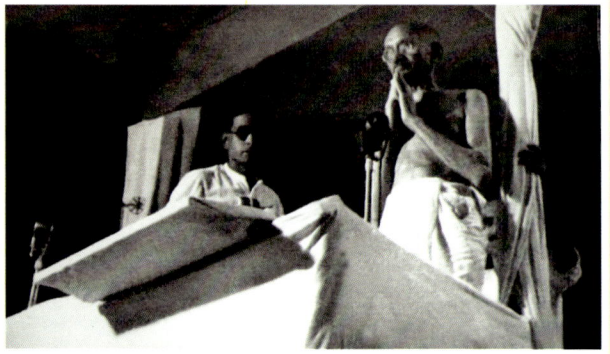

Gandhi with Jawaharlal Nehru and J.B. Kripalani at the
Quit India session, Bombay, 1942.

many parts of the country, leading the police to resort to firing. The press was muzzled. With the Congress leaders in jail, the civilian and military police reigned supreme.

Gandhi, in detention at the Aga Khan Palace in Poona, began a three-week fast, but the British government, in turn, came out with a white paper blaming the Congress for the disorders. The British government stood firm and repudiated the Congress stand on 'Quit India'.

The Hindu right-wing parties and the Communists did not support the Quit India movement, although for different reasons. The Communist Party of India (CPI) asked its cadres to stay away, although many local-level workers did join the movement.

Tear gassing and shooting of Indians in 1942.

Above: Rajendra Prasad, Sardar Patel, Pattabhi Sitaramayya, Shankar Rao Deo, Prof Ranga, and other leaders shortly before their arrest on 9 August 1942.

Left: Aga Khan Palace, Poona, where Gandhi was confined, soon after he gave the call 'Do or Die.'

Gandhi with political prisoners at Dum Dum Central Jail,
Calcutta, December 1945.

END OF WAR AND THE WAVELL PLAN, 1945

Lord Wavell assumed the viceroyalty in October 1943. On the eastern frontier, Subhas Chandra Bose, who had left India in January 1941 to organise the INA with Japanese help, was preparing for an armed entry into India. In Bangkok, he had announced the formation of the Provincial Government of Free India. At this time of uncertainty, Wavell appealed to the Congress for cooperation.

Gandhi suffered a huge personal loss when his wife, Kasturba, passed away in February 1944. Soon after, he was released on medical grounds. Gandhi assured Wavell of cooperation if the British would make an immediate declaration of Indian independence and form a national government. Gandhi also held talks with Jinnah in September 1944, trying to bring about a resolution for a Congress–League understanding of India's future after independence. However, the talks did not succeed.

The war in Europe ended in 1945. Through April and May 1945, talks continued on finding a solution to India's status after the war. In England, following the resignation of Prime Minister Winston Churchill, who was unsympathetic to the Indian nationalist cause, significant changes took place. The Liberal and Labour parties put pressure on the British government to end the stalemate on India and resolve the issue. The Labour Party eventually came to power. In June 1945, it announced the Wavell Plan, proposing a move for India's advance towards full self-government. Simultaneously, members of the CWC who had spent the war years in prison were released. Nehru observed, *'I am coming out of jail after 1,041 days.'*

At the Shimla conference in the summer of 1945, Lord Wavell and the All India Parties' representatives met to discuss the British proposals, but the negotiations failed as the Congress was unwilling to accept the Muslim League's claim to nominate only its members to the Executive Council and not any Muslim outside the League.

Within the country, passions ran high when, after the fall of Japan, thousands of INA soldiers fell into British hands, facing trial for having waged war against the King. The famous revolt of the Indian naval ratings at Bombay in February 1946 showed that even the military forces were affected by the events of the day. The INA trials of Col Shah Nawaz, Captain Sehgal, and Lt Dhillon provoked such deep anger and resentment that eventually the men had to be released.

Gandhi, Jawaharlal Nehru, and Sardar Patel with
INA officers at the Bhangi Colony, Delhi, April 1946.

Talks with members of the British Cabinet Mission *(left to right)*: Lord Pethwick-Lawrence, Maulana Azad, Asaf Ali, A.V. Alexander, and Sir Stafford Cripps.

CABINET MISSION, 1946

In January 1946, the British government sent an all-party British parliamentary delegation known as the Cabinet Mission to meet the leaders of different parties in India with the aim of resolving the issue of independence. The Congress position was clear—that the basis of any dialogue could only be acceptance of the demand for independence, along with the plan for its implementation. The Cabinet Mission finally recommended that a constitution-making body should be formed to frame a new constitution, with an interim government in place. The Congress decided to accept the proposal for the formation of an interim government. In September 1946, Jawaharlal Nehru assumed the office of prime minister in the interim government, along with an interim cabinet.

Fearing isolation, Jinnah and the Muslim League agreed to join the cabinet in October, but decided to boycott the Constituent Assembly. They called for observing 11 August as 'Direct Action Day' to achieve Pakistan.

Throughout 1946, communal disturbances took place in various parts of the country. Bengal was hit particularly hard, with acts of violence in Noakhali and Tipperah. It was becoming increasingly clear that as India was moving towards independence, one of the most pressing problems facing the country was the danger of large-scale violence in areas with a mixed population of Muslims and Hindus.

Gandhi with Jawaharlal Nehru, the Congress president, at
the AICC meeting in Bombay, 6 July 1946.

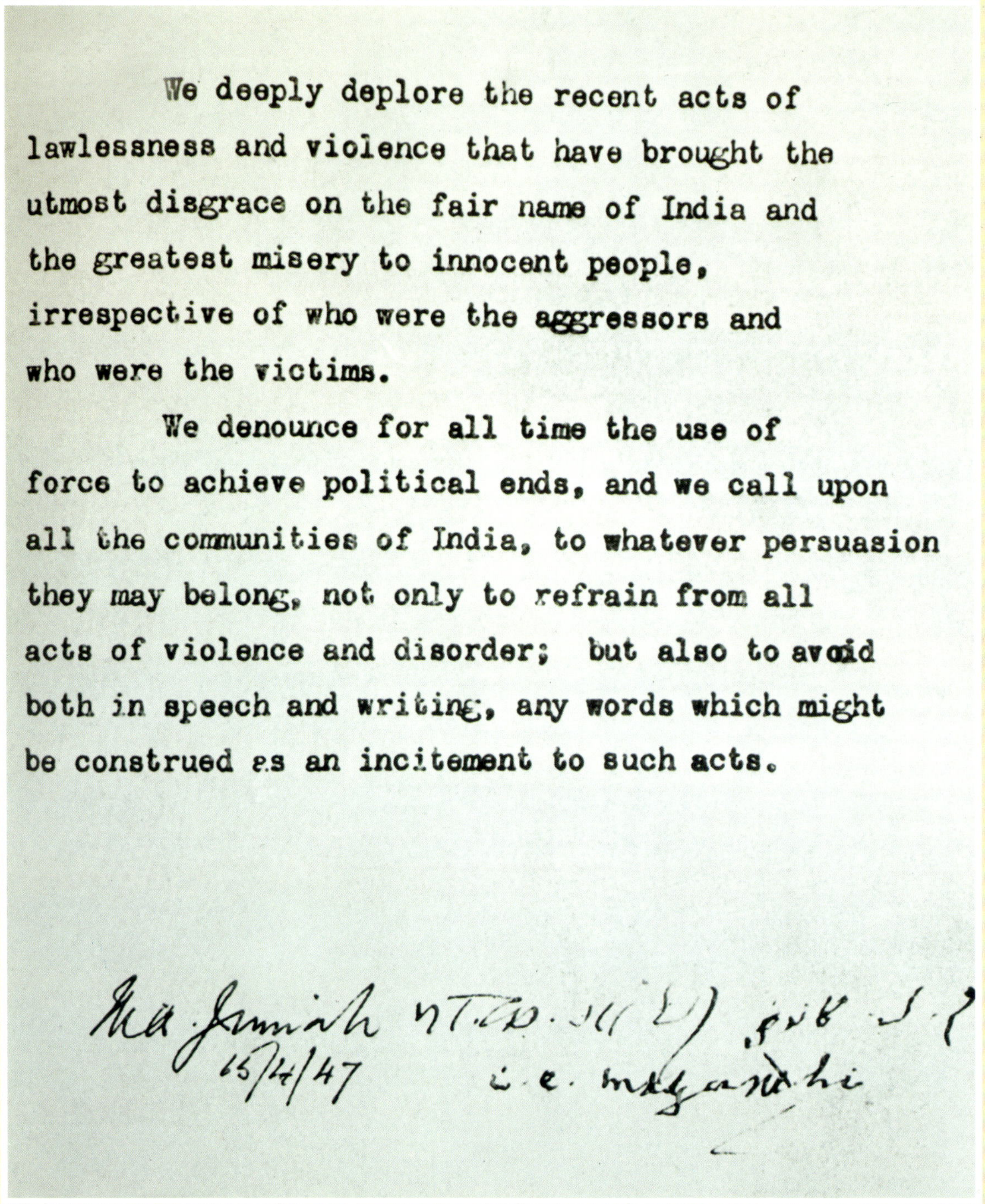

We deeply deplore the recent acts of lawlessness and violence that have brought the utmost disgrace on the fair name of India and the greatest misery to innocent people, irrespective of who were the aggressors and who were the victims.

We denounce for all time the use of force to achieve political ends, and we call upon all the communities of India, to whatever persuasion they may belong, not only to refrain from all acts of violence and disorder; but also to avoid both in speech and writing, any words which might be construed as an incitement to such acts.

M.A. Jinnah
15/4/47

M.K. Gandhi

The joint appeal for peace signed by Mohammed Ali Jinnah in English and by Gandhi in Hindi, Urdu, and English, Delhi, 15 April 1947.

Gandhi on his 'a village a day' tour of riot-stricken Noakhali, Bengal. During this tour, Gandhi walked 116 miles and covered 47 villages in the districts of Noakhali and Tipperah, January-March, 1947.

Communal riots throughout the country compelled the leaders to accept the partition plan in 1947. *Left to right:* Sardar Baldev Singh, J.B. Kripalani, Sardar Vallabhbhai Patel, Jawaharlal Nehru, Lord Mountbatten, Mohammed Ali Jinnah, and B.R. Ambedkar.

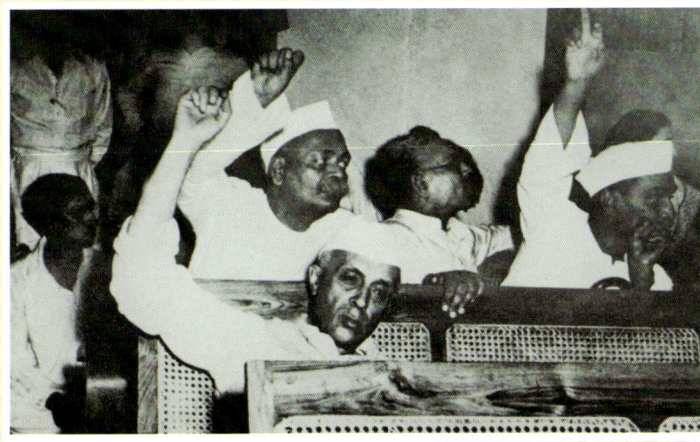

AICC meeting, New Delhi, 15 June 1947. The picture below shows Jawaharlal Nehru amongst others voting for the partition of India.

MOUNTBATTEN PLAN, 1947

On 20 February 1947, the British government declared that it would leave India not later than June 1948. It also announced the appointment of Lord Mountbatten as the Viceroy of India with responsibility for arranging the transfer of power to Indian hands. The Mountbatten Plan, approved by the British cabinet, became the final verdict on India in respect of partition and independence. It envisaged that while the existing Constituent Assembly would frame the constitution of India, this would not apply to those parts of India that were unwilling to accept it. The country was to be free but not united. India was to be partitioned and a new state, Pakistan, was to be created along with a free India. It became clear that in this volatile situation, partition was the price that had to be paid for independence. In June 1947, the CWC accepted the Mountbatten Plan. It was a bitter pill to swallow for the Congress, which had been fighting constantly against the division of the country. But eventually they could not delay the matter, particularly in view of the announcement by the British government that the transfer of power had to be finalised not later than June 1948. Cyril Radcliffe was tasked with drawing the line of partition through Punjab, Bengal, and Assam.

Prime Minister Jawaharlal Nehru addressing the midnight session
of the Constituent Assembly of India, on 14-15 August 1947.

INDEPENDENCE, 1947

On 7 August 1947, Jinnah left Delhi for Karachi to await the birth of Pakistan. On 14 August, Rajendra Prasad, the president of the Constituent Assembly, announced that India had assumed power for the governance of India. At the stroke of midnight, Jawaharlal Nehru, as the prime minister of independent India, eloquently announced to the nation and the world that India's tryst with destiny had now been achieved:

At the stroke of the midnight hour when the world sleeps, India will wake to life and freedom. A moment comes, which comes but rarely in history, when we step out from the old to the new, when an age ends and when the soul of a nation, long suppressed, finds utterance.

And so ended one of the most momentous phases in the history of the Indian National Congress—its long and relentless struggle for the liberation of the country from imperialist rule. The Congress, led by commanding personalities fully committed to the nationalist cause, represented the dreams and aspirations of a nation long enslaved. It had taken six decades of single-minded focus and unwavering determination, the vision of extraordinary men and women, but India finally triumphed over the world's mightiest imperial power. The unique nature of the Indian freedom struggle set a shining example for the rest of the world. Above all, it immortalised the one who *'marched for freedom, clad in the robe of truth with non-violence for his staff, the "naked fakir."'* Gandhi demonstrated that through love and non-violence, and with the dedication and sacrifice of many, even a seemingly impossible goal could be achieved.

The Times of India

for CARPETS and FURS, visit

ESTABLISHED 1838

OPTICIANS
BY APPOINTMENT TO
H.E. SIR JOHN COLVILLE GOVERNOR OF BOMBAY

BALIWALLA & HOMI Ltd.
255, HORNBY RD. ETC.
BOMBAY

LARGEST NET SALES of any Daily Newspaper Printed in Northern, Southern, Central or Western India.

REGD. No. B111

NO. 193. VOL. CIX.   BOMBAY: FRIDAY, AUGUST 15, 1947   PRICE TWO ANNAS   DO NOT PAY MORE

BIRTH OF INDIA'S FREEDOM

NATION WAKES TO NEW LIFE

Mr. Nehru Calls For Big Effort From People

"INCESSANT STRIVING TASK OF FUTURE"

Assembly Members Take Solemn Pledge

Pandit Nehru

NEW CABINET OF INDIA

Fourteen Members

PANDIT NEHRU TO BE PREMIER

NEW DELHI, August 14.

Mrs. Naidu's Message

STATE VISIT TO KARACHI

FRENZIED ENTHUSIASM IN BOMBAY

Crowds In Festive Mood

"MAY BOMBAY PROSPER"

Governor's Message

WISHES TO INDIA

WILD SCENES OF JUBILATION IN DELHI

From Our Special Representative
NEW DELHI, AUGUST 14.
ENTIRE DELHI KEPT AWAKE TO WITNESS THE HISTORIC EVENT OF USHERING IN THE FREEDOM OF INDIA AT THE HOUR OF MIDNIGHT

"Go Forward In Tranquillity And Prosperity"

MR. ATTLEE'S MESSAGE TO FREE INDIA

NEW DELHI, August 14.

The Hindustan Times

LARGEST CIRCULATION IN NORTHERN, NORTH-WESTERN AND CENTRAL INDIA.

NEW DELHI, SATURDAY, JULY 19, 1947.

VOL. XXIV. NO. 198.   PRICE TWO ANNAS

END OF 200-YEAR-OLD BRITISH RULE IN INDIA

ROYAL ASSENT TO INDEPENDENCE BILL

BRIEF BUT COLOURFUL CEREMONY IN LORDS

Two Dominions Created

King George VI

FREE INDIA FLAG

LONDON, July 18.

CONSTITUENT ASSEMBLY

UNION'S RELATIONSHIP WITH RULERS

PROVISION FOR PROVINCES' JURISDICTION IN STATES

By Our Special Representative
NEW DELHI, Friday

MESSAGE FROM PREMIER

Equality Of Status With Britain

Sir Shafaat Ahmed Khan Dead

FOUNDED GANDHI TEMPLE

Provisional Govt. For Burma

ANNOUNCEMENT LIKELY NEXT WEEK

Return Of Bollaert Welcomed

TRAVANCORE WILL BE INDEPENDENT ON AUG. 15

Indonesia's Rice Offer Holds

UNION JACK DOWN

Lucknow Result

Gandhiji's Visitors

VICEROY TO VISIT LAHORE

ON TERMS

On Other Pages

The birth of the Dominion of India: celebration in London, 23 August 1947. The scene outside India House as the new flag of the Dominion of India was unfurled besides the Union Jack on a corner of the building (The Illustrated London News).

1947

Nehru and Nation Building

1964

Nehru and
Nation Building

1947 - 1964

The struggle for independence had been a difficult journey for those who had led the country selflessly, demanding sacrifice and commitment. Recalling the time he had spent in jail, Jawaharlal Nehru observed, *'Prison is not a pleasant place to live in even for a short period, much less for long years.'* What sustained him, as indeed many others, was the recognition, to quote one of Nehru's favourite passages from George Bernard Shaw, *'This is the true joy of life, the being used for a purpose recognised by yourself as a mighty one.'* And what could be mightier or nobler than laying the foundations of a new nation taking its first steps on the path of democracy and freedom? In Nehru's own words, *'We are little men serving great causes, but because the cause is great, something of that greatness falls upon us also.'*

RECONSTRUCTION

At last independence arrived, but it brought in its wake monumental challenges. In the months preceding 15 August 1947, it had become evident that the division of the country was inevitable. Riots and clashes between Hindus and Muslims erupted across Bengal, Bihar, and Punjab. Faced with the immediate prospect of losing their homes and livelihood, and with their security at risk, people took to the streets as wanton killings and violence escalated along communal lines. Millions of Hindus and Sikhs migrated to India, and millions of Muslims left for what is now Pakistan.

Nehru was conscious of the grave threat posed by communalism to the unity and integrity of India, and he personally carried out a massive campaign against it through radio broadcasts and public speeches. He demonstrated through personal example the fearless response to communal violence.

With the establishment of Pakistan, Hindu communal forces became increasingly strident, declaring 15 August as a day of mourning and attacking the government for what they saw as a policy of Muslim appeasement. Soon riots broke out in Delhi. When Gandhi said that Pakistan should be given its share of immovable assets despite the ongoing hostility in Kashmir, Hindu communal forces sharpened their attack on him.

Anguished by the brutality and violence of the partition riots, Gandhi undertook an indefinite fast on 13 January 1948 for peace and communal harmony. On 15 January, the representatives of all communities, led by Jawaharlal Nehru, Rajendra Prasad, and Maulana

Partition led to millions crossing the border to the other side of the India-Pakistan divide, making it the greatest trek in the history of human migration. Sadly, it was associated with horrific communal bloodshed of equally gigantic proportions.

Azad, gave an assurance in this regard. On 17 January, a Central Peace Committee was formed under the leadership of the Congress president to ensure that all efforts would be made to normalise the situation. On 18 January, Gandhi called off his fast. But in the surcharged atmosphere, not everyone appreciated Gandhi's efforts to speak for all, Hindus and Muslims alike.

GANDHI'S ASSASSINATION

On 30 January 1948, as Gandhi came for his usual prayer meeting, he was assassinated by a fanatic young man, Nathuram Godse, a member of the Hindu Mahasabha and the RSS, and a close associate of V.D. Savarkar. Gandhi's assassination shocked the entire nation because the man who himself had espoused communal harmony had fallen to the merciless bullets of the very same communal forces. Thus tragically ended the life of one of the most remarkable men of our times, who was loved and revered as Bapu (father) and honoured as the Mahatma by the people of his country.

For more than three decades, Gandhi had dominated the national movement with the strength of his moral force and his firm conviction in standing up for a just cause. People from all walks of life, regions, and communities rallied behind him. Not only did he attract widespread support for the national movement and the Congress Party, but he also fundamentally

altered the character of the movement. Addressing the nation after Gandhi's assassination, Nehru said:

. . . the light has gone out of our lives . . . the light that shone on this country was no ordinary light . . . For that light represented more than the immediate present, it represented living the eternal truths, reminding us of the right path, drawing us from error, taking this ancient country to freedom.

Nehru realised that Gandhi's assassination was not merely an act of a lone fanatic but was also backed by the ideology of the RSS, which he described as a fascist organisation. Sardar Patel, with Nehru's support, banned the RSS and the Hindu Mahasabha. The ban on the RSS was lifted only in July 1949 when it gave an undertaking that it would function under severe restrictions. The Hindu Mahasabha was dissolved.

Left: Jawaharlal Nehru climbs the fence of Birla House and breaks the news of Gandhi's death to the sorrow striken people, 30 January 1948.

Above: The UN flag at half mast.

Right: Newsflashes from Delhi.

GANDHI CRUCIFIED BY FANATICISM

THE BOMBAY SAMACHAR

જગતની સર્વોત્તમ વિભૂતિ મહાત્મા ગાંધીજી

Amrita Bazar Patrika

GANDHIJI SHOT DEAD

Light Gone Out.

નૂતન ગુજરાત

આ પુ ગયા... બાપુ ઘણું

The Times of India

DAILY PRABHAT

પ્રભાત

MAHATMA GANDHI ASSASSINATED AT DELHI

MARATHA FROM POONA FIRES AT POINT-BLANK RANGE

IRREPARABLE LOSS TO MANKIND

The King's Message

FUNERAL TODAY AT JUMNA GHAT; COUNTRY-WIDE GRIEF

માનવતેંચી જીવનજ્યોત માવળ્ળી !
સારें જગ નિબિડ અંધःकारांत बुडालें !!

भारताचा महात्मा राष्ट्रपिता

NATIONAL HERALD

MAHATMA GANDHI PASSES

Shot On Way To Prayer Meeting

The Bombay Chronicle

MAHATMA SUCCUMBS TO ASSASSIN'S BULLET

On Way To Meeting

BOMBAY'S MILLION CITIZENS STUNNED

Premier Appeals For Peace

આપણા જીવનનો પ્રકાશ બુઝાયો છે અને હવે સર્વત્ર

ગુજરાત સમાચાર

હતભાગી રાષ્ટ્ર પર વજ્રઘાત

જનતાની આંખડીનું અજવાળું જ્યારે આંખ

The Hindustan Times

MAHATMA GANDHI KILLED BY ASSASSIN'S BULLET

THE LIGHT HAS GONE FROM OUR LIVES

AT POINT

Left: Mahatma Gandhi's funeral procession on way to Rajghat.

Above: People's homage to the Mahatma.

Top right: Nehru contemplates before the lighted pyre.

Bottom right: Indira Gandhi on the train which took the ashes of Mahatma Gandhi, 1948.

J.B. KRIPALANI (1888-1982)

President, 54th Session, Meerut-1946.

A Gandhian socialist, Acharya J.B. Kripalani was all his life a critic of the establishment. He was prominently involved for over a decade in important Congress Party affairs, and in the organisation of the Salt Satyagraha and the Quit India Movement; served in the interim government of India (1946–1947) and the Constituent Assembly of India. After drifting away from the Congress Party in 1951, he started an English newspaper *Vigil* and formed the Krishak Mazdoor Praja Party. He wrote a number of books on Gandhian philosophy.

REHABILITATION

Independent India faced the immense challenge of reconstruction, consolidation, and nation building, which now began in right earnest. The immediate problem facing the new government was the rehabilitation of six million refugees. A huge relief camp was set up in Nilokheri near Delhi to resettle the refugees from Punjab. In East Bengal, large camps provided immediate relief to refugees. J.B. Kripalani, the Congress president, established a Central Relief Committee in July 1947, with Sucheta Kripalani as its secretary.

Many dedicated people worked hard to prevent the spread of violence and to resettle the refugees. Notable among them were Sardar Tarlok Singh at the Punjab Rural Rehabilitation Centre, Premvati Thapar at the Jalandhar Women's Camp, S.K. Dey at Nilokheri, and S.K. Ghosh at Faridabad. Sushila Nayar was put in charge of rescuing and recovering abandoned and abducted women, and in Uttar Pradesh, Sarojini Naidu did commendable work in limiting the violence.

INTEGRATION

When the British departed, they left behind not only India and Pakistan, but also a large number of states constituting princely India. India under British rule had included approximately 562 princely states, ranging in size from a few square miles to a state as large as Hyderabad with a population of approximately 17 million. The government headed by Pandit Nehru faced the urgent task of integrating the states that had earlier accepted British paramountcy. Sardar Vallabhbhai Patel, the deputy prime minister, headed the newly created States Department, and along with Nehru he ensured the integration of the country in a remarkably short period between 1947 and 1950.

On the eve of the transfer of power, Lord Mountbatten and Sardar Patel appealed to the princes to accede to the Indian Union. On 5 July 1947, Patel reminded the states that:

By common endeavours we can raise the country to a new greatness, while lack of unity will expose us to fresh calamities. I hope the Indian states will bear in mind that the alternative to cooperation in general interest is anarchy and chaos which will overwhelm great and small in a common ruin.

Princely States

Sardar Patel succeeded in getting the majority of the princes to join the Indian Union, through appeals, coercion, and a 'carrot and stick' approach. All states except Jammu & Kashmir, Junagadh, and Hyderabad signed the Instrument of Accession. The Nawab of Junagadh acceded to Pakistan on 15 August 1947, but the people of the state rose in revolt

VALLABHBHAI PATEL (1875-1950)

President, 45th Session, Karachi-1931.

Sardar Vallabhbhai Patel, often described as the 'Iron Man of India', played a leading role in the Indian freedom struggle. The Kheda Satyagraha turned Patel into a national hero. He became the first Deputy Prime Minister and the Home Minister of India, and is credited with achieving the political integration of India. He sorted out the problems of partition and restored law and order with great courage and foresight, and with the ruthless efficiency of a great administrator.

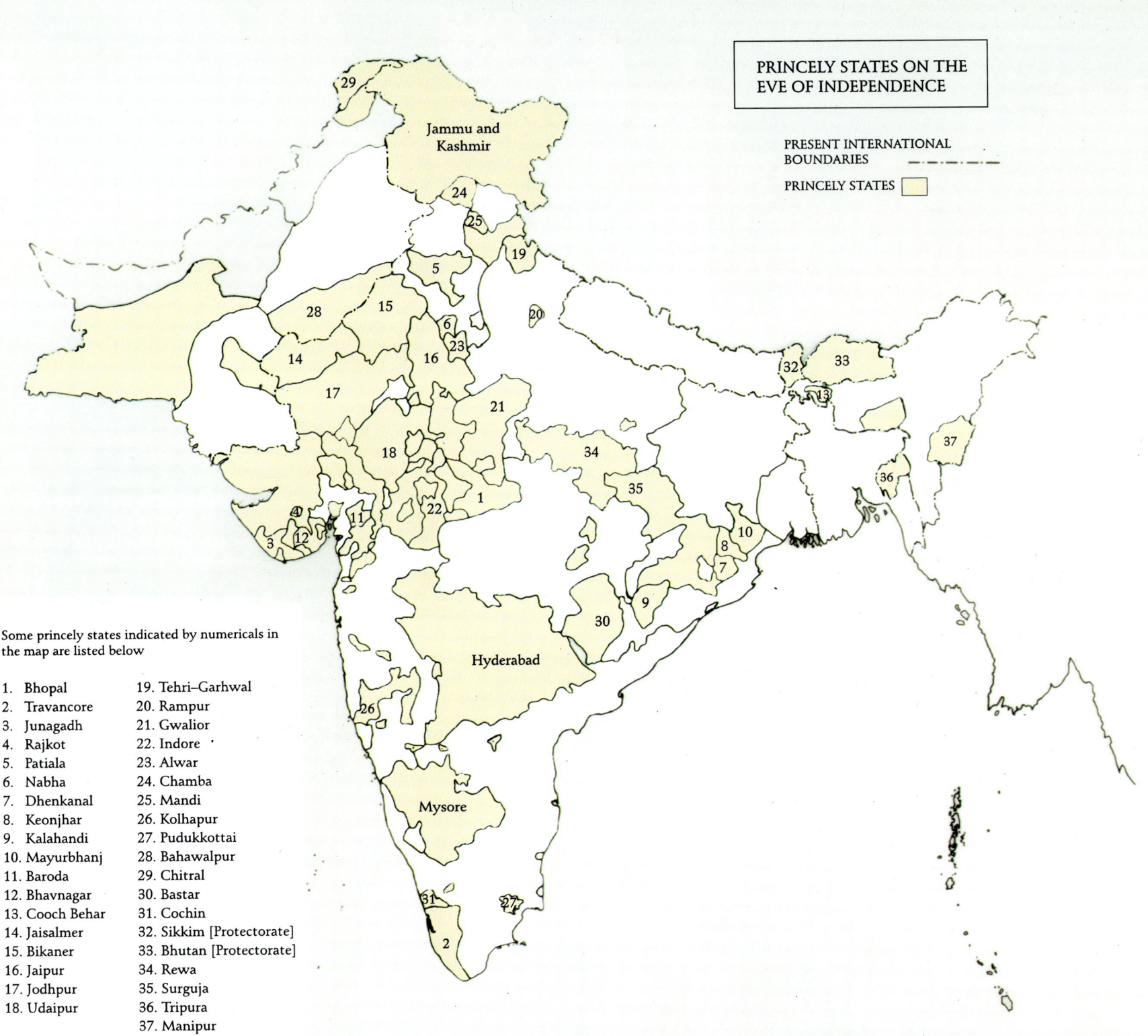

PRINCELY STATES ON THE
EVE OF INDEPENDENCE

PRESENT INTERNATIONAL
BOUNDARIES

PRINCELY STATES

Jammu and
Kashmir

Hyderabad

Mysore

Some princely states indicated by numericals in
the map are listed below

1.	Bhopal	19.	Tehri–Garhwal
2.	Travancore	20.	Rampur
3.	Junagadh	21.	Gwalior
4.	Rajkot	22.	Indore
5.	Patiala	23.	Alwar
6.	Nabha	24.	Chamba
7.	Dhenkanal	25.	Mandi
8.	Keonjhar	26.	Kolhapur
9.	Kalahandi	27.	Pudukkottai
10.	Mayurbhanj	28.	Bahawalpur
11.	Baroda	29.	Chitral
12.	Bhavnagar	30.	Bastar
13.	Cooch Behar	31.	Cochin
14.	Jaisalmer	32.	Sikkim [Protectorate]
15.	Bikaner	33.	Bhutan [Protectorate]
16.	Jaipur	34.	Rewa
17.	Jodhpur	35.	Surguja
18.	Udaipur	36.	Tripura
		37.	Manipur

and formed a provisional government. At their request, the Government of India took over the administration of Junagadh in November 1947. In Hyderabad, the Nizam declared that it would be an independent state, and here Patel had to resort to police action, and Hyderabad eventually acceded to the Indian Union in September 1948.

Kashmir

Jammu & Kashmir presented a very special problem because it was a Muslim-majority state ruled by a Hindu maharaja. The Kashmiri Muslim Conference urged Jammu & Kashmir to accede to Pakistan, but the National Conference, affiliated to the All India States People's Conference, under the leadership of Sheikh Abdullah, was inclined otherwise. On 15 October 1947, the prime minister of Jammu & Kashmir in a telegram to the British prime minister complained of an economic blockade and a virulent press and radio campaign by Pakistan aimed at coercing the state to accede.

On 22 October, the Pakistani attack on Kashmir began. The valley was subjected to pillage and plunder by the marauding invaders. They reached Baramullah on 27 October, placing Srinagar in danger. Faced with this situation, Maharaja Hari Singh acceded to India by signing the Instrument of Accession, under the Union of India Act. Indian troops were flown in and Srinagar was saved. India approached the United Nations Security Council in December 1947, and a ceasefire was effected between India and Pakistan in 1948.

After 1948, India and Pakistan accepted the United Nations ceasefire line, leaving a part of Kashmir under Pakistani occupation. Kashmir, however, continued to remain a delicate and sensitive matter. In 1950, Article 370 of the Constitution of India granted Kashmir a special status within the Union of India. Kashmir's own constitution, which was adopted in 1956, declared Kashmir as an integral part of the Union of India.

In December 1961, Goa was liberated from the Portuguese, thereby completing the task of the integration of India.

The most significant and enduring achievements of the Congress leadership in the aftermath of the country's partition were the rapid unification of India and the rehabilitation of millions of refugees. Nehru, Patel, Maulana Azad, G.B. Pant, B.C. Roy, B.G. Kher, and others, backed by the grass-roots functionaries of the *praja mandals* and other bodies affiliated to the All India States People's Conference, worked hard to realise these goals.

CONSTITUTENT ASSEMBLY
(December 1946 – December 1949)

The first decade of Congress rule in independent India shaped the vision of the new nation and laid the foundation of its democratic institutions and secular character. The party brought together exceptional people of different ideologies to unite in the task of nation building. The composition of Nehru's cabinet, which included five non-Congress members— Dr B.R. Ambedkar, S.P. Mookerjee, John Mathai, C.H. Bhabha, and Shanmukham Chetty—was truly representative of India's secular, flexible, and all-encompassing character.

These principles were integral to the framing of the Constitution of India, which was a truly daunting enterprise.

The Constituent Assembly made efforts to include people of all shades of opinion. There were 292 Congress members, 72 Muslim League members, and the rest belonged to other parties. Apart from members sent by the provinces of British India, there were also representatives of the princely states. Even though the majority of members were from the Congress, every effort was made to work through consensus and broad agreement. The Congress also nominated independent members to represent civil society and also appointed legal luminaries.

The Congress leadership had maintained since the 1930s that the constitution would reflect the aspirations of the Indian people. The basic principles and the broad structure of the Constitution bore the distinct imprint of Congress ideology. The CWC discussed and ratified every important resolution before placing it before the Constituent Assembly. The first meeting of the Constituent Assembly on 9 December 1946 was a historic day as the people's representatives came together to determine the future constitution of the country.

By the time the Constituent Assembly met for its third session in April-May 1947, it had become clear that the Muslim League would not participate in the work of the body. The process was, however, made more participatory by asking for submissions from the public at large.

OBJECTIVES RESOLUTION, 1946

On the fifth day of the first session of the Constituent Assembly, 13 December 1946, Jawaharlal Nehru moved the historic Objectives Resolution, which created the framework of the Constitution. It firmly resolved to proclaim India as a sovereign republic, securing for its citizens justice and equity, social, economic, and political, equal status of opportunity before the law, freedom of thought, expression, belief, faith, worship, vocation, association, and action, with adequate safeguards for minorities, backward and tribal areas, and depressed and other backward classes.

The Congress chose Dr Ambedkar, a non-Congress member and a prominent Dalit leader, as the chairman of the Drafting Committee, who played a pivotal role in the drafting of the Constitution. He was ably assisted by formidable legal minds, K.M. Munshi, Alladi Krishnaswami Aiyar, B.N. Rau, and S.N. Mukherjee. The Congress leadership tapped the best talent—irrespective of party affiliation, political background, or considerations of caste, community, region or religion—to join in the task of drafting a constitution for free India.

Congress leaders Jawaharlal Nehru, Vallabhbhai Patel, and Rajendra Prasad, the president of the Constituent Assembly, made the most substantial contributions. Nehru and Patel headed various important committees and both worked hard to ensure consensus, allowing free and frank debate to guide the deliberations. On controversial issues, all members were given an opportunity to express their opinions. Nehru remarked that in this task they had to balance two factors: *'the urgent necessity in reaching our goal and the other that we should reach it in proper time and with as great unanimity as possible.'*

BHIMRAO RAMJI AMBEDKAR (1891-1956)

Dr B.R. Ambedkar, popularly known as Babasaheb, was the chief architect of the Indian Constitution. A well-known political leader and an eminent jurist, Ambedkar's efforts to eradicate social evils like untouchablity and caste restrictions were remarkable. Throughout his life, he fought for the rights of the Dalits and other socially backward classes. In 1932, he signed the famous Poona Pact with Mahatma Gandhi. In 1936, he founded the Independent Labour Party. Ambedkar was appointed as the nation's first Law Minister in the cabinet of Jawaharlal Nehru. A Buddhist convert, he founded the Bharatiya Bauddha Mahasabha in 1955. He was posthumously awarded the Bharat Ratna in 1990.

Dr Ambedkar acknowledged the Congress contribution in his speech to the Constituent Assembly on 25 November 1949, giving credit to the party:

The task of the Drafting Committee would have been a very difficult one, if this Constituent Assembly had been merely a motley crowd, a tessellated pavement without cement, a black stone here and [a] white stone there on which each member or each group was a law unto itself. There would have been nothing else but chaos. This possibility of chaos was reduced to nil by the existence of the Congress Party inside the Assembly[,] which brought into its proceedings [the] essence of order and discipline. It is because of the discipline of the Congress Party that the Drafting Committee was able to pilot the Constitution in the Assembly with the sure knowledge as to the faith of each Article and each amendment. The Congress Party is therefore entitled to all the credit for the smooth sailing of the draft Constitution in the Assembly.

THE CONSTITUTION OF INDIA

The Constitution of India was amongst the largest in the world, with 395 Articles and 9 Schedules. The Preamble of the Constitution, which spells out its basic philosophy, was carved out of the Objectives Resolution and speaks of the solemn resolve of the people of India to secure to all citizens justice, liberty, equality, and fraternity. India was proclaimed to be a democratic republic with a parliamentary system based on universal adult franchise. This had been a consistent demand of the Congress since the late nineteenth century and was a significant step in empowering the marginalised sections of society. That India embraced democracy within the institutional framework of the Constitution is testimony to the fore-sightedness and sagacity of its founding fathers. The Republic of India guarantees to all Indian citizens fundamental rights of speech and expression, freedom to assemble peaceably, to form associations, and to acquire and hold property, and equality before the law. The Constitution became an instrument for the removal of social injustice. Untouchability was abolished, and its practise penalised in 1955. Affirmative action formed the cornerstone of the social agenda. Seats were reserved in the legislature and in educational institutions for the Scheduled Castes and Scheduled Tribes, and government jobs were reserved for them. The Constitution also laid down certain Directive Principles of State Policy to guide the states in the framing of laws.

The Constitution of India came into force on 26 January 1950. The date had a special significance. At midnight on 31 December 1929, at a massive public gathering in Lahore, Jawaharlal Nehru had hoisted India's tricolour flag on the banks of the river Ravi and declared

Above: Prime Minister Nehru signing the Constitution of India, 24 January 1950.

Across: A facsimile of the Preamble to the Constitution of India.

THE REPUBLIC OF INDIA
26th January 1950

WE, THE PEOPLE OF INDIA, having solemnly resolved to constitute India into a SOVEREIGN DEMOCRATIC REPUBLIC and to secure to all its citizens:

JUSTICE, social, economic and political;

LIBERTY of thought, expression, belief, faith and worship;

EQUALITY of status and of opportunity; and to promote among them all

FRATERNITY assuring the dignity of the individual and the unity of the Nation:

IN OUR CONSTITUENT ASSEMBLY DO HEREBY ADOPT, ENACT AND GIVE TO OURSELVES THIS CONSTITUTION.

C. RAJAGOPALACHARI (1878-1972)

Chakravarti Rajagopalachari, informally called Rajaji, served as the last Governor-General of India. A lawyer, politician, writer, statesman, and leader of the Indian National Congress, he participated in the agitations against the Rowlatt Act, the Non-Cooperation movement, the Vykom Satyagraha, and the Civil Disobedience movement. He was the founder of the Swatantra Party and the first recipient of India's highest civilian award, the Bharat Ratna (1954). Rajaji vehemently opposed the use of nuclear weapons and was a proponent of world peace and disarmament.

RAJENDRA PRASAD (1884-1963)

President, 48th Session, Bombay-1934.

Dr Rajendra Prasad served as the first president of independent India (1950-1962). As president, he exercised his moderating influence and moulded policies and actions silently and unobtrusively. He was the first leading political figure in the eastern provinces and played a prominent role during the Champaran Satyagraha. In 1934, Rajendra 'Babu' played a significant role in organising huge funds for earthquake relief in Bihar. When the Congress ministries were formed in 1937, it was the Parliamentary Board, consisting of Sardar Patel, Rajendra Babu, and Maulana Azad, that effectively provided guidance and control. He was awarded the Bharat Ratna in 1962.

poorna swaraj or complete independence, asking Indians to observe 26 January as Independence Day.

It had taken three years and the collective wisdom of remarkable individuals imbued with *'moral vision, political skill, and legal acumen'* to complete the task. The remarkable feat of laying the foundations of what is today the world's largest democracy has been hailed as the greatest political venture since the framing of the US Constitution.

Following the transfer of power in 1947, C.R. Rajagopalachari succeeded Lord Mountbatten as Governor-General. After the Constitution came into force, the office of the Governor-General was replaced by that of the President. C.R. Rajagopalachari relinquished the office of Governor-General and Rajendra Prasad became the first President of India, with Jawaharlal Nehru as the first Prime Minister.

Linguistic Reorganisation of the States and the Official Language

The demand for the reorganisation of the states on the basis of language was a major problem facing the new government. In its early years, the Congress had supported the demand for the linguistic demarcation of provincial boundaries at its sessions in 1927, 1928, and 1937. Increasingly, however, doubts rose about the wisdom of promoting linguistic divisions.

The issue came to a head when leaders from Andhra, including Swami Potti Sriramulu, a respected Gandhian, undertook a fast unto death for the recognition of Andhra as a separate state, provoking unprecedented violence. Eventually, Nehru announced the formation of Andhra Pradesh, as well as the appointment of a State Reorganisation Commission in 1953, which recommended the linguistic reorganisation of the states.

The Constitution had declared Hindi in the Devanagari script as the administrative language to be used throughout the country. However, the non-Hindi-speaking states saw the decision to do away with English and an endorsement of Hindi as evidence of the domination of the Hindi-speaking north over the rest of the country. It was regarded as a move to edge out non-Hindi-speaking Indians from jobs and other positions. In 1963, the Dravida Munnettra Kazhagam (DMK), based in Tamil Nadu, launched a massive movement against Hindi, which spread to other parts of the country. Eventually, Nehru gave an assurance that English would continue to be an associated language for official purposes until the non-Hindi-speaking states voluntarily agreed to implement constitutional provisions for making Hindi the lingua franca of the country.

GENERAL ELECTIONS, 1952

The first general elections of free India were held in February 1952. The Congress won comfortably, securing 364 out of 489 seats in Parliament, and 2,247 out of 3,280 seats in the state assemblies. Nehru led the election campaign, covering 40,000 kilometres and addressing over 35 million people, and the results were a testimony to his personal charisma and popular appeal. The main plank of the Congress campaign was the fight against communalism. It was an empowering experience for the rural masses to exercise their franchise, and the elections came to personify a festival of democracy. It is a great tribute to the secular ideology and leadership of the Congress that despite the cataclysmic events surrounding the partition of the country, peaceful elections were held within the framework of India's secular constitution.

In the next two general elections, too, the Congress performed far better than the other parties. It commanded a stable majority in the Lok Sabha, but the number of Congress representatives in the state assemblies declined to some extent. Until the 1960s, however, the Congress remained the dominant party, demonstrating its plurality and flexibility by representing different groupings.

PARTY ORGANISATION

The character of the Indian National Congress changed after independence. The AICC resolved in 1948 to retain the Congress as the only organisational body to administer the country. The new party constitution was approved at the Jaipur session in December 1948. A three-tier membership was envisaged to broaden the base of the party, which was later amended to two types of membership—primary and active. Congress committees were established at the *mandal* level to strengthen the grass-roots organisation. The Congress was the only pan-India party not just in terms of its geographic reach but also in the universality of its appeal to all sections of society. As Nehru said, the Congress was *'the mirror of the nation.'*

During this period, Parliament under Nehru's leadership resolved many conflicts and promoted national integration. The mature functioning of Parliament was amply demonstrated on several occasions, such as the debates on the States Reorganisation Commission, Lal Bahadur Shastri's resignation as Railway Minister in 1958 following the rail accident at Ariyalur (Tamil Nadu), and V.K. Krishna Menon's resignation as Defence Minister after China's invasion in 1962. G.V. Mavalankar, the Lok Sabha speaker, distinguished himself as an able parliamentary authority, setting an example for his successors.

The national movement had brought together diverse individuals and groups in the pursuit of a common goal—seeking independence from British rule. The Congress had successfully assimilated various views, internal conflicts, and ideological differences within the framework of a larger national vision. After independence, many political groups emerged from the fold of the Congress to branch off into distinct parties such as the Swatantra, the Samyukta Socialist, the Jana Sangh, and the Communist Party of India.

Within the Congress, too, healthy ideological differences persisted between Nehru and Sardar Patel. This was perhaps most strongly manifested at the Nasik session in 1950 over the issue of the presidentship of the Congress. Nehru supported the candidature of J.B. Kripalani, while Patel supported that of Purshottam Das Tandon, who won. Tandon constituted the CWC in a manner not quite to the liking of Nehru. The latter resigned from the CWC, followed by Maulana Azad as well as many others, forcing Tandon to resign. J.B. Kripalani quit the Congress along with his followers because of differences with Nehru regarding the role of the party in governance. Nehru's view was that the government and the party should maintain an arm's length distance from each other, allowing for an independent structure of governance.

Members of the Executive Committee and the staff of the Congress Party in Parliament, 8 February 1952.

PURSHOTTAM DAS TANDON (1882-1961)

President, 56th Session, Nasik-1950. He is widely remembered for his efforts to make Hindi the official language of India; was called Rajarshi because of his austere life and philanthropy; was awarded the Bharat Ratna in 1961.

U.N. DHEBAR (1905-1977)

President, 60th-64th Sessions (Avadi-1955, Amritsar-1956, Indore-1957, Gauhati-1958, and Nagpur-1959); offered individual *satyagraha* (Viramgam-1941); played a prominent role in the merger of the state of Kathiawad in the Indian Union; was awarded the Padma Vibhushan in 1973.

Nehru tried to ensure that the Congress remained an inclusive party that welcomed diversity. He was concerned that the Congress should ideologically maintain a socialist orientation, and he took the initiative of radically altering party policies in the spheres of social equality, equity, and economic development.

Sardar Patel died in 1950, and Nehru remained as the towering leader of the Congress and the government. The AICC elected Nehru as the Congress president, and he continued in this office until the Avadi session in 1955 where the 'socialistic pattern of society' was adopted as an objective of the party. He also presided over three sessions of the Congress—at New Delhi in 1951, at Hyderabad in 1953, and at Kalyani in 1954.

The transformation of the Congress from being a party that had led the national movement to a party now heading the government inevitably brought, over a period of time, problems of factionalism, weakening contact with the masses, internal power struggles, and corruption. A resolution adopted at the Avadi session in 1955 directed the CWC to take firm measures to ensure organisational discipline. In 1963, the loss of three by-elections did not go unnoticed, and the party leadership decided to take firm action.

K. Kamaraj and Nehru put together a plan for reorganising and reinvigorating the party with a clear agenda and clearly defined party and parliamentary wings. The Kamaraj Plan asked leaders to relinquish official positions and to approach the masses to restore confidence in the Congress. Three hundred resignations from ministerial posts, including from all members of the union cabinet and from the state chief ministers, followed. Nehru accepted the resignations of six union cabinet members and six chief ministers. This was seen by some as an attempt to purge some powerful right-wing colleagues.

NEHRU'S VISION FOR A NEW INDIA

Planning for Growth

Long before independence, the Congress Party had been deeply aware of the many problems that needed attention for improving the quality of life of ordinary Indians. Nehru in particular had a clear understanding of the challenges confronting the nation in its early years. As far back as 1936, in his presidential address to the Lucknow session, he had stated his views, outlining his policy for ensuring social justice and the welfare of the masses. Nehru was steadfast in pursuing the ideology of planning, and the National Planning Committee was set up in 1938, almost entirely on his initiative.

In November 1947, the Congress set up an Economic Programme Committee under the chairmanship of Nehru to draw up an economic policy for the Congress. The report of this committee, submitted in January 1948, emphasised the importance of establishing a just social order to ensure the equitable distribution of income and wealth. It proposed the creation of a permanent Planning Commission, which was established on 15 March 1950, with Nehru as chairman. In the planning process, Nehru was ably assisted by Prasanta Chandra Mahalanobis, a Cambridge-trained physicist and statistician, the man who introduced modern statistics to India and who used data collection and analysis effectively for the planning process.

In July 1951, Nehru presented a report to the AICC emphasising the need for laying the foundations of a welfare state in India. The Avadi session in 1955 resolved that:

. . . planning should take place with a view to the establishment of a socialistic pattern of society where the principal means of production are under social ownership or control, production is progressively speeded up and there is equitable distribution of the national wealth.

Nehru maintained that planning was essential to the development needs of a poor country with scarce resources, which needed to be managed optimally and which could be ensured only through effective national planning. He also felt that India would continue to face unforeseen crises and calamities—invasions, droughts, floods—and hence the country must have the ability to respond to these situations in

Above: Nehru signing the report of the Planning Commission on the First Five-Year Plan, New Delhi, 7 July 1951.

Next page, centrespread: Nehru addressing the first meeting of the National Development Council, New Delhi, 8 November 1952.

a planned and systematic manner. He also felt that state intervention in economic policy (what he called 'the commanding heights of the economy') was imperative for developing the country's infrastructure and for ensuring that large projects were taken up so that the country could reap the benefits of the economies of scale. The state alone could mobilise the resources required for such ambitious projects. Nehru felt that ownership of key industries should not be allowed to fall into the hands of private individuals.

Land Reforms

Unequal access to land was a fundamental problem in rural India. Land reform legislation had long been on the agenda of the Congress. After independence, this issue was prioritised, and by 1949 different states had passed major legislation to abolish the *zamindari* system. This step at one stroke led to an economic and social revolution in rural India, empowering the rural peasantry. The state vested the right of ownership in tenants, doing away with age-old exploitation represented by the imposition of rents and cesses. It freed land for redistribution to the landless. Tenants and sharecroppers got occupancy rights and now paid reduced fixed rents.

Nehru strongly backed the implementation of land reforms, believing them to be necessary because, as he said:

We felt that this [was the] inner urge of our people because we heard the cry of millions of people and sometimes deep murmurs and rumblings which, if not listened to and if not answered, create big revolutions and changes in the country.

He viewed land reforms not only in terms of social equity but also within the larger perspective of economic development. In a letter to chief ministers in 1954, he observed:

The whole policy of land reforms apart from moving the burden of the actual tiller was to spread the income from the land more evenly among the peasantry and thus give them the purchasing power. In this way the internal market would expand and productive forces of the country would grow.

Community Development

The needs of peasants, most of whom lacked the material resources, education, and knowledge necessary to negotiate the major changes taking place in rural areas, also received attention.

On 2 October 1952, under the First Five-Year Plan, a nationwide Community Development Programme (CDP) was launched that envisaged the village as a basic unit of development. The programme was especially aimed at improving the conditions of backward groups and backward areas. Under this programme, community development schemes were launched focusing on improved road connectivity, cattle welfare,

Nehru visiting villages near Delhi to inspect the progress of community development, 13 June 1955.

improved methods of cultivation, canal irrigation, and the introduction of scientific methods of agriculture. At the first CDP conference in 1952, Nehru expressed the hope that:

These community centres will not merely pick out the best and most favourable spots and help them start but also try to work out the problems of the other spots which are backward, economically, socially, and in other respects.

Self-reliance

The economic policy of the Congress emphasised *swadeshi* or self-reliance, clearly recognising that underdevelopment was a result of a lack of technological progress. To remedy this, major initiatives to foster self-sufficiency were introduced. The Industrial Policy Resolution of 1948 stressed the role of the state in the development of industry. The New Industrial Policy Resolution of 1956 emphasised the vital role of the state in planning, developing, and exercising overall control of resources. It committed the state to undertaking the expansion of the public sector, which would cover basic industries and public utility services. In pursuing a policy of a mixed economy, Nehru envisaged that while basic industries would remain under state control, other industries could continue to be privately managed.

The country's modernisation depended crucially on planning, a mixed economy, and rapid industrialisation guided by the state.

Public Sector Undertakings: 'Temples of Modern India'

The New Industrial Policy Resolution of 1956 classified new industries into three categories. The first was the exclusive responsibility of the state and included energy, power, iron, coal, steel, electricity, telephone, defence-related industries, and aviation. The second covered both public and private sector participation and included chemicals, fertilisers, pharmaceuticals, and road transport. The third was the private sector, which primarily covered consumer industries.

Nehru identified the production of power and steel as essential for self-sufficiency and planning. India collaborated with other countries, and the result was the establishment of steel plants in Rourkela (Orissa) with German help, in Bhilai (Madhya Pradesh) with Russian help, and in Durgapur (West Bengal) with British help. The Indian steel industry symbolised India's ambition to forge ahead on a self-reliant, productive industrial path.

Power generation was the other major area identified as crucial. Dam projects were undertaken on the Mahanadi, Rihand, Tungabhadra, Damodar, and Satluj rivers. The most prestigious of these was the Bhakra Nangal dam in Punjab, the second highest in the world. Inaugurated in July 1954, it was a symbol of what Nehru called *'the temples of modern India'*. The first state-owned oil refinery was inaugurated in Noonmati, Assam in 1962.

Nehru as an Institution Builder

Nehru was determined to foster the 'scientific temper', which he considered the driver of progress. Many new engineering institutes were established, the most important being the premier Indian Institutes of Technology, five of which were started between 1957 and 1964. The Indian Institute of Science, Bangalore, was granted deemed university status in 1959. In 1950, the Council of Scientific and Industrial Research was set up with a chain of national and regional laboratories, including the National Physical Laboratory. In 1954, Nehru laid the foundation stone of the Tata Institute of Fundamental Research in Bombay. In 1958, the Defence Research and Development Organisation was set up. The many institutions established in the early post-independence years are testimony to the farsightedness of Nehru, who hoped that these would become the *'visible symbols of building up the new India and of providing life and sustenance to our people.'*

Nuclear Energy and Space Research

Soon after independence, India embarked upon a nuclear programme aimed at developing its nuclear capacity for peaceful purposes. The Atomic Energy Act of 1948 paved the way for the creation of the Atomic Energy Commission on 3 January 1954. Dr Homi Bhabha's pioneering work helped set India on the road to developing a nuclear programme devoted to peaceful

Previous page: Jawaharlal Nehru at Tata Iron and Steel Company, Jamshedpur, 25 November 1950.

Above: Nehru's visit to the Bhakra Nangal Dam under construction, 28 September 1959.

Across: Nehru at the Indian Standards Institution.

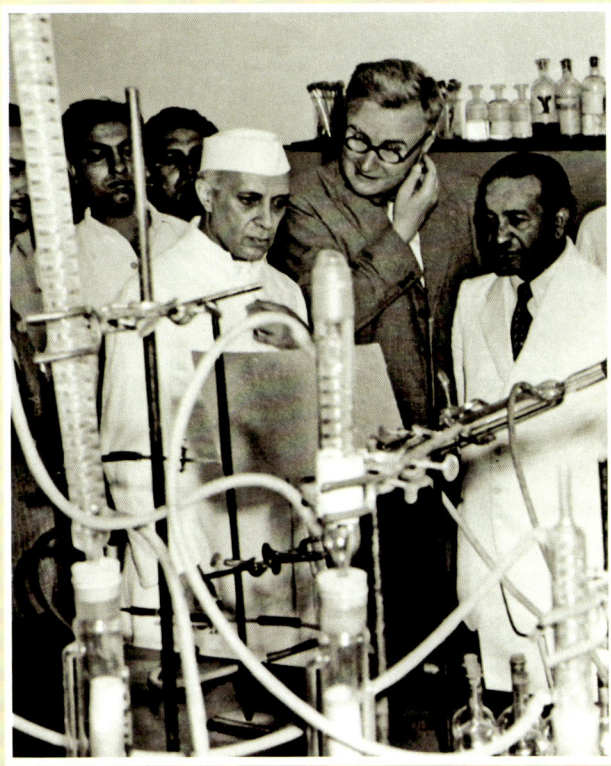

Above: Nehru at the National Chemical Laboratory, Poona, 3 January 1950. G.I. Finch and S.S. Bhatnagar are also seen in the picture.

Across: Nehru with Homi Jehangir Bhabha at the inauguration of the atomic reactor 'Apsara', Trombay, Bombay, 20 January 1957.

purposes. The Bhabha Atomic Research Centre was created to enhance India's capabilities in this area. Nehru believed that India had to harness its scientific and technological talent to build 'atoms for peace'. But he also stressed that nuclear, chemical, and biological knowledge and power should not be used to manufacture weapons of mass destruction. In furtherance of this policy, India consistently supported nuclear disarmament.

Dr Vikram Sarabhai, the father of the Indian space programme, helped establish the Indian Space Research Organisation.

Education as a Tool for Empowerment

The major concerns in the 1950s were the removal of adult illiteracy, universalisation of primary education, and the training of man-power in different areas. Maulana Abul Kalam Azad was given charge of the education portfolio at the centre. The Indian Council for Cultural Relations was set up in 1950 under Maulana Azad to help formulate and implement policies pertaining to India's external cultural relations, to foster mutual understanding between India and other countries, and to promote cultural exchanges with other peoples.

The establishment of the University Education Commission under the chairmanship of Dr S. Radhakrishnan in 1948, and the Secondary Education Commission under the chairmanship

of Dr A.L. Mudaliar in 1952, laid the foundations of school education and higher education.

NEHRU: A GLOBAL STATESMAN

Nehru, with his deep understanding of the country, the world, and the international scenario, played a vital role in shaping India's foreign policy in the post-independence period. His charismatic personality made him a natural leader for the countries of the South. He believed Indian culture to be an integral instrument in strengthening India's diplomatic relations with the rest of the world. Drawing on his experience, he laid the foundations of a policy that came to be known as Non-Alignment.

Non-Alignment

India gained freedom in a polarised world in which two major power blocs competed for ideological, political, and military dominance. Against the backdrop of Cold War tensions and increased nuclear capabilities, Nehru formulated a policy that would enable India, and indeed many of the newly decolonised nations of Asia and Africa, to oppose foreign dominance and to maintain their independence. He took the lead in defining the concept of non-alignment. In a speech at Columbia University, in New York City, in 1949, Nehru stated:

The goals of Indian Foreign Policy were combining idealism with national interest, . . . the pursuit of peace[,] not through alignment with any major power or group of powers, but through an independent approach to each controversial or disputed issue, liberation of subject peoples, the maintenance of freedom[,] both national and international.

The five principles of coexistence ('Panchsheel') between sovereign states as enunciated by Nehru became the basis of the Non-Aligned Movement. These were mutual respect for sovereignty and territorial integrity, mutual non-aggression, non-interference in the internal affairs of sovereign states, equality and mutual benefit, and peaceful coexistence. The movement was further strengthened at the Non-Aligned meeting in Belgrade in 1961.

In 1953, Nehru, Khrushchev, and Bulganin signed the Indo-Soviet Trade Agreement. The first Indian MIGs were manufactured in 1968 with Russian aid.

Nehru also sought to maintain good relations with the USA, but strains developed between the two countries after 1954 when Pakistan and the USA signed the Mutual Defence Treaty. However, Indo-US relations improved in the late 1950s and 1960s.

Jawaharlal Nehru addressing the First Conference of
Non-Aligned Nations, Belgrade, 2 September 1961.

Nehru's Vision for South-South Cooperation

On the eve of India's independence, Gandhi had said, '*India's freedom will remain incomplete so long as Africa remains in bondage.*' Nehru, a visionary statesman and the architect of India's foreign policy, carried forward this commitment by supporting liberation movements across Africa. India played a major role in the decolonisation of many African nations. Even in the early years of the decolonisation movement, he remained optimistic about the future of the continent:

Whatever the immediate future may be in Africa, it is clear that the whole continent of Africa has got a big future and changes will take place there fairly rapidly. These changes will be governed by the new political consciousness of the African people. We welcome this consciousness and wish to cooperate with this.

He embraced the newly independent nations of Asia and Africa, pointing to their shared experience of colonial subjugation, economic exploitation, and racial discrimination. Addressing the Bandung Conference in 1955, Nehru said:

It is up to Asia to help Africa to the best of our ability because we are sister continents. We are determined not to be dominated by any country or continent. We are determined to bring happiness and prosperity to our people and to discard age-old

shackles that have tied us, not only politically but [also] economically to the shackles of colonialism.

In 1962, hailing the spirit and potential of Africa and expressing India's solidarity with the continent, Nehru said:

Of one thing there can be no doubt, and that is the vitality of the people of Africa. Therefore, with the vitality of her people and the great resources available in this great continent, there can be no doubt that the future holds a great promise for the people of Africa.

The Asian Relations Conference, convened by Nehru in March-April 1947 in New Delhi, focused on the problems of Asian and African peoples under colonial rule. In line with this policy, India took an active interest in the liberation of the states of Indochina from colonial rule. Nehru obtained the support of several Asian leaders at a meeting in Colombo in April 1954 for these states to be allowed to determine their own destiny without the involvement of external actors. In January 1964, a conference of Indian Ocean states in New Delhi supported Indonesia's independence from Dutch rule. Subsequently, four Indochina supervisory commissions under India's chairmanship were set up. India under Nehru exerted a moral force for international peace and cooperation, and became involved in mediation and peacekeeping operations in Korea, Congo, and Cyprus.

China

India cultivated friendship with China from 1954 to 1959, and Nehru visited Peking in 1954. India was amongst the first to recognise the People's Republic of China and to campaign for a seat for China at the United Nations. In 1959, however, the flight of the Dalai Lama from Tibet to India created tensions between the two countries. Another area of misunderstanding was China's claim to areas of the North-East Frontier Agency (NEFA) and the Aksai Chin plain in eastern Ladakh in Kashmir. In 1960, the two countries held talks on this issue, but China pushed India to give up Aksai Chin. On 20 October 1962, China encroached onto Indian territory without any provocation. China's aggression was not only a political but also a personal setback for Nehru, and it was condemned by people both within and outside the country.

Nehru's Legacy

Nehru, who had not been in the best of health for some time, passed away on 27 May 1964. Some years before, in July 1955, at an impressive ceremony at the Rashtrapati Bhavan, the President, Dr Rajendra Prasad, had conferred the highest national award, the Bharat Ratna, on Nehru.

Nehru's vision and leadership shaped the post-independence years. He laid the founda-

Jawaharlal Nehru receiving India's highest civilian award, the Bharat Ratna, from President Rajendra Prasad, New Delhi, 7 September 1955.

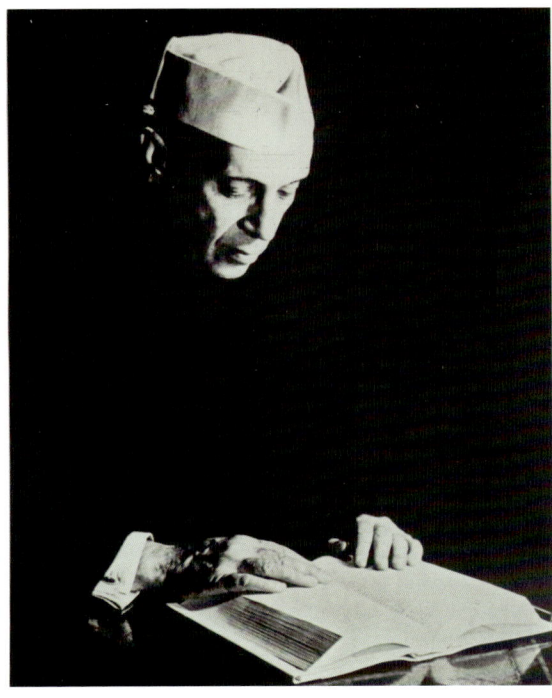

tions of a self-reliant, productive, and confident India, creating many of its institutions and leaving an indelible stamp on every aspect of the country. A socialist and a democrat, he was, above all, an Indian who deeply loved his country and his people. In his own words:

*If any people choose to think of me . . . ,
I should like them to say this man with all
his mind and heart loved India and the
Indian people and they were indulgent to him
and gave him of their love most abundantly
and extravagantly.*

Nehru's last journey, New Delhi, 28 May 1964.

1964

An Era of Decisive Leadership

1984

5

An Era of Decisive Leadership

1964 - 1984

AFTER NEHRU, WHO?

Jawaharlal Nehru's demise brought to the fore many tensions that had remained hidden because of his tall stature and unquestioned leadership. By 1964, the serious challenges of governing a large and diverse country were becoming evident. An increasingly articulate electorate demanded results. Regional pressures manifested themselves, and the ambitions of regional leaders became more visible and vocal. These developments have to be seen as a historical process in the unprecedented task of democratising a large population and of mobilising a diverse electorate divided along the lines of caste, religion, region, and language.

In 1964, the passing away of Nehru raised the question of finding an able successor. One of the senior-most ministers in Nehru's cabinet, Gulzari Lal Nanda, took charge as the interim prime minister.

There were at least four aspirants—G.L. Nanda, Morarji Desai, Jagjivan Ram, and Lal Bahadur Shastri. Kamaraj, the Congress president, adopted the 'consensus' method and informally consulted some CWC members and state chief ministers to choose Shastri.

The choice of Shastri as prime minister was widely accepted, but deeply resented by Morarji Desai and his supporters, who argued that only the Congress Parliamentary Party had the prerogative of choosing the leader.

THE SYNDICATE

Even during Nehru's time, an informal group of powerful Congress leaders had emerged known as the Syndicate. The group initially consisted of K. Kamaraj, N. Sanjeeva Reddy, S. Nijalingappa, Atulya Ghosh, and S.K. Patil. Later C.B. Gupta and others also joined them. Morarji Desai, known for his conservative ideas, also moved closer to the Syndicate at a later stage.

LAL BAHADUR SHASTRI

Shastri, a mild-mannered and soft-spoken man, became prime minister on 2 June 1964. He had enjoyed Nehru's trust, serving in his cabinet as Railway Minister. An experienced minister and skilled negotiator, he was the first choice of the party leadership to resolve intra-party conflicts.

While the country had taken giant strides under Nehru, more needed to be done for socio-economic development to achieve the objectives of self-reliance, eradication of poverty, removal

Lal Bahadur Shastri with Ayub Khan, Tashkent, 1966.

of illiteracy, providing basic health care. Shastri, in continuation with Nehru's policies, proclaimed his commitment to the principles of socialism and rural development. He turned his attention to reinvigorating rural society and economy, taking forward the agenda of agrarian reforms, the foundations for which had been laid in the Nehru period. Shastri's famous slogan *'Jai Jawan, Jai Kisan'* (Hail the soldier, hail the farmer), recognising the invaluable contribution of India's farmers and soldiers, the sentinels at the country's borders, stirred the emotions of the people.

WAR WITH PAKISTAN, 1965

Mounting tensions with Pakistan presented a serious problem for India's second prime minister. In the autumn of 1965, Pakistan engaged in military action in some border areas in Gujarat and followed this up with full-scale war. Under Shastri's leadership, India met the challenge effectively, pushing back the Pakistani troops across the Punjab plains, following them up to Lahore. However, under sustained pressure from world leaders and the United Nations Security Council, the war was brought to an end. India and Pakistan accepted a ceasefire in September 1965. The Soviet premier, Aleksei N. Kosygin, used his good offices to bring together the prime ministers of India and Pakistan, Shastri and Ayub Khan respectively, at Tashkent in January 1966. Sadly, while in Tashkent, Shastri suffered a massive heart attack and passed away, plunging the country into gloom.

LAL BAHADUR SHASTRI (1904-1966)

Abandoned his studies to take part in the Non-cooperation movement; played a leading role in the Salt Satyagraha; gave the slogan *'Jai Jawan, Jai Kisan';* prime minister of India,1964-66. Humble, tolerant, with great inner strength and resoluteness, he was a man of the people who understood their language.

NEELAM SANJEEVA REDDY (1913-1996)

President, Bangalore-1960; Bhavnagar-1961; Patna-1962.

Took part in the Civil Disobedience Movement; an influential peasant leader; took an active part in the Quit India Movement; held various important positions in the Congress. In 1977, elected as the president of the Republic.

S. NIJALINGAPPA (1902-2000)

President, Hyderabad-1968; Faridabad-1969.

Starting as a volunteer, he rose to be the president of the Pradesh Congress Committee and finally the president of the AICC. Known for his unique services rendered for the unification of Karnataka. He served as the state's first chief minister.

GULZARI LAL NANDA (1989-1998)

Imprisoned for offering *satyagraha* in 1932, 1942-44; instrumental in organising the Indian National Trade Union Congress; later became its president; held various portfolios in Congress government; sworn in as acting prime minister of India in 1964 and in 1966; awarded the Bharat Ratna in 1997.

JAGJIVAN RAM (1908-1986)

President, Bombay-1969.

Active participant in the Satyagraha and the Quit India movement; was inducted into the interim government at the centre in 1946; spokesman of the depressed classes. With a characteristic combination of shrewdness and adaptability, he made his political career a success.

K. KAMARAJ (1903-1975)

President, Bhubaneswar-1964; Durgapur-1965; Jaipur-1966.

Freedom fighter Kamaraj was elected president of the Tamilnad Congress Committee in 1940; became chief minister of Madras in 1954. Famous for his 'Kamaraj Plan'. He worked quietly among the masses; honoured posthumously with the Bharat Ratna.

BATTLE FOR SUCCESSION

Once again, the question of leadership arose. G.L. Nanda was again made the interim prime minister, but the situation was more complex as Morarji Desai remained a strong contender and ideological differences between the various groups in the party had grown sharper. However, the younger radical leaders were opposed to Desai's conservative policies and began to look to Indira Gandhi. The preference was not merely because she was Nehru's daughter. She had demonstrated her political skills as Congress president in 1959 and as Minister In-charge of Information and Broadcasting in Shastri's cabinet.

In the contest for leadership after Shastri's death, the Congress president, Kamaraj, did not follow the 'consensus' method. He allowed the Congress Parliamentary Party to choose their leader through the ballot. Indira Gandhi won decisively, defeating Morarji Desai by 355 votes to 169. She became prime minister at the age of 48.

INDIRA GANDHI

Indira Priyadarshini, born on 19 November 1917, was the only child of Jawaharlal and Kamala Nehru. She spent her childhood at Anand Bhavan in Allahabad, witnessing the nationalistic fervour of the times at a very close range. Her mother was in ill health, and her

INDIRA GANDHI (1917-1984)

President, 1959, 76th Session (1978-83, Delhi) and 77th Session (1983-84, Calcutta).

Indira Gandhi was the Prime Minister of India from 1966 to 1977 and from 1980-1984, a total of fifteen years. She is India's only woman prime minister to date and the world's all-time longest serving woman prime minister. She implemented programmes like Garibi Hatao, nuclear projects, family planning, bank nationalisation, food security. She led India to victory in the Indo-Pak war in 1971. Indira Gandhi launched Operation Blue Star in Punjab for stopping the Sikh secessionist movement. She was assassinated by her own bodyguards in 1984. She was awarded the Bharat Ratna in 1971.

Top: Indira Gandhi during a visit to Maharashtra as Congress president, 1959. *Centre:* With Nehru at a Congress meeting, Madurai, 1961. *Bottom:* Being sworn in as Union Minister of Information and Broadcasting, 1964.

father often absent for long periods. Although Nehru spent much of his time away from home, he lovingly educated his daughter through a series of letters that he wrote to her during his long imprisonment, later published as *Letters from a Father to a Daughter.* In addition to the invaluable education that young Indira received from her father, she also attended Shantiniketan and Somerville College, Oxford University. She married Feroze Gandhi on 26 March 1942, but Feroze died young in 1957. They had two sons, Rajiv and Sanjay.

Early Phase

Indira Gandhi played an important role in Nehru's household, acting as his social hostess. But she did much more than that. She chaired the Central Social Welfare Board from 1953 to 1957, served on the Central Parliamentary Board in 1956, and presided over the All India Youth Congress between 1956 and 1960. She was Congress president in 1959, and also the Minister In-charge of Information and Broadcasting in Shastri's cabinet.

Challenges before Indira Gandhi

As prime minister, Indira Gandhi faced a number of domestic and international challenges, but she handled most of them with considerable skill and statesmanship.

Visiting forward positions in Kashmir during the
Indo-Pakistan conflict, September 1965.

She defused movements for regional autonomy by accepting the demand for a Punjabi *suba* and the Naga demand for autonomy. Economic recession, worsened by drought, was handled effectively.

GENERAL ELECTIONS, 1967

The campaign for the general elections of 1967 was conducted in a difficult time of rising prices and food scarcities. Factionalism within the Congress and the widespread 'anti-Congressism' of the opposition parties compounded problems.

The Congress suffered an unexpected defeat at the polls in many states, which reduced its majority in the Lok Sabha. The vote share of the party went down to 41 per cent, while the number of seats now stood at 284 in a house of 520. Nine union ministers and four state chief ministers were defeated.

This election also brought about a near-rout of the Syndicate leaders. In a class by itself was the fall of Kamaraj. He had lost not only his state, of which he was 'uncrowned king' until then, but also his seat. The only prominent Syndicate leader to be elected was Sanjeeva Reddy. However, the electoral setback did not affect the stature of Indira Gandhi. She was unanimously re-elected prime minister and Morarji Desai became deputy prime minister. In May 1967, the AICC met for the first time after the electoral shock. The rank and file, especially the radicals among them, promptly nicknamed 'Young Turks', denounced the 'old and reactionary leaders' for having alienated the traditional voters of the Congress, especially the

Right: Indira Gandhi being sworn in as the prime minister by President Radhakrishnan, 24 January 1966.

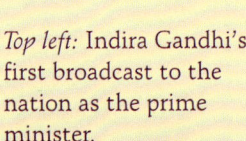

Top left: Indira Gandhi's first broadcast to the nation as the prime minister.

Top right: Addressing the nation from the ramparts of the Red Fort, Delhi, 15 August 1966.

Bottom right: Indira Gandhi with senior Congress leaders.

Harijans (now called Dalits), religious minorities and the poor in general. The party, they thundered, would never be able to recover the lost ground until it returned to earlier socialistic policies diluted by 'pragmatism' in recent years. The attention at the AICC was focused on giving the government's economic policies a leftwards push. But despite the din and noise, neither side, least of all Indira Gandhi, wanted to force the issue. Consequently, the leadership drafted a Ten-point programme on which the radicals and the Conservatives could agree. The only point of contention in it was the key issue of nationalisation of private banks for which there was considerable sentiment within the political class.

ELECTION OF THE CONGRESS PRESIDENT

The Congress president, Kamaraj, had held the office for nearly five years and it was time for change. Different groups in the party supported different candidates. Eventually, S. Nijalingappa was made party president with the support of Kamaraj and Indira Gandhi. The president, however, appointed some of his own supporters to the CWC. Indira Gandhi and the young radicals of the Congress, the Young Turks, objected to this. These leaders pushed for more aggressive economic policies aimed at realising the welfare state that had been envisaged by Nehru.

MID-TERM POLLS OF FEBRUARY 1969 AND THE AFTERMATH

Mid-term polls took place in four states in February 1969 and the position of the Congress weakened further. Against the backdrop of slow economic growth, rampant corruption, rural unrest, and urban discontent, internal differences within the Congress came to a head. The election results had shocked Congressmen. The leftist 'Young Turks' criticised senior leaders for the failure to implement the Ten-point programme for socioeconomic development. The Congress Forum for Socialist Action indicted the party leadership. C. Subramaniam, president of the Tamil Nadu Congress Committee, wanted the party to adopt a radical programme of socialist action and to declare democratic socialism as its goal ahead of the 1972 elections.

IDEOLOGICAL DEBATE WITHIN THE PARTY

Indira Gandhi sent a note of 'stray thoughts' to the CWC, urging the members to adopt more people-oriented policies such as nationalisation of major commercial banks, implementation of land reforms, ceilings on urban income and property, and curbs on industrial monopolies.

The 72nd session of the Congress in 1969 in Faridabad proved to be a significant event. On the eve of the session, Indira Gandhi expressed the view that the Congress should not lean to the extreme left or the extreme right, but should adopt a middle course with democratic socialism as its objective. Both she and the party president were against the idea of coalition.

Ideological differences within the party led to sharp polarisation. After its electoral defeat, the Congress leaned leftward. The right-wing Syndicate did not see merit in these socialist policies and instead advocated better ties with the USA and the suppression of leftist groups. At Faridabad, the intra-party wrangles set the stage for a split.

The leftists and the Young Turks attacked Morarji Desai. Bhagwat Jha Azad, a member of Indira Gandhi's cabinet, accused some of his ministerial colleagues of sabotaging the implementation of the Ten-point programme. Indira Gandhi defended Morarji Desai, but she and Nijalingappa differed over issues like the linguistic reorganisation of the country, the mixed economy, and the role of the public sector. The action taken by Nijalingappa against some of the Young Turks for attacking Desai exacerbated the situation.

The pressure for change was building up. Indira Gandhi relieved Morarji Desai, known for

Top left:
The historic meeting of the AICC at Bangalore in July 1969 witnessed a collision between the old guard and the prime minister over the question of the nominee for the presidentship of the Congress. The clash led to the exit of Morarji Desai from the government and to the nationalisation of the major banks.

his conservative stance, of the finance portfolio and assumed control of it herself. On 19 July, she declared the nationalisation of 14 leading banks by a presidential ordinance, along with steps for the effective implementation of land reforms, ceilings on income and property, and curbs on industrial monopolies. Mrs Gandhi stated, *'This is only the beginning of a bitter struggle between the common people and the vested interests of the country.'* People welcomed this step enthusiastically. This was also a strong message to the Syndicate and a firm assertion of her leadership. Morarji Desai resigned from the cabinet.

SPLIT IN THE PARTY

The demise of Zakir Hussain, President of India, on 3 May 1969, and the question of his successor led to a rift between the government and some Congress members. The party president, Nijalingappa, and his supporters upheld the claim of N. Sanjeeva Reddy, Speaker of the Lok Sabha. Indira Gandhi, however, preferred a president of her choice.

A surprise candidate emerged when the Acting President, V. V. Giri, put forward his claim as an independent candidate. A clash was imminent, with the party president calling for unity in support of N. Sanjeeva Reddy, while many other senior Congress leaders like Jagjivan Ram and Fakhruddin Ali Ahmed advocated the right to vote according to one's conscience.

V. V. Giri called for a 'conscience vote', probably the first time that such an appeal had been made. This presented a crisis situation since a conscience vote would be a breach of party discipline, with serious consequences for the stability of the Congress government, if the party happened to be in power. Mrs Gandhi supported the conscience vote. On 20 August 1969, V. V. Giri, the conscience candidate, backed by Mrs Gandhi and her supporters, became the president, defeating N. Sanjeeva Reddy, and thus turning the course of the history of the Congress Party.

The party president called a meeting of the CWC, which passed a resolution seeking disciplinary action against Indira Gandhi. Following the breakdown of all talks, the CWC under Nijalingappa met and expelled Indira Gandhi as party leader on 12 November 1969. But one large group of Congress Members of Parliament rejected the CWC directive. In all, 220 Congress Lok Sabha MPs supported Indira Gandhi and only 68 went with the Syndicate.

The result was a major split in the party, both at the centre and in the states. The Congress formally split into two factions, Congress (O), led by Nijalingappa and Morarji Desai, and Congress (R), led by Indira Gandhi. In the AICC, 466 out of 705 members joined the Congress (R).

Aftermath of the Congress Split

Indira Gandhi's group, the Congress (R), called for an AICC meeting at which C. Subramaniam was chosen the interim president until regular elections could take place.

Garibi Hatao

At its 73rd session in Bombay, on 1 December 1969, Jagjivan Ram was made the president of the Congress (R). The Bombay session was also significant for the adoption of the slogan 'Garibi Hatao' (Remove Poverty) and of the socioeconomic action plan to remove poverty and hunger.

Indira Gandhi, who no longer had a majority in the Lok Sabha, depended on support from the Dravida Munnettra Kazhagam (DMK) and the Communist Party of India (CPI). Nevertheless, throughout the 1970s, she took action on many fronts in pursuance of Congress Party resolutions. The Essential Commodities Act and the Monopolies and Restrictive Trade Practices Act, 1969 were designed to check concentration of economic power. The implementation of land reforms gained momentum.

Abolition of Privy Purses

On 5 September 1970, a bill was introduced for the abolition of privy purses and princely privileges. This secured support in the Lok Sabha, but failed to get a two-thirds majority in the Rajya Sabha. On 7 September, a presidential order was passed seeking to derecognise the princes. This was challenged in the Supreme Court, which then struck down the order.

On 27 December 1970, the Lok Sabha was dissolved and Indira Gandhi went to the electorate to seek a fresh mandate.

GENERAL ELECTIONS, 1971

The growing popularity of Mrs Gandhi and the Congress was resented by the opposition parties, particularly by those individuals who had left the Congress, and the rightist groups. Inspired solely by anti-Congress sentiment, the leftist and rightist groups—the Jana Sangh, the Swatantra Party, the Samyukta Socialist Party, and the Congress (O)—came together in an unnatural grouping called the Grand Alliance on the eve of the 1971 elections.

General elections were held in 1971, a year ahead of schedule. Indira Gandhi, who was contesting the elections on her own for the first time, went to the electorate with the pro-poor slogan of 'Garibi Hatao', highlighting the need to remove poverty and hunger. The four-party Grand Alliance went with the slogan of 'Indira Hatao'. However, the Grand Alliance parties did not fare well in the elections. This was not surprising since apart from their dislike of the

Congress and Indira Gandhi, they had no other meeting ground in terms of agenda or ideology.

People supported Indira Gandhi and gave her an overwhelming mandate. Her party won 352 of 518 seats in the Lok Sabha. The number of seats held by the Congress (O) fell from 65 to 16. The Election Commission recognised Indira Gandhi's group as the real Congress with the right to call itself the Indian National Congress without the suffix (R), and restored the frozen Congress symbol of two bullocks to it. But Indira Gandhi's supporters preferred the 'calf and cow' symbol that it had adopted after the 1969 split.

Left: Indira Gandhi on being re-elected as the leader of the Congress Parliamentary Party after the elections of 1971.

1971 WAR AND THE BIRTH OF BANGLADESH

In East Pakistan, Sheikh Mujibur Rahman was engaged in a liberation movement to achieve independence from Pakistan. He had won the elections but the Punjabi-dominated West Pakistan government and army refused to accept him as the legitimate leader, which then led to an uprising in East Pakistan and saw the emergence of the Mukti Bahini. This movement grew in strength. On 25 March 1971, the Pakistan army cracked down on the civilians of East Pakistan and perpetrated unprecedented genocide, leading to an influx of about 10 million refugees into India. While pointing out that *'an internal problem of Pakistan has become an internal problem of India also'*, Indira Gandhi stood by the suffering people.

On 3 December 1971, Pakistan launched air strikes on nine Indian air fields in the Western sector. India reacted by recognising the provisional government of Bangladesh on 6 December and joined the Mukti Bahini to resist Pakistan. War broke out on both the Eastern and North-western fronts. After a short but decisive engagement, Indian troops entered Dhaka on 16 December, and the Pakistani army under General Niazi in East Bengal surrendered. East Pakistan was liberated and a new nation, Bangladesh, was born. With the surrender of Pakistan on the Eastern front, Indira Gandhi declared a unilateral ceasefire. Pakistan had no option but to accept.

Left page: Scenes from Indo-Pakistan war of Dember 1971; bottom picture shows General A.A.K. Niazi (right), Commander-in-Chief of the Pakistan forces, surrendering to Lt. Gen. J.S. Aurora, Dacca, 16 December 1971.

Indira Gandhi and Zulfikar Ali Bhutto signing the historic Shimla Agreement, 2 July 1972.

Aftermath of the 1971 war

Indira Gandhi's popularity and stature soared following her strong and decisive leadership during the 1971 war. Even the opposition leaders hailed her as Durga, an incarnation of Shakti, and the war was seen as her personal success. She mobilised world opinion on Bangladesh, travelling to all the major countries, except the USA, which was avowedly hostile.

Military victory paid rich electoral dividends as the Congress won the assembly elections of March 1972, including in West Bengal.

Shimla Agreement, 1972

By the early 1970s, India had emerged as the leader of the subcontinent. On 2 July 1972, Indira Gandhi and Zulfiqar Ali Bhutto, prime ministers of India and Pakistan respectively, signed the famous Shimla Accord. It sought to provide the basis of a durable peace by confirming the new line of control (LoC) in Kashmir and by accepting the principle that problems would be settled through bilateral negotiations.

In March 1972, legislative assembly elections were held in all but four states. The Congress won a landslide victory, capturing more than 70 per cent of assembly seats. A veritable 'Indira wave' had swept the country.

Top: Indira Gandhi during her visit to Dacca in March 1972.

Bottom: A part of the gathering at the public rally in Dacca.

185

INDIRA GANDHI'S VISION FOR SUSTAINABLE DEVELOPMENT

Green Revolution

Indira Gandhi was committed to ensuring India's self-sufficiency in food grain production. This was indeed a remarkable achievement as India turned from being a net food importer to a food-surplus country. The Food Corporation of India (1964) and the Agricultural Prices Commission (1965) were set up to combat food scarcity and to ameliorate the effects of bad droughts. New high-yielding seed varieties of wheat from Mexico were introduced, which ushered in the 'Green Revolution'. The technology was extended to rice production in Bengal and Bihar. A multi-pronged effort involving public investment in fertilisers, power, and irrigation, and a proactive credit and pricing policy, helped India achieve self-sufficiency in food grain production by 1971-72.

Environmental Issues

Indira Gandhi recognised the imperative to maintain harmony between man and nature, and was deeply committed to environmental protection. She was one of two heads of state to attend the First United Nations Conference on the Human Environment on 5 June 1972 at Stockholm, where she highlighted the importance of environmental conservation. The Wildlife Protection Act, 1972 was passed during her tenure, as was the Forest Conservation Act, 1980. Project Tiger, 1973 was launched as a measure for the protection of the endangered tiger.

NUCLEAR POLICY

The Congress had been committed to a policy of strategic and political independence since the country gained freedom. Indira Gandhi's nuclear policy has to be seen within this context. In her words, *'India does not accept the principle of apartheid in any matter, and technology is no exception.'* In 1968, India did not sign the Non-Proliferation Treaty since it did not assure equality to all nations.

Pokharan

On 18 May 1974, India conducted an underground nuclear explosion at a depth of 100 metres at Pokharan in the Rajasthan desert as part of the research and development work of the Atomic Energy Commission. Mrs Gandhi told the Rajya Sabha that India was committed to using nuclear energy for peaceful purposes, adding, *'We must keep our eyes and ears open and be on top with the latest technology.'*

At the same time, Indira Gandhi led the disarmament initiative in the 1980s. She launched the Six-Nation Five-Continent Initiative to bring pressure on the superpowers to reduce their conventional weapons and to eliminate nuclear weapons.

SHANKAR DAYAL SHARMA (1918 -1999)
President, 74th Session, 1972-Calcutta.

A scholar and politician. Shankar Dayal Sharma participated in state people's movement against feudal tyranny. He took part in the Quit India Movement. He was President of India from 1992-1997.

D.K. BAROOAH (1918 -1999)
President, 75th Session, 1975-Chandigarh.

A veteran of India's struggle for independence, Barooah served in Indira Gandhi's Cabinet from 1949-51. He edited *Dainik Assamiya* and *Natun Assamiya* and also wrote *Sagar Dekhisa*.

DIFFICULT TIMES

The huge number of Bangladeshi refugees imposed a heavy economic burden on India, which was still reeling under the cost of the recent war. Rising prices, food shortages, and growing unemployment caused much disaffection. The severe drought of 1972-73, the oil shock of 1973, and the drain of foreign currency reserves compounded matters. India faced serious economic and political unrest, with the outbreak of food riots, campus disturbances, student protests, industrial strikes, and agitations. In May 1974, a 22-day nationwide railway strike and a mutiny by the Armed Constabulary in Uttar Pradesh resulting in violence added to the turmoil. The President of India described the situation as an unprecedented national crisis.

Two mass agitations in Bihar and Gujarat converted the socioeconomic discontent into a political movement.

In Gujarat, in January 1974, widespread anger over high food prices led to anarchic conditions, marked by strikes, arson, looting, rioting, and student protests. President's rule was imposed on the state, followed by the dissolution of the state assembly. Fresh assembly elections were announced for June 1975.

In Bihar, an anti-government student movement led by Jaiprakash Narayan, who called for a 'total revolution', was launched in March 1974. He demanded the resignation of the Congress government in Bihar and asked people to pay no taxes and to establish parallel people's governments across the state. The movement was supported by students, traders, the middle class, and a section of the intelligentsia. Indira Gandhi refused to succumb to the pressure and did not dissolve the assembly.

A Setback

Against this backdrop, Indira Gandhi suffered two major blows. In April 1971, Raj Narain, her socialist opponent from the Rae Bareilly constituency in Uttar Pradesh, brought an election petition against her in the Allahabad High Court. On 12 June 1975, the High Court set aside Mrs Gandhi's election on relatively minor technical violations of the law. She was disallowed from contesting elections for six years and had 20 days to appeal to the Supreme Court.

On the same day, the results of the state assembly elections in Gujarat were announced. The Janata Party won 87 seats, while the Congress got 75 in a house of 182. The opposition parties now demanded Mrs Gandhi's resignation. Her instinct was to resign in the wake of the judicial verdict and to await the decision on her appeal in the Supreme Court. But she was persuaded against this step by her close supporters in the party. On 24 June, Justice Krishna Iyer, the Vacation Judge in the Supreme Court, rejected Mrs Gandhi's plea for a complete and absolute stay of the judgment, granting only a conditional stay until the court convened to consider her appeal.

Indira Gandhi accepting felicitations from the people after the Supreme Court upheld her election to the Lok Sabha, November 1975.

Emergency, 1975

On 25 June, the opposition parties led by Jaiprakash Narayan announced that a nation-wide campaign of mass agitation and civil disobedience to force Mrs Gandhi to resign would be launched on 29 June. At a mass rally, he called on the people to obstruct the functioning of the government and asked the police, the armed forces, and the bureaucracy to defy the government, terming the same as 'illegal'. This was tantamount to a call for revolt. In response, on 26 June, the president of India declared a state of grave emergency resulting from a threat to the security of India from internal disturbances.

In July, Parliament formally approved the imposition of the Emergency by a vote of 336 to 59. This was followed by the large-scale arrests of a number of opposition leaders and the banning of some organisations like the RSS, Naxal bodies, and the Jamaat-i-Islami. The Emergency lasted 19 months.

The 42nd Amendment Act of 3 January 1976 denied the power of judicial review, altering the basic structure of the Constitution.

In 1976, Sanjay Gandhi through the Youth Congress outlined his Five-point programme, which laid emphasis on literacy, banning of dowry, family planning, environmental protection, and slum clearance. He also laid the foundations for the production and sale of the people's car, Maruti.

In the months following the proclamation of the Emergency, inflation, which had reached 30 per cent, was brought under control. Food and essential commodities were made readily available. Industrial production increased and the country enjoyed favourable foreign exchange reserves.

However, curbs on freedom of expression and personal liberties aroused great opposition. Population control and slum clearance programmes were deeply resented by the people.

TWENTY-POINT PROGRAMME

On 1 July 1975, Indira Gandhi announced her government's Twenty-point Programme of economic reconstruction. She said, '*What has been done is not an abrogation of democracy, but an effort to safeguard it.*' She added, '*The emergency provides us with a new opportunity to go ahead with our economic tasks.*' The Twenty-point Programme had a wide-reaching impact on poverty alleviation. It addressed rising prices and inflation; undertook redistribution of surplus land; adopted measures to improve the conditions of the landless, small peasants, and artisans; extended protection to weavers and support to the handloom industry; abolished bonded labour; liquidated rural indebtedness; introduced new minimum agricultural wages; simplified licensing procedures; and ensured supply of essential commodities at controlled prices.

The Twenty-point Programme, which continued until March 1977, was revitalised in January 1980 under the theme *'Shram eva jayate'* (Work alone wins). Many new initiatives were taken up, including primary health care, universal elementary education, fair-price shops, integrated rural development, a National Rural Employment Programme, land ceiling measures, and programmes for Scheduled Castes and Scheduled Tribes.

END OF THE EMERGENCY AND GENERAL ELECTIONS, 1977

Indira Gandhi in a conversation with her childhood friend, Pupul Jayakar, spoke of the tremendous sense of responsibility that she had carried since the age of three when she felt she needed to look after her parents, as her mother was very ill and her father in jail. Pupul Jayakar quotes her as saying:

In moments of crisis when my back is to the wall, I let go. I do not know what operates. I listen, see all the facts and a solution emerges. I then examine the solution in the harsh light of reality. When I have to do a thing which is right, I do it without concerning myself with the consequences to me!

On 18 January 1977, Indira Gandhi announced that general elections would be held in March 1977. She lifted the Emergency, and all political leaders were released and press censorship and curbs on freedom of expression were removed to prepare the ground for the elections. The elections were conducted in a free and fair manner. The world applauded India's commitment to democracy.

The opposition parties of the Grand Alliance—the Congress (O), the Jana Sangh, the Socialist Party, and the Bharatiya Lok Dal—allied themselves as the Janata Party and fought on the platform of reviving democracy. The message of the Congress was progress and stability.

Jagjivan Ram and some other Congress members left the party in February 1977 and formed a new party called Congress for Democracy, which joined forces with the Janata Party.

The results shocked the Congress as it suffered a major defeat, winning only 154 seats in the Lok Sabha, while the combined opposition secured 330 of the 542 seats. Indira Gandhi lost in Rae Bareilly, and Sanjay Gandhi lost in Amethi.

Following the election results, the Janata Party adopted a policy of political vendetta against Indira Gandhi, foisting cases and instituting enquiries. Sanjay Gandhi mobilised the youth in a sustained agitation against the Janata government and its politics of vendetta.

In the Wilderness

Following electoral defeat, many leaders demanded the resignation of the Congress president and the CWC members. Indira Gandhi accepted the verdict of the people and assumed responsibility for the party's defeat. She resigned as prime minister on 22 March.

The CWC met to elect a new president and a new committee. K. Brahmanand Reddy was elected Congress president, defeating Siddhartha Shankar Ray. Ten members were elected to the CWC. Y.B. Chavan was chosen the leader of the Congress Party in Parliament.

JANATA GOVERNMENT

In March 1977, the Janata Party formed the next government with Morarji Desai, then 81 years old, as prime minister. In July 1977, Sanjeeva Reddy was elected president with the support of the Janata Party and its allies.

The Janata government arrested Mrs Gandhi on 3 October 1977 on the charge of abusing the office of prime minister by obtaining illegal funds for the purchase of Jeeps for use by her party's candidates in the 1977 elections. However, the Chief Metropolitan Magistrate ordered her release the next day as there was no real case against her.

The AICC was summoned to condemn the vindictive act of the Janata government, but instead they criticised Mrs Gandhi and her supporters like P.V. Narasimha Rao, A.R. Antulay, Pranab Mukherjee, Buta Singh, Vasant Sathe, R. Gundu Rao, and Kalpnath Rai.

Second Split and Indira Gandhi's Return to Power

The younger leaders began a move to elect Indira Gandhi as the Congress president. In January 1978, four CWC members called a national convention of Congress workers. This converted itself into the 76th plenary session of the Congress where Indira Gandhi was named president on the proposal of Kamlapati Tripathi. Mrs Gandhi formed the new CWC, which decided to fight the forthcoming state assembly elections. Ultimately, the party split formally.

The Election Commission did not recognise Indira Gandhi's group as the Congress. The 'cow and calf' symbol was retained by the other faction led by Brahmanand Reddy, and the suffix (I) was used by the faction led by Mrs Gandhi. A new reserved symbol 'hand' was allotted to it. A new party headquarters was established at 24, Akbar Road in New Delhi. The Congress (I) continued to be called by this name until it was recognised as the Congress by a court verdict in 1982.

Shah Commission

One of the first acts of the new Janata government was the dismissal of Congress ministries in nine states and the setting up of the Shah Commission to look into the alleged excesses of the Emergency. Former senior Congress ministers were summoned before the

Above: 'A part of the massive crowd at Ludhiana's Guru Nanak Stadium with Mrs Gandhi at the microphone on Wednesday. The time was soon after 1.30 pm and the sun beat down mercilessly on the gathering,' read the caption in The Tribune, 13 April 1978.

Across: Prem Bhatia's article *'Punjab At Her Feet?'* in the same newspaper, reproduced.

The Tribune, 13 April 1978

PUNJAB AT HER FEET?

From **Prem Bhatia**

Ludhiana, April 12—She is back, not yet as Prime Minister nor even as an M.P., but she has recovered lost political ground at a pace and in a measure which would have appeared like a pipe dream a year ago. At Ludhiana today Indira Gandhi seemed to have Punjab at her feet. From 9 a.m. to 1.30 p.m. a crowd of eager and excited men, women and children waited at the local Guru Nanak Stadium to see her and to hear her speak. The stadium has no cover, and by 11 a.m. the sun had already become uncomfortably hot. By the time she finally arrived, after several false alarms, the sun was unbearable. There were nearly 5,00,000 people in that crowd. Almost no one had an umbrella and there were no arrangements for drinking water. Since the gates were closed by 12.30 p.m., it was not easy to get out of the stadium to look for water either. And yet they sat on the hot and dusty ground—thirsty, and mopping their faces. They looked too tired even to shout "zindabad" with audible zest.

Indira Gandhi arrived soon after 1.30 p.m.—over two hours late and then bedlam broke. Those near the high rostrum pushed their way towards the raised platform to have a look at her. No one near where we sat died but dozens looked close to suffocation. Indira Gandhi herself seemed a trifle surprised at the welcome as she climbed the steps to the rostrum and had a clearer view of the crowd. Who were the people in this mass of humanity? They were not all local citizens. In fact most had come from outside Ludhiana—from Amritsar, Jullundur, Ferozepore, small townships and little hamlets. Some did indeed look like men who came for an outing in trucks someone else paid for. But there were many others who looked dead serious as Indira Gandhi's supporters.

Flags held aloft, shouting slogans in her favour and curses against the Home Minister, hundreds of small groups had marched to the stadium and taken their places. This was no unorganised "mela". It was a well-arranged exhibition of strength and support for the former Prime Minister.

One had heard of the great receptions she was given at Patna, at Calcutta and less populous places in recent days and one had taken the reports with a pinch of salt. But here in Ludhiana was evidence that could not be ignored "Indira Gandhi, zindabad, zindabad" from thousands of throats was more than the work only of cheer leaders.

What is the matter with this country, you might well ask. Only a year ago they wanted to lynch her; many still presumably do. But at least the 5,00,000 who gathered in Guru Nanak Stadium today treated her as a hero. They had come not to sing panegyrics in favour of the Congress (I) but to see her. Quite a few began to leave the stadium immediately thereafter and without waiting for her speech.

Two lessons emerge. First, there is no future in Punjab for the "other" Congress: only Indira Gandhi's Congress now matters. Secondly, her return does not mean the end of the Akali Party or even of the Akali-Janata combine. Well, not yet anyway. More than 50 per cent of today's audience at the Guru Nanak Stadium were Sikhs, which means that her support is wide-based, but it does not mean that all the Sikhs present will vote for Indira Gandhi's Congress. It is again the repetition of an old Indian political phenomenon. We usually accept leaders but not necessarily the parties they lead. And therein lies Indira Gandhi's strength and weakness. She was never very good at organising a strong initiative-oriented team. She is even less likely to do so in the immediate future. Meanwhile she reigns as the Empress of the Congress of her own choice. She is still a long way from recovering the title of Empress of India.

commission, and many of them blamed Indira Gandhi, claiming that they had only acted on her advice and direction. A number of chief ministers who were called on to depose before the commission also did the same.

Indira Gandhi was summoned by the Shah Commission and prosecuted under Section 178 of the Indian Penal Code. She refused to give evidence before the commission, maintaining that the procedure followed was incorrect and illegal.

On 8 November 1978, Mrs Gandhi won the by-election from the Chikmagalur constituency in Karnataka and returned to the Lok Sabha as the leader of the opposition. On 18 December, the Janata government accepted the findings of the Shah Commission and took a series of measures against Mrs Gandhi and her supporters. The next day, 19 December, the Lok Sabha expelled Indira Gandhi and sentenced her to imprisonment for a term to last until the prorogation of the House. She was sent to Tihar Jail, and released on 26 December.

All these actions of the Janata Party only helped to generate popular sympathy for Mrs Gandhi.

Breakup of the Janata Party

The issue of dual membership involving the leaders of the former Jana Sangh who continued as members of the RSS resulted in infighting in the Janata Party. Infighting resulted in the eventual breakup of the Janata Party. On 15 July 1979, Morarji Desai resigned. On 28 July, Charan Singh formed the government, but it lasted for only a few months. At the end of 1979, midterm elections to the Lok Sabha were announced—two years ahead of schedule. Jaiprakash Narayan—the architect of the Janata Party—died a few months earlier. His dream of ushering in the total revolution was never realised.

GENERAL ELECTIONS, 1980

Indira Gandhi launched a countrywide campaign, touring for 63 days, covering over 40,000 miles, visiting 384 constituencies, and

Indira Gandhi amongst jubilant supporters following her landslide election victory, New Delhi, 1980.

addressing more than 1,500 meetings. Her appeal to the people was simple—elect a government that works. She asked the nation to vote for the Congress (I) for order, stability, and progress as against the Janata Party's record of infighting and non-governance. Sanjay Gandhi mobilised the Youth Congress to garner support for the party.

In January 1980, Indira Gandhi returned to power in a landslide victory, 33 months after the electoral defeat of the party that had ended 30 years of Congress rule. The Congress (I) won 353 out of 529 seats, giving it a two-third majority.

The Congress (I) also emerged victorious in eight out of nine states, the opposition winning only in Tamil Nadu, under the AIADMK. The victory was solely attributable to the leadership and charisma of Indira Gandhi. The election showed the genuinely national character of Indira Gandhi's victory, with the people reposing confidence in her to form and lead an effective government for the next five years.

On 23 June 1980, in a tragic accident, Sanjay Gandhi, at the young age of 33, died in an air crash of the single-engine plane he was piloting.

A WORLD LEADER

Indira Gandhi adopted a firm and pragmatic approach to foreign policy. Despite American pressure, she decried the US bombing of Vietnam. With the USA, there remained some areas of tension, though Indira Gandhi's visit to Washington D.C. in 1982 was an important breakthrough. She also strengthened relations with the Soviet Union in order to build a counter-alliance to the US-China-Pakistan axis by signing, in 1971, the 20-year Indo-Soviet Treaty of Peace, Friendship and Cooperation.

Non-Aligned Movement

Indira Gandhi played a leading role in the Non-Aligned Movement, while maintaining good relations with both the superpowers. At the Algiers Conference, held on 5-9 September 1973, Indira Gandhi stated:

We are here because of our convictions and response to the inspiration which initially brought us together and which is still valid in the contemporary world. We have a very important part to play in the remaking of the world.

Left: Indira Gandhi chairing the meeting of the Commonwealth Heads of Government (CHOGM), New Delhi, November, 1983.

In March 1983, the Seventh Non-Aligned Conference held in New Delhi was attended by about 100 member states and was keenly watched by the bigger powers. Indira Gandhi, who was elected chairperson, made a significant contribution in shaping the NAM agenda. She emphasised the importance of maintaining freedom from outside interference as the watchword of the movement, which rested on five major principles: decolonisation, development, disarmament, détente, and democratisation. Nehru had set the stage for NAM, and his daughter took it forward. Describing it as *'history's biggest peace movement'*, she brought a new sense of purpose and optimism to NAM, which was recognised by many world leaders, including Fidel Castro of Cuba. India's role in awakening and strengthening Asian-African consciousness was also widely recognised at the conference.

Indira Gandhi played an active role at the meeting of the Commonwealth Heads of Government and at many other international fora.

PUNJAB CRISIS

Meanwhile, the situation in Punjab was growing increasingly tense as the Akali Dal presented a series of demands, including the formation of a separate Sikh state called Khalistan. The government was prepared to concede anything but secession. In dealing with legitimate demands, Indira Gandhi had earlier accepted the Sikh demand for a separate Punjabi-speaking state in March 1966, and had made Chandigarh a union territory, which would be the capital of both Punjab and Haryana.

However, the Akalis asked for greater autonomy as stated in the 1973 Anandpur Sahib Resolution. A violent agitation began in the state after the Akali Dal lost power in 1980. The extremists in Punjab, led by Sant Jarnail Singh Bhindranwale, launched a

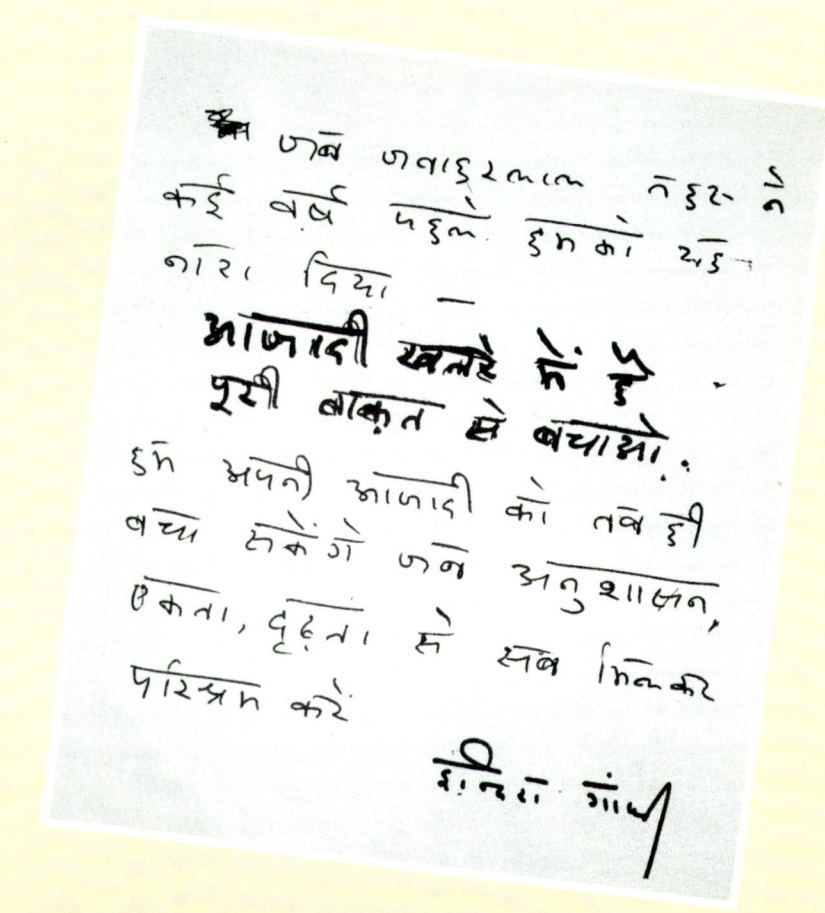

terrorist movement for Khalistan, with backing from Pakistan. From their safe haven in the Golden Temple in Amritsar, they started amassing arms and spreading violence and terror, targeting Hindus and destroying public property. Punjab suffered immensely as terrorism spread.

Eventually, the government launched Operation Blue Star, sending in the army in June 1984 to liberate the Sikh holy shrine from the control of armed terrorists. A three-day siege resulted in many people being killed, including Bhindranwale, and the hold of the terrorists was broken. The Golden Temple was restored to the head priests, but in Punjab and elsewhere there was great resentment and bitterness at what was seen as the desecration of the holiest shrine of Sikhism.

On 31 October 1984, Indira Gandhi, while walking from her home to her office at 1 Safdarjung Road, was assassinated by two Sikh members of her security guard. She paid the ultimate price in the service of the nation, while trying to preserve its integrity and secular character.

INDIRA GANDHI'S LEGACY

Indira Gandhi dominated the Indian political scene like a colossus regardless of whether she was in power or in opposition. She is remembered for being a firm and decisive leader with an abiding commitment to the welfare of the poor and the marginalised. During her tenure, the government introduced far-reaching legislation for social justice and economic equity, and she also strengthened India's presence in the international arena. Nehru was prime minister for 16 years and nine months. Indira Gandhi, too, was prime minister for almost as long, holding office for two stretches, from January 1966 to March 1977, and then from January 1980 to October 1984. Both were genuinely secular and nationalist, representing all Indians regardless of gender, class, caste, or region. Above all, they loved India deeply, a love that the people of India reciprocated in full measure. Indira Gandhi was a role model for women in India, and indeed for women around the world. She demonstrated the possibilities for women in the political arena by holding her own in a hitherto largely male-dominated domain. She successfully steered the country through some very difficult times. She won the hearts of the poor as their protector and champion. They mourned her death as they would that of a family member.

1984

Leading Towards 21st Century

1991

Leading Towards 21st Century

1984 - 1991

A NEW LEADER

Following Indira Gandhi's assassination, senior Congress leaders turned to Rajiv Gandhi in an hour of need to lead the party.

Unlike the past two occasions when Nehru and Shastri had died, the choice of a successor to Indira Gandhi did not prove too difficult. For one, most of the older leaders were no longer in the Congress. The party's stewardship was now in the hands of comparatively younger leaders who felt that only someone from Indira Gandhi's family could keep the party and the country united.

Rajiv Gandhi, the elder son of Indira Gandhi, had entered politics after the death of his younger brother, Sanjay, to support his mother during a difficult time. After attending Doon School and studying engineering at Cambridge University, he returned to India and became a pilot with Indian Airlines. Following Sanjay's death, he reluctantly contested the election from Amethi in 1981 and won. A few months later, he assumed the leadership of the Youth Congress. As his mother's advisor and confidant, he took

an increasing interest in the reorganisation of the Congress Party. In February 1983, he became one of the seven new general secretaries of the Congress, tasked with revitalising the party.

At a time of national crisis, Rajiv Gandhi, who stood for stability and continuity, was the unanimous choice of the Congress and was sworn in as prime minister on 31 October 1984.

EARLY YEARS

As Rajiv Gandhi entered politics, he prepared himself for meeting new challenges. At the Congress centenary celebrations in 1985 in Bombay, he said:

When I started my political work, it was only with the motive of being by the side of my mother… She gave me no directions, no formulae, no prescriptions. She just said, 'Understand the real India, its people, its problems.' So I plunged into work. Millions of faces in varying moods of joy and sorrow, of eager expectation, of triumph and defeat, filled my being, till they merged into the face of Mother India, proud, defiant, confident…

Rajiv Gandhi, at 40, was India's youngest prime minister, representing the modern face of the Congress and of the Indian polity. His openness, charm, earnestness, and honesty endeared him to the people, especially the youth. His idealism and vision for a modern and dynamic India struck a chord with the masses. He rallied the people with his promise *'Together we will build an India of the twenty-first century.'* He spent the first year of his term in office travelling widely, discovering his country, meeting ordinary Indians, receiving their petitions, and connecting with them.

CHALLENGES BEFORE THE NATION

Indira Gandhi's assassination had produced an emotional reaction in the country, with nation-wide riots against the Sikh community. The situation was particularly grave in New Delhi where hundreds died in the riots. Rajiv Gandhi's immediate task was to quell the violence and restore calm. This was not easy as the wound inflicted on the Sikh community's psyche was deep and would take time to heal.

The Bhopal gas tragedy, perhaps the biggest industrial accident ever seen in India, erupted in early December 1984 on the eve of elections. Thousands died and many more were severely incapacitated for life in a deadly gas leak at the Union Carbide factory in Bhopal.

GENERAL ELECTIONS, 1984

In December 1984, Rajiv Gandhi, believing that it was essential to hold the elections on schedule, went to the people with a promise of stability. The Congress won with an overwhelming majority, securing 415 out of 543 seats. This unprecedented victory was in great part a tribute to the late Indira Gandhi, and a vote for India's

RAJIV GANDHI (1944 - 1991)
President, 78th Session (Centenary), Bombay-1985.

Rajiv Gandhi, at 40, became the youngest prime minister of India. Besides being the harbinger of a generational change in the country, he received the biggest mandate in the nation's history in the elections to the Lok Sabha (1984). It was during his tenure as prime minister that concrete steps were taken to draw the youth more closely into nation-building activities, and the country saw a tremendous growth in its stature in international affairs. He dismantled the Licence Raj, modernised tele-communications and the education system, strengthened the *panchayati raj* system, encouraged science and technology initiatives, and improved relations with the United States. Rajiv Gandhi was assassinated in a bomb blast at an election rally at Sriperumbudur, Tamil Nadu, in May 1991.

Historic victory for Congress-I

Three-fourths majority in Lok Sabha achieved

Record win for Rajiv

Hindustan Times Correspondent

NEW DELHI, Dec. 29—The Congress-I avalanche has written India's electoral history anew bringing for the party an unprecedented three-fourths majority in the Lok Sabha and a tally which was only six short of the dizzy figure of 469.

Late tonight with reports yet to come in from 15 constituencies, the Congress-I had bagged 394 of the 495 results declared. The party, under Mr Rajiv Gandhi, improved upon the previous record of 371 seats set in 1957 with his grandfather, Jawaharlal Nehru spearheading the Congress.

The Congress-I made a clean sweep in Madhya Pradesh, Rajasthan, Haryana and Delhi and nearly so in the rest of the Hindi region like Uttar Pradesh, Bihar and Himachal Pradesh as well as in Maharashtra and Gujarat. In the South, it staged a powerful comeback in Karnataka and re-established itself as a force to reckon with in Tamil Nadu and Kerala.

With the results for 15 seats remaining to be declared, the party position was as follows: Congress-I 393, CPI-M 18, Janata 10, BJP 2, CPI 5, Congress-S 4, Telugu Desam 24, AIADMK 12, other parties 17, and independents 5.

Mr Rajiv Gandhi capped his party's success with a personal triumph, retaining the Amethi seat and defeating Rashtriya Sanjay Manch president Menaka Gandhi by the staggering margin of 3,14,878 votes—so far the widest margin in the current election. Mrs Menaka Gandhi lost her security deposit.

The Congress-I Parliamentary Party is going to present itself with a New Year gift on Monday by electing Mr Rajiv Gandhi its president. The same day, the Election Commission is expected to notify constitution of the Lok Sabha. The customary...

corded substantial ground to the Congress-I in West Bengal, especially in the urban areas, though it retained its prestigious seats in Calcutta.

It has been estimated, on the basis of the flattering winning margins, that the Congress-I will collect for the first time more than 50 per cent of the popular votes. A preliminary analysis reveals that the bulk of the Congress-I party's gains of 72 seats over the first estimate declared had been extracted from the Janata, the Communists, parties and the BJP, in that order. The analysis also showed that the Congress lost 37 of the Telugu Desam held, the bulk to the AIADMK. The BJP, the CPI-M, the Janata and the independents the party's gain thus was 35.

Among the important Opposition

Continued on page 16 col 1

Party position

Congress-I	394
Telugu Desam	25
CPI-M	18
Janata	10
CPI	4
Congress-S	5
Independents	21
Others	

A MASSIVE MANDATE

What the Congress-I has inflicted on a stunned Opposition is not just a defeat. It is a regular rout. The massive landslide with which the Congress-I has won has put almost every pollster and pundit to shame. Indeed, some of them had confidently predicted less than a bare majority for the ruling party in what was obviously a case of the wish being father to the thought. Prime Minister Rajiv Gandhi had predicted several times during his hectic campaign blitz that his party would sweep the poll. He had also forecast that once the people declared their preference, the Opposition would not be visible. All that was taken as election rhetoric, but to the dismay of the Opposition, his words became tragically true.

Even the Congress-I could not have foreseen the magnitude of its victory. And it is mind-boggling. Janata Party President Chandra Shekhar fell by the wayside; his weighty associate Era Sezhian in Tamil Nadu was dealt a politically fatal blow at the hands of former film star Vyjayanthimala Bali, a mere novice in politics; the Bharatiya Janata Party lost both President Atal Behari Vajpayee and Vice-President Ram Jethmalani, the latter ignominiously biting the dust in a clash with yet another star of the cine world; Hemwati Nandan Bahuguna, the man who never lost an election, was

Sympathy tide did the trick, says Shekhar

Times Correspondent

...DELHI, Dec. 29—The ...Communist (Marxist)...

First task to preserve national unity: PM

Hindustan Times Correspondent

NEW DELHI, Dec. 29 — Prime Minister Rajiv Gandhi, who will be leader of the new Congress Parliamentary Party on...

today that his economic, fiscal... the out-... be of...

He indicated that he would give his message to the nation and also spell out his Government's policies in the first week of January after the new Government takes over.

...ested certain ideas ...ues in 1977. "It ...over ...Asker ...olicy.

A close race in Bengal

Hindustan Times Correspondent

CALCUTTA, Dec. 29 — The Congress-I is maintaining its steady march in West Bengal. The Left Front and the Congress-I were running neck-and-neck with... won by each at 7.30 p.m. to...

Declaration of...

the Janata govern-...iss-...

CONGRESS SET FOR A SWEEP

Tidal wave few could see

By GIRILAL JAIN

Apparently the Congress logical sentiment should have party under Mr Gandhi's been the heroes of today at a leadership is set to win a land... of victory not a few people...

N. Rao elected. Vajpayee is defeated from Ramtek ◆

NEW DELHI Dec 28

THE Congress party led by Mr Rajiv Gandhi is all set to sweep the polls...

THE HINDUSTAN TIMES

New Delhi Saturday December 29 1984

Eighty Paise

RAJIV WAVE SWEEPS INDIA

Rao, Buta Singh, Patil romp home

Vajpayee defeated Shekhar trails

Inroads into Left citadels

NEW DELHI, Dec. — Hindustan Times Correspondent

206   JOURNEY OF A NATION

Left: Newspaper headlines, 29-30 December 1984.

Above: Rajiv Gandhi taking the oath of office as prime minister of
India at the swearing-in ceremony, Rashtrapati Bhavan, New Delhi.

unity and integrity. The massive victory of the Congress led by Rajiv Gandhi in the December 1984 elections engendered a spirit of optimism and hope, marking the beginning of a new phase in the history of post-independence India.

PARTY AFFAIRS

After four decades of Congress rule, the changes and tensions inherent in a vibrant democracy began surfacing. The Congress as well as other parties suffered from defections or 'floor-crossings', a practice that started in 1967-1968 when legitimately elected governments were brought down through defections. It came to be used as an expedient tool over the years to destabilise elected governments and undermine democracy. In an attempt to cleanse public life, the new government passed the Anti-Defection Act in January 1985, which gave the party leadership a powerful instrument to enforce discipline.

In March 1985, state assembly elections were due, and under Rajiv Gandhi's guidance, many non-performing candidates were dropped in favour of young educated professionals. As the challenges of governance mounted, some close aides of Indira Gandhi were gradually brought back to work for the government and the party.

In 1988, the 61st Amendment to the Representation of People's Act, 1950 lowered the voting age from 21 to 18, allowing all Indians above 18 to exercise their franchise.

PREPARING INDIA FOR THE TWENTY-FIRST CENTURY

Rajiv Gandhi was a visionary leader who dreamt of ushering in a technology-led revolution to prepare India for the twenty-first century. He said:

India is an old country but a young nation. . . I am young, and I too have a dream. I dream of a strong India—self-reliant and in the front rank of the nations of the world in the service of mankind.

He established six technology missions to apply the power of science in severely under-developed areas—drinking water, literacy, immunisation and health of pregnant women and children, White Revolution or improved milk production, edible oil production, and tele-communication. He brought in professionals from the developed world to advise him on the new technologies, laying the foundations of the technology revolution in India. The Centre for Development of Telematics (C-DOT) was established with the aim of providing telecom-munication access to every village in the country by the end of the twentieth century. The information highway was expanded, led by the National Informatic Centre (NIC), as every district was sought to be connected to the central government through a computer network.

Above: Rajiv Gandhi inaugurating the Urdu Computer, July 1986.

Across: Rajiv Gandhi speaking at the Congress centenary celebrations, 6 May 1985.

Rajiv Gandhi spearheaded the country's computerisation programme even in the face of stiff opposition. His vision ensured that India prepared itself as a leader in software development.

SETTING THE ECONOMIC AGENDA

In addition to deploying modern technology for administrative efficiency and decentralising decision-making at the community level, Rajiv Gandhi sought to remove controls over industries and to demystify the budget process. He took forward the economic reforms that began with Indira Gandhi's return to power in 1980, preparing the ground for the major programme of economic liberalisation launched later in 1991. During his tenure, the Indian economy grew at 5.5 per cent, breaking the barrier of 3-3.5 per cent at which it had stagnated for several years.

The first budget announced by Rajiv Gandhi's Finance Minister, V.P. Singh, was a break with the past in several respects. It heralded the decontrol and deregulation of key industries, such as textiles, machine tools, computers, and drugs, to catalyse production, making way for diversification and modernisation. It unshackled the entrepreneurial spirit of the private sector from the stranglehold of bureaucratic red tape. Rajiv Gandhi outlined his economic vision in an interview to the *Financial Express* in 1985:

The Indian economy had got caught in a vicious circle of creating more and more controls. Controls really lead to all the corruption, to all the delays, and that is what we want to cut out.

Many people saw Rajiv Gandhi as being ahead of his times and he was often described as a man in a hurry. The business sector and the large and growing middle class responded enthusiastically to the steps he proposed. New trades and businesses opened, and the housing and real estate market boomed. The second half of the 1980s was indeed a good time for Indian industry, with robust economic growth and stable industrial production.

REFORMING THE CONGRESS PARTY

Unconventional and dynamic in his approach, Rajiv Gandhi was keen to democratise the Congress and to bring young people into the party. He articulated his desire to ensure efficiency and root out corruption in his address at the Congress centenary celebrations in Bombay in 1985, warning against the machinations of 'power brokers' and vested interests:

We have looked at others. Now let us look at ourselves. What has become of our great organisation? Instead of a party that fired the imagination of the masses throughout the length and breadth of India, we have shrunk, losing touch with the toiling millions. It is not a question of victories and defeats in elections. For a democratic party, victories and defeats are part

of its continuing political existence. But what does matter is whether or not we work among the masses, whether or not we are in tune with their struggles, their hopes and aspirations. We are a party of social transformation, but in our preoccupation with governance we are drifting away from the people. Thereby, we have weakened ourselves and fallen prey to the ills that the loss of invigorating mass contact brings.

Exhorting Congress workers to undertake internal party reform, he said:

The revitalisation of our organisation is a historical necessity. At this critical juncture, there is no other political party capable of defending the unity and integrity of the country. There is no other party

Congress centenary
celebrations, 6 May 1985.

*capable of taking the country forward to progress
and prosperity. All other parties are shot through
with internal contradictions. The sorry, unedifying
spectacle of their total incapacity, corruption,
nepotism, hypocrisy has disfigured our political
landscape. They have shown a cynical disregard for
sensitive issues of national security. Some have not
hesitated even to collude with anti-national
elements. Their ideological roots are shallow, their
political outlook circumscribed by region, caste, and
religion. Wherever they have come to power, they
have retarded social and economic progress. They
have no sense of history. Those who campaign for a
weak centre, campaign against the unity and
integrity of India.*

The old guard of the Congress Party found
Rajiv Gandhi's style of functioning with
meticulous professionalism out of tune with
their own approach. Rajiv Gandhi infused fresh
blood into his team, which was a mix of youth
and experience. Some leaders who had acted as
his advisors in the early years of his term left
on account of some differences. Rajiv Gandhi's
dream of ushering in party reform could not
be fulfilled, and party elections were put off
repeatedly due to internal pressures.

SETTING THE SOCIAL AGENDA

On 15 August 1986, Rajiv Gandhi announced his Twenty-Point Programme, which focused on schemes aimed at ameliorating rural poverty, raising productivity, reducing income inequalities, removing social and economic disparities, and improving the quality of life. The Twenty-Point Programme deepened the process of land reforms, encouraged the two-child norm for population control, and had a special thrust for the empowerment of women and the weaker sections of society.

Rajiv Gandhi was deeply concerned that the funds earmarked for development often did not reach the poor and were appropriated by middlemen. He sought to plug the leakages in the delivery mechanism through the direct transfer of resources to the village *panchayats*, a step that was also ensured through a constitutional amendment. Though these measures provoked opposition from vested interest groups, Rajiv Gandhi remained steadfast in his desire for the reform of village institutions.

Rajiv Gandhi recognised the imperative for the economic empowerment of the rural masses and launched the Jawahar Rozgar Yojana, a rural employment scheme, as a measure of poverty alleviation. This assured employment to at least one member of every rural household for 50-100 days in a year.

Rajiv Gandhi understood the importance of primary education in rural areas. The New Education Policy had a special focus on the rural poor, and Model Schools or Navodaya Vidyalayas were established in each district to provide affordable quality education to poor rural children.

Rajiv Gandhi also launched the Indira Mahila Yojana scheme, which recognised the rights of women as equal partners in society and provided them the opportunity of participating equally in nation-building.

Rajiv Gandhi was a firm believer in the devolution of power to the grassroots level and in strengthening the institution of the village *panchayat,* the traditional village republic of India, drawing inspiration from Mahatma Gandhi's commitment to creating institutions for self-governance in every village of the country. He introduced legislation to make elections to *panchayats* mandatory, having the backing of the Constitution. He believed that political participation of women in rural areas would perhaps be the greatest empowering force. The National Perspective Plan, drafted in 1988, proposed the reservation of 30 per cent of elected seats for women in all *panchayati raj* bodies. This, however, did not pass in the Rajya Sabha in the face of stiff opposition given that elections were imminent. While piloting the constitutional amendment bills in the Rajya Sabha, Rajiv Gandhi said:

The Panchayati Raj and Nagarpalika Bills are not only instruments for bringing democracy and devolution to every chaupal and every chabutra, to every aangan and every dalaan. They are also a charter for ending bureaucratic oppression, technocratic tyranny, crass inefficiency, bribery, red-tapeism, nepotism, corruption, and the million other malfeasances that afflict the poor of our villages, towns, and cities.

It, however, remained high on the Congress agenda for the next election, and after the return of the Congress to power, the historic legislation empowering Indian women was enacted.

Like his mother, Rajiv Gandhi was deeply conscious of the importance of environmental sustainability. He established a new Ministry of Environment and Forests to strike a balance between the imperative of development while ensuring environmental sustainability.

Bill aims at ending the hold of power brokers, says Rajiv

NEW DELHI, May 15 that these institutions have been leached of their ability to stand on their own as representative forums of the people's will. Their existence has depended less on the mandate of people than the whims of State Governments.

Introducing the Constitution (64th Amendment) Bill in the Lok Sabha on Monday, Prime Minister Rajiv Gandhi said.

Democracy was the greatest gift of our freedom struggle to the people of India. Independence made the nation free. Democracy made our people free.

SUSPENSION GROUNDS: Our Bill leaves it to the States to determine the grounds and conditions on which Panchayats may be suspended or dissolved. We expect State Legislatures to specify the grounds on which the Panchayat. That is a matter for the Governor acting, in accordance with the Constitution, on the aid and advice of the State Government. Our concern is with ensuring that a dissolved Panchayat is reconstituted within a reasonable period of time.

GOVERNORS' ROLE: Our proposed Constitutional amendment lays the Constitutional injunction upon the State Legislatures. It is for the State law. A quite unnecessary controversy has been raised about the role of the Governor in the proposed Panchayati Raj system. The Constitution is unambiguous on this point. Articles 154(1) states that:

"The executive power of the State shall be vested in the Governor."

Article 163(1) clarifies that:

"There shall be a Council of Ministers with the Chief Minister at the head to aid and advise the Governor in the exercise of his functions..."

Continued from page 1 col 3

Panchayat Bill moved in House

The Prime Minister said it was the purpose of the Bill to ensure that powers delegated to panchayats remained within the panchayats and were not channelled outside the system.

To end any role for powerbrokers in the system, the Bill provides for direct election of members to panchayats, at...

chayati Raj were overshadowed by Ministers appointed by the State Government or, as in the case of Karnataka, by the MLA becoming the ex-officio chairman of the Taluka Panchayat samiti, the Prime Minister said.

"We are asking of the State Legisla-...

attention to recasting, revamping and rejuvenating the cooperative movement which had been termed by late Jawaharlal Nehru as the essential complement to Panchayati Raj.

Mr Gandhi also denied that there was any move to change the basic structure of the Constitution...

Reliving the Dandi March, 11-12 March 1988.

REGIONAL ISSUES

Rajiv Gandhi addressed many long-standing issues, both within and outside the country. In West Bengal, the Gorkhas were demanding greater independence. In Bihar, the Jharkhand agitation needed attention. In Jammu & Kashmir, unrest was assuming serious proportions and after 1987, the secessionist movement became active in the state.

Punjab

Soon after assuming office in January 1985, Rajiv Gandhi ordered the release of key Akali leaders who had been detained since Operation Blue Star and lifted the ban on the All India Sikh Students Federation. In November 1984, he ordered an inquiry into the anti-Sikh riots in Delhi and elsewhere, and soon began talks with Akali leaders to find a settlement to the Punjab problem.

In August 1985, he announced a settlement with the Shiromani Akali Dal, led by Sant H.S. Longowal, famously known as the Rajiv-Longowal Accord, even though some Akali leaders were opposed to it. The state assembly elections were fixed for September 1985. Unfortunately, Longowal was assassinated on 20 August, the very same day that he announced that the Akalis would take part in the elections. The Akali Dal, now led by Surjit Singh Barnala, formed the government, but it faced internal

problems and had to quit office. Punjab faced instability and a breakdown of law and order, and eventually president's rule was imposed in the state.

Rajiv Gandhi believed that the problem of terrorism in Punjab must be tackled by engaging with the Sikhs of India. He advocated restraint and caution in reacting to violent situations, while demonstrating firmness in dealing with actions that caused instability or threatened the unity of the nation. In a debate in Parliament, he said:

We can almost go back to biblical times, and when we work backwards, we see that whenever India has had a secular attitude, India has risen; and whenever we have had a communal outlook, India has crumbled and fallen. . . . If India is to remain strong, we cannot allow communal forces to mix religion with politics . . . Our genius through the ages has been the way in which we have assimilated, in the way in which we have absorbed, in the way in which we have synthesised, how we have tolerated differences, how we have produced a harmony out of different groups of people in our country.

The Punjab problem called for fresh initiatives. A new action plan, Operation Black Thunder, was launched to clear the Golden Temple in Amritsar of arms and gunmen. The National Security Guard and the Special Action Group were created, which, instead of the army, surrounded the Golden Temple in May 1988 and

in a 10-day siege cleared the holy shrine of the extremists. A number of initiatives were introduced to tackle the problem of continuing terrorism. While some problems persisted, the rapidly deteriorating situation in Punjab was now firmly halted. Operation Black Thunder effectively demonstrated the will of Rajiv Gandhi's government to take firm action to bring peace to Punjab.

Rajiv Gandhi with Sant Longowal, August 1985.

Northeast

In the northeast, the Naga tribes in the hills along the Assam-Burma border had never been completely brought under control by the British, and they were eager to assert their independence. Many Nagas converted to Christianity under the influence of American Baptist missionaries. The state of Nagaland was formed in 1963, but violence against the tribes in the region continued. In 1972, the northeastern region was reorganised in an attempt to secure the support of urban tribal leaders. The union territories of Manipur and Tripura and the Meghalaya region of Assam gained full statehood. The North East Frontier Agency became the union territory of Arunachal Pradesh and the Mizo district of Assam became the union territory of Mizoram. However, the Mizo National Front called for an independent Mizoram. In 1987, Rajiv Gandhi addressed this problem and both Mizoram and Arunachal Pradesh were granted statehood.

Assam, too, experienced periods of instability. In addition to the general grievance of underdevelopment, the agitation was also against the influx of illegal Bengali-speaking immigrants who had reduced the Assamese to a minority in their own state. Some tribal groups in Assam had long asked for a separate state within India. The large-scale influx of Bangladeshis into this area further complicated the situation. The discovery of 'foreigners' on the electoral rolls in 1979 created a movement that assumed serious proportions. The occupation of tribal lands by the Assamese and the Bengalis resulted in continued unrest and killings, in particular the massacre of hundreds of Bengali-speaking Muslims at Nellie in 1983.

Under the Assam Accord of 15 August 1985, Rajiv Gandhi's government reached an agreement with the leaders of the movement. Foreigners who had come between 1951 and 1961 were to be given full citizenship, including the right to vote, and those who came between 1961 and 1971 would not have voting rights for ten years, while the rest would be deported. Following this agreement, state assembly elections were held, and the Asom Gana Parishad took office in 1985.

Rajiv Gandhi thus succeeded in defusing unrest in the northeast, resulting in the end of the 20-year insurgency in the region. The Assam and Mizo accords were shining examples of a new approach to resolving intractable issues through an accommodating and conciliatory approach.

RAJIV GANDHI'S WORLD VISION

Rajiv Gandhi dreamt of a new world order and international cooperation based on a restructured United Nations, on the principles of democracy and sovereign equality.

Prime Minister Rajiv Gandhi and Sonia Gandhi being given a traditional welcome by the people on their arrival in Aizwal, Mizoram, July 1986.

In the neighbourhood, Rajiv Gandhi wanted to maintain cordial and cooperative relations with Pakistan, based on a shared history and built through enhanced people-to-people exchanges. He welcomed the Geneva Accord for the cessation of interference in Afghanistan. He endeavoured to create a climate of trust with China, recognising the need for a resolution to the vexed border problem through dialogue. He advocated enhanced engagement with ASEAN and the countries of East Asia, including Japan. He strived to build upon India's historic relations with the Soviet Union, enhancing economic engagement between the two countries.

Rajiv Gandhi supported the just cause of the Palestinians, condemning the brutal Israeli attack on the occupied territories.

Sri Lanka

In Sri Lanka, the long-standing ethnic conflict between the Sinhalese and the Sri Lankan Tamils was assuming serious proportions. The Liberation Tigers of Tamil Eelam (LTTE), founded by the more radical Tamils, demanded separation from Sri Lanka and the creation of an independent Tamil Eelam by using violence and terror.

Rajiv Gandhi used the forum of the South Asian Association for Regional Cooperation (SAARC) to discuss the situation with the Sri Lankan prime minister. When the Sri Lankan army ordered a blockade of the northern district of Jaffna, largely inhabited by Tamils, Rajiv Gandhi ordered relief supplies to be paradropped to this area when the Sri Lankan navy prevented Indian vessels from reaching the shore.

Ultimately, the Sri Lankan government agreed to let India play a role in finding a solution to the ethnic problem. The Indo-Sri Lanka Agreement of 27 July 1987 envisaged a devolution of power to the Tamil-majority areas, dissolution of the LTTE, and designation of Tamil as an official language of Sri Lanka. Addressing Parliament on the implementation of the agreement, Rajiv Gandhi stated:

The Government of India believe that, despite some problems and delays, many of which were foreseen but unavoidable in the resolution of an issue of this magnitude and complexity, this Agreement represents the only way of safeguarding legitimate Tamil interests and ensuring a durable peace in Sri Lanka. Some have chosen to criticise the Agreement. None has shown a better way of meeting the legitimate aspirations of the Tamils in Sri Lanka, restoring peace in that country and of meeting our own security concern in the region. We have accepted a role which is difficult, but which is in our national interests to discharge. We shall not shrink our obligations and commitments. This is a national endeavour.

The agreement was acclaimed internationally as it struck a balance between meeting the aspirations of the Tamil people and maintaining the unity and integrity of Sri Lanka. Prabhakaran, the LTTE leader, beguiled by first agreeing to the accord, but resiled on return to Sri Lanka. The LTTE, however, refused to give up violence and started a propaganda against India, threatening Tamils who disagreed with its stance. An Indian Peace Keeping Force (IPKF) was sent to Sri Lanka with a mandate to protect the civilians and to apprehend anyone carrying arms. The LTTE aggressively pursued a policy of military conflict and attacked the IPKF, which was then forced to disarm the LTTE. The repudiation of an agreement that held out the promise of lasting peace in Sri Lanka led to a humanitarian crisis, and amidst a growing perception that the Indian government was siding with the Sri Lankan government, the forces were withdrawn in 1989.

Pakistan

Relations with Pakistan, marked by a high degree of mutual suspicion, were strained further when routine military exercises conducted by the Indian army in the deserts of Rajasthan in late 1986 were seen as hostile activity by Pakistan. It retaliated by increasing its troop movements at the border across Rajasthan and Punjab. In February 1987, the president of Pakistan visited India and an effort was made in a meeting between Prime Minister Rajiv Gandhi and President Zia-ul-Haq to defuse the crisis diplomatically. A few months later, Rajiv Gandhi visited Islamabad and met Benazir Bhutto, his

Top: Rajiv Gandhi exchanging the Indo-Sri Lanka Accord with President J.R. Jayawardene, 29 July 1987.

Below: Rajiv Gandhi with Benazir Bhutto, the prime minister of Pakistan.

Pakistani counterpart, and both signed accords reaffirming the Shimla Agreement. Nevertheless, Pakistan continued to support terrorism in Punjab and Jammu & Kashmir. Rajiv Gandhi had a special understanding with Benazir Bhutto, and the two families remain cordial with each other even till date.

A Democratic World Order

Rajiv Gandhi's foreign policy drew upon Nehru's ethical foundations, and he believed in the indispensability of non-violence, of freedom from nuclear weapons and the need for disarmament, and in peaceful coexistence. As part of the Five Continents Initiative, he continued efforts for disarmament, creating a positive environment for the dismantling of nuclear weapons.

Nuclear Disarmament

Soon after becoming prime minister, Rajiv Gandhi held the first summit of the six nations—Greece, Mexico, Sweden, Tanzania, Argentina, and India—to mobilise support for a move calling on the superpowers to reduce weapons and to eliminate nuclear armaments.

During the visit of the Soviet leader Mikhail Gorbachev to India in November 1986, the two leaders formulated a plan for nuclear disarmament known as the Delhi Declaration.

Rajiv Gandhi said that the *'ideals of Gandhiji and Lenin have found expression in the Delhi Declaration.'* This matured into the Action Plan for Nuclear Disarmament, presented by Rajiv Gandhi to the United Nations General Assembly Special Session on Disarmament on 9 June 1988. In a moving address, he said:

Non-violence in international relations cannot be considered a Utopian goal. It is the only available basis for civilised survival, for the maintenance of peace through peaceful coexistence, for a new, just, equitable and democratic world order.

The Action Plan called for a binding commitment by all nations to eliminate nuclear weapons by 2010, for the establishment of a Comprehensive Global Security System under the aegis of the United Nations, and for a plan for radical and comprehensive disarmament.

Left: Rajiv Gandhi with Mikhail Gorbachev after signing the Soviet-Indian document, Moscow, 22 May 1985

Right: Rajiv Gandhi addressing the UN General Assembly on the occasion of its 40th Aniversary in New York, 24 October 1985.

Anti-Apartheid Struggle and the Decolonisation of Namibia

Rajiv Gandhi reaffirmed the solidarity of the Indian people and the INC with the people of South Africa in their just struggle against apartheid, believing in the inalienable right of all human beings to lead a life of dignity and freedom. He was outraged by the inhuman repression of the racist Pretoria regime. He was seriously concerned about the continuing illegality of Namibia's colonisation and declared his resolve to work with other world leaders to bring an end to its repression.

While replying to a debate in Parliament, he said:

What is happening in South Africa, in Namibia, is much worse than anything that is happening anywhere else in the globe. It is a shame for all of humanity that such treatment to our brother humans still exists, still goes on towards the end of the twentieth century. We must raise our voices and fight for the freedom of these brave people. We must give them all the help we can to fight their battle. . . . We must raise our voices till action is taken. . . .We find today that the US has put an embargo on Nicaragua. If it really wanted to strike it out for humanity, they should have put an embargo on trade with Namibia.

As prime minister, Rajiv Gandhi extended strong political, material, and moral support to the African National Congress (ANC) and South West Africa People's Organization (SWAPO) of Namibia. On the global stage, he emerged as a leading crusader in the struggle against apartheid. At the Bahamas Commonwealth meet, he proposed economic and trade sanctions against a racist South Africa to mobilise support in isolating a repressive regime. At the Nassau Commonwealth meet, a decision was taken to constitute an Eminent Persons Group (EPG), to facilitate a political dialogue on South Africa, co-chaired by President Olusegun Obasanjo of Nigeria and the former prime minister of Australia, Malcolm Fraser. The initiative was aimed at forestalling a bloodbath in South Africa, although it failed to make Pretoria see reason.

At the London Commonwealth Heads of Government Meeting (CHOGM) summit, the EPG report stirred the conscience of all nations, and a decision was taken to adopt measures listed in the Nassau Accord and additional steps to mount pressure on South Africa. The British government opposed the move, and Rajiv Gandhi created history by taking on Margaret Thatcher head on; Britain was reduced to a minority of one, with all the other Commonwealth nations steadfastly behind him. Later, the UN General Assembly passed a resolution imposing comprehensive mandatory sanctions against South Africa.

Rajiv Gandhi was in touch with ANC President Oliver Tambo and other leaders of the struggle. He supported the International Youth Conference Against Apartheid convened by the

Top left: Rajiv Gandhi with Sam Nujoma, Moscow, 9 January 1986.

Top right: Rajiv Gandhi with Alfred Nzo, Archbishop Trevor Huddleston, and Anand Sharma at the International Youth Conference Against Apartheid, New Delhi, January 1987.

Below: Belgrade Summit.

Top left: Rajiv Gandhi with Nelson Mandela, October 1990.

Top right: Rajiv Gandhi with Kenneth Kaunda.

Bottom left: Rajiv Gandhi with Africa Fund Committee members, 1989.

Bottom right: Rajiv Gandhi and Sonia Gandhi with Zenani Mandela and her husband, New Delhi, 1985.

Indian Youth Congress to commemorate the 75th anniversary of the ANC in January 1987, which was attended by representative leadership delegations from 82 countries. ANC Secretary General Alfred Nzo, who later on became the foreign minister of independent South Africa after the historic transition, and the iconic leader Archbishop Trevor Huddleston were prominent among those who attended the conference.

In 1988, India supported the 'Freedom at 70' campaign on the occasion of Nelson Mandela's 70th birthday, and Rajiv Gandhi made a fervent plea for Mandela's release, urging intervention by the United Nations Security Council. In the same year, Rajiv Gandhi refused visas to the English cricket team, the names of seven of whose players figured on the UN register on apartheid links. His strong decision, supported by a petition of Members of Parliament (MPs), reverberated in all the major capitals of the world.

Rajiv Gandhi was equally supportive of the cause of the SWAPO, and he raised the issue at the NAM Bureau meeting, which passed a resolution that echoed across the world. SWAPO was granted full diplomatic status in India. Rajiv Gandhi's role was considered of such significance that the Namibian government, in a memorable gesture, invited him to the country's independence day celebrations even though he was the leader of the Opposition. It was here in

Windhoek that he first met Nelson Mandela and the two developed a deeply emotional relationship.

Rajiv Gandhi as chairman of the Non-Aligned Movement met a number of NAM leaders. He described it as *'an alternative vision of world stability and security based on cooperation and the renunciation of force.'* At the Non-Aligned Summit at Harare in 1986, he took up the cause of South Africa, urging the establishment of the AFRICA (Action for Resisting Invasion, Colonialism and Apartheid) Fund, and the resolution was adopted. The AFRICA Fund had India as its chair and Zambia as vice-chair, and served as a measure of solidarity for the frontline states and for the liberation movements in southern Africa

Engaging with All Major Powers

In dealing with all the major powers, Rajiv Gandhi showed great maturity and a deep understanding of the changes that had overtaken the world in the post-Cold War period. He recognised that it was important for India to engage meaningfully both with the USA and the USSR. He was at equal ease with President Ronald Reagan as with General Secretary Mikhail Gorbachev. Rajiv Gandhi's visit to the USA in 1985 helped improve relations, and the USA agreed to give India a supercomputer for processing weather forecasting data.

His landmark visit to China in 1988 was aimed at improving trade relations and establishing a mechanism for resolving long-standing problems and disputes between the two countries in a spirit of cooperation. He was the first prime minister since Nehru to visit China.

He advocated greater linkages with the countries of Latin America and especially supported the efforts of Daniel Ortega to maintain the independence of Nicaragua from interference by other countries.

Rajiv Gandhi was the first Indian prime minister to visit Cuba and struck a personal rapport with Fidel Castro. He received the Order of Jose Marti, posthumously conferred upon Indira Gandhi in tribute to her stature as a world leader.

At the centre of his world view was India itself and the need for enhancing India's political unity and building its economic and military strengths. In India's external engagements, he represented a blend of the idealism of the Nehruvian era and the pragmatism of Indira Gandhi.

Top: Rajiv Gandhi with world leaders at a dinner hosted by the Swedish prime minister, Ingvar Carlsson, Stockholm, January 1988.

Bottom right: Rajiv Gandhi and Margaret Thatcher, May 1985.

233

ORGANISATIONAL ISSUES

Problems within the Congress were also growing. Electoral defeat in Haryana, Kerala, and West Bengal damaged the image of the party. Many of Rajiv Gandhi's early supporters and advisers were young and were not very familiar with the politics of the country. Some of them left the Congress, including V.P. Singh, Arun Singh, Arun Nehru, and Arif Mohammad Khan, and joined the opposition parties.

Political Challenges and Resurgence of Opportunistic Anti-Congressism

The five-year term of Rajiv Gandhi's government was coming to an end. The first half of his tenure had been relatively smooth. He was projected as a leader with a clean image, as a man of vision, eager to prepare India technologically to meet the challenges of the twenty-first century. However, the second half of his term saw some turbulence.

By far the most serious problem was the one created by the Bofors arms deal controversy. The government had purchased the latest weapons to strengthen and modernise the Indian defence forces. Amongst these was the purchase of Howitzer guns from the Swedish firm Bofors. Following allegations that bribes were paid to Indian officials to get the contract, the opposition launched a nationwide agitation for an enquiry, demanding action against those found guilty. Other allegations also surfaced concerning the purchase of submarines from West Germany and the appointment of an American international detective agency, Fairfax, to investigate the dealings of some industrialists.

The opposition in the Lok Sabha resigned *en masse*, forcing an early election. This revived the practice of opportunistic anti-Congressism as a central mode of political mobilisation rather than a debate on substantive ideological issues, and paved the way for electoral adjustment amongst the non-Congress parties.

Rajiv Gandhi announced general elections in November 1989.

NATIONAL FRONT

The right-wing opposition parties that had earlier combined and broken up now moved closer in the new context to give a united fight to the Congress, under the banner of the National Front, while maintaining their separate identities. The National Front arrived at electoral adjustments with the Left Front and the BJP. By then, V.P. Singh had left the Congress and joined the Janata Dal, which was a constituent party of the National Front.

During this period, many diverse anti-Congress groups like the Left and the BJP came together to support V.P. Singh. This association lent legitimacy and credibility to the BJP and also softened its hard-line communalism to some extent. Regional and national secular non-Congress parties also combined politically with the Left parties and the BJP. By October 1988, the Janata Dal came into being with the merger of the Jan Morcha, the Janata Dal, the Lok Dal, and the Congress (S).

The Bofors deal and the Nehruvian concept of secularism were both under attack by some of these parties, and became the main electoral issues.

The right-wing parties came to the fore with the Vishwa Hindu Parishad's (VHP) claims over the Babri Masjid site and its moves to build a temple for Lord Rama there. This led to communal clashes, but the VHP went ahead with the laying of the foundation stone for the temple a few days prior to the Lok Sabha elections. Consequently, the BJP gained electoral advantage among some sections.

GENERAL ELECTIONS, 1989

The 1989 general elections were marked by unprecedented violence and the results went against the Congress Party. No single party got a majority.

The Congress emerged as the single largest party and was invited to form the government with the help of its allies. However, Rajiv Gandhi chose to stay in the opposition as the Congress had not obtained a clear majority. The Congress reposed its faith in Rajiv Gandhi's leadership, unaffected by the election reverses.

JANATA DAL GOVERNMENT

On 2 December 1989, the National Front formed the government with V.P. Singh as prime minister. However, there was continuing instability due to both internal and external crises. Since the government was formed with outside support, it was inherently unstable and lacked popular support.

V.P. Singh's move, on 7 August 1990, to implement the recommendations of the Mandal Commission in respect of reservation quotas for the Scheduled Castes, Scheduled Tribes, and Other Backward Classes in educational institutions and in government jobs led to a massive and violent countrywide agitation.

TOTAL BANDH IN HP; STUDENT SUCCUMBS TO BURNS

Firing in Delhi claims one

Policemen carrying away one of the student injured in firing in New Delhi on Tuesday. This student later succumbed to his injury. — TOI photo by Sondeep Shankar.

Top: Rajiv Gandhi's *Sadbhavana Yatra* to Bhagalpur,
October 1990.

Right: Rajiv Gandhi releasing the Congress Party
election manifesto, April 1991.

Collapse of V.P. Singh Government

Terrorism in Punjab and Jammu & Kashmir continued unabated. V.P. Singh withdrew the IPKF from Sri Lanka. Following this, the LTTE infiltrated into Tamil Nadu, creating a serious law and order problem.

The V.P. Singh government did not last long. On the Ram Mandir (temple) issue, the withdrawal of support by the BJP resulted in the collapse of the government. One of the constituent parties of the National Front headed by Chandrashekhar broke away and formed the next government with the backing of the Congress. However, it lasted for only a few months, and general elections were ordered in May 1991.

GENERAL ELECTIONS, 1991

The Congress spent this period addressing organisational issues in order to be well prepared for the polls. Organisational elections had not taken place in the party for two decades, despite periodic attempts. The PCCs were set up with nominated members, and the central leaders decided the PCC presidents. Training camps and workshops were organised to promote more effective interaction between grassroots-level party workers and the leadership. This helped the central leadership to respond to the needs and aspirations of people in each constituency.

RAJIV GANDHI'S TRAGIC ASSASSINATION

Rajiv Gandhi planned the Congress election strategy on the basis of a sound assessment of the prospects in each state and chose the party candidates with great care. He undertook an extensive campaign tour for Congress candidates, which also took him to Sriperumbudur in Tamil Nadu. On the fateful evening of 21 May, while greeting people at the election meeting venue, a human suicide bomb suddenly exploded close to him, and he died a violent death.

the price for trying to bring peace to Punjab, and he, too, paid the price for trying to resolve the Tamil issue in Sri Lanka.

Rajiv Gandhi was no more, but his dedication and hard work during the campaign resulted in a massive victory for the Congress in the elections. The Congress emerged as the single largest party, winning 227 seats, just 29 short of a majority.

Rajiv Gandhi's term as the prime minister was brief, but many of his policies and initiatives have had a lasting impact on the country, laying the foundations for many significant changes that took place in the next few years, propelling the Indian economy to new heights.

ELECTING A NEW LEADER

After Rajiv Gandhi, many eyes turned to his wife, Sonia Gandhi, but she made it abundantly clear that she would not like to be considered. Senior Congress leaders chose, in the first elections held in two decades, P.V. Narasimha Rao as the Congress president at the 79th session of the Congress in Tirupati, Andhra Pradesh, in 1992. After the election results were announced, through a process of consultation and consensus, Narasimha Rao was chosen unanimously as the leader of the Congress Parliamentary Party and the prime minister of the country.

The LTTE, which had harboured a grouse against Rajiv Gandhi ever since the IPKF had been sent to Sri Lanka, was later identified as the perpetrator of this dastardly assassination.

Rajiv Gandhi sacrificed his life for the cause of the country, seeking to uphold secularism, national unity, and communal harmony. His mother paid

THE HINDUSTAN TIMES

RAJIV ASSASSINATED

Bomb blast at meeting near Madras; 20 others killed

leader of international stature

stormy life lost in prime

Nation is stunned

Tearful farewell to Rajiv

Thousands join last journey

Another crusader dies for peace

1991

A New Political Reality

2004

A New Political Reality

1991 - 2004

In 1991, India stood at the cusp of a major change. The stability of the earlier years had given way to volatile politics and shifting political arrangements. In these uneasy times, the Narasimha Rao government was formed with the outside support of the Jharkhand Mukti Morcha and a few independents, and completed its full term.

P.V. Narasimha Rao (1921-2004)

President, 79th Session, Tirupati (1992-96).

P.V. Narasimha Rao, Prime Minister (1991-96), oversaw a major economic transformation and handled various national security crises during his tenure. He broke convention by appointing a non-political economist and future prime minister, Dr Manmohan Singh, as his finance minister. A polyglot, he could speak 17 languages.

A BOLD AGENDA OF ECONOMIC REFORMS

Rajiv Gandhi understood the changed economic reality of a globalised world and undertook several economic reforms for deregulating industry, introducing flexible exchange rates, and partially lifting import controls. The Congress manifesto for the general elections of 1991 outlined his vision and the benefits of a measured and calibrated liberalisation.

The summer of 1991 presented a grim economic situation, with alarming domestic inflation, declining exports, and disrupted industrial production. Foreign exchange reserves were at their lowest ebb, sufficing only for seven days of imports. India faced a crisis of balance of payment and repayment of foreign debt. Dr Manmohan Singh, an acclaimed economist and a former Governor of the Reserve Bank of India, was the finance minister. He rose to the challenge, introducing a series of bold and pragmatic measures and created a liberal economic environment.

Economic liberalisation had a dramatic impact on the Indian economy. Foreign investments grew exponentially. Within a year, inflation was brought down to nine per cent, providing much relief to the common people. An open economy, which was slowly integrating with the world, saw enhanced capital flows even as industrial licencing was hugely reduced and government controls were restricted only to the strategic sector. Private enterprise was allowed to invest in key sectors of the economy like aviation and telecommunications, generating considerable competition.

A hitherto insular economy was transformed into one with a liberal outlook, and unshackled entrepreneurial spirit from the licence-quota permit raj.

The story of India's economic transformation and rapid economic recovery is a unique one. While the economic reforms had a far-reaching impact on the Indian economy, the process was not devoid of criticism, particularly from the socialist nationalists who perceived the reforms as a departure from the Nehruvian vision and a move towards neocolonial policies.

It was, therefore, important to reconcile the bold agenda of the economic reforms with the ideal of Nehruvian socialism from the Congress Party's perspective. The party outlined the nuances, clearly showing that there were deep synergies between the Nehruvian ideology and economic reforms. The Congress stood firm in its commitment to socialism and to the creation of a society that provided equal opportunities to all, while remaining in tune with the changing realities of the globalised world. Achieving self-reliance required making Indian industry globally competitive. After decades of state support, Indian industry had finally come of age, acquiring the ability to compete internationally. The

MANMOHAN SINGH (b. 1932)

India's fourteenth prime minister, Dr Manmohan Singh, is rightly acclaimed as a thinker and a scholar. An economist by profession, he was the Governor, Reserve Bank of India (1982-85), Deputy Chairman, Planning Commission (1985-87) and Finance Minister (1991-96). In 2010, *Newsweek* magazine listed him as the leader who is most respected by other leaders. He was described as 'the leader other leaders love.' In 2005 and 2010, he was chosen to be among *Time's* 100 most influential people. He is well regarded for his diligence and his academic approach to work, as well as his accessibility and his unassuming demeanour.

economic ideology of the Congress was, therefore, imbued with the philosophy of change with continuity.

GROWTH WITH EQUITY

The Congress retained its abiding commitment to achieving social and economic justice and to empowering the poor, the backward sections, and the minorities. The economic reforms and the concomitant growth had a 'trickle-down' effect, lifting millions of people out of poverty. A number of schemes targeting the empowerment of the poor were launched to achieve these objectives. Investment in rural development and poverty alleviation programmes in the five years of this period was to the tune of Rs. 340 billion, three times the amount spent in the previous five years.

Watershed budget on the cards

NEW DELHI, July 23.

THE finance minister, Dr Manmohan Singh, will present the 1991-92 Union budget to Parliament tomorrow. It is expected to mark a turning point in India's fiscal history, reports PTI.

The budget, as Dr Singh has himself indicated, would spell out the measures through which the Narasimha Rao government would strive to put the crisis-ridden economy back on the rails. It may hark back on the fiscal and the disequilibrium...

subsidy which has gone up from Rs 375 crores in 1981-82 to a whopping Rs 4,592 crores in 1989-90.

The devaluation of the rupee would enhance the subsidy burden for both domestic and imported fertilisers by making imports dearer and by raising the price of petroleum, which is the major...

economy in the first part of his speech. The exact implications of these measures would have to await fresh...

RBI guidelines for private banks

BOMBAY, Jan. 22 (HTC)

After giving free field to nationalised banks which account for 91 per cent of total bank branches and handle 86 per cent of the bank business in the country for over two decades now, the Reserve Bank has decided to permit setting up of new private sector banks.

It today laid down detailed conditions for setting up of new private banks. Such banks must subserve the underlying goals of financial sector reforms which are to provide competitive, efficient and low cost financial intermediation services for the society at large. They should be financially viable. Their presence should result in upgradation of technology in the banking sector. They should...

Act, 1934 at the appropriate time. The decision of the RBI in these matters shall be final.

The bank will be governed by the provisions of the Banking Regulation Act, 1949 in regard to its authorised, paid up capital. The...up capital for such a... 100 crore. The prom...tion for such a bank...ined by the RBI and...ct to other applicable...shares of the bank...on stock exchanges.

...ar relations is not good at the moment", says Mr Kutzenkov.

granted under Section 53 of the said Act, to public financial institutions.

The new bank shall not be allowed to have as a director any person who is a director of any other banking company, or of companies which among themselves are entitled to exercise voting rights in excess of 20 per cent of the total voting rights of all the shareholders of the banking company, as laid down in the Banking Regulation Act, 1949. The bank will be governed by the provisions of the Reserve Bank of India Act, 1934, the Banking Regulation Act, 1949 and other relevant statutes, in regard to its management set-up, liquidity requirements and the scope of its activity. The directives, instructions, guidelines and advices given by...

Rupee partly convertible, I-T reduced

Worthy Sequel

Dr Manmohan Singh's second budget is less a historic breakthrough than a worthy sequel to his first. It carries forward the logic and philosophy of his first budget, which aimed to convert India from a control-bound, inward-looking economy into a market-friendly, outward-looking one. The country is being opened up and integrated into the global economy through partial convertibility of the rupee, lower import duties and the abolition of import licensing, a relaxation of FERA, permission to foreign investors to buy shares in the Indian stock markets, and the liberalisation of the philosophy of investment. Serious attempts are being made to get out of the stagflation that characterised this year. The one per cent cut on lending rates, cut in income-tax rates, lower import duty on capital goods, slashing of the statutory liquidity ratio (thus easing the credit squeeze), and abolition of import licensing and greater scope for foreign investment should all help pour additional growth, as well as melt away the pressure on inflation control. If welfare failed to do so in 1991-92 when budgeting went haywire, thanks principally to shortfalls in customs revenue and to credit to the former Soviet Union...

The Times of India News Service and PTI

NEW DELHI, Feb. 29.

THE Union finance minister, Dr Manmohan Singh, who has been on the defensive in Parliament for the past week, rebutting charges of having leaked the 1992-93 Union budget to the World Bank, today presented budget proposals which seek to give relief to income tax payers and investors while raising excise duties on various products.

The taxation proposals, which were not entirely in line with the prescriptions reportedly made by the World Bank, were partially in the line of proposals to make the Indian rupee partially convertible to create a small farmers' agriculture corporation and to slash the statutory liquidity ratio for banks, which followed since last year and provide a boost to industrial production.

In his second budget, the finance minister, Dr Manmohan Singh, raised the excise duty on cigarettes depending on length to net a hefty Rs 325 crores and spread his net wide to cover cement, paints, watches, non-ferrous metals, plastics and watches.

on expenditure tax will result in a revenue loss of Rs 100 crores while the customs duty reliefs amount to a substantial Rs 2,023 crores.

Following widespread criticism, the finance minister announced withdrawal of the scheme of tax deduction at source on term deposits. He proposed to allow import of gold up to 5 kg by NRIs and thus returning from abroad. A sum of excise import duty ad valorem. A surcharge scheme of gold bond for raising resources and idle gold holding was also announced...

Singh proposed a ten per cent tax rebate on the incomes above Rs 50,000. In the case of working women having a total income up to Rs 75,000, the standard slab of Rs 12,000 to Rs 15,000. The general slab... Authors, playwrights, artists, musicians, actors and sportsmen will get a tax rebate of 25 per cent in respect of specified savings as compared to 20...

More budget reports,
Pages 7, 8, 9, 10, 11

HIGHLIGHTS

Announcing major concessions on direct and indirect taxes, the finance minister...

convertible on trade account replacing the exim scrips.

The government also proposes to introduce comprehensive amendment to the Foreign Exchange Regulation Act to bring it in line with the requirements of the new policy.

As a concession to the fourth estate, the minister proposed to exempt fully import of newsprint from import duty. At present it is attracting Rs 560 of duty per tonne.

Contrary to fears, Dr Singh has decided to maintain a system of food crores...

Foreign in...

NEW DELHI, Sept. 14 (PTI).

FOLLOWING are the highlights of the major policy guidelines issued by the finance ministry today to attract the flow of foreign...from institutional in...

of securities from t...
- FIIs to obtain a...tration with SEBI...latory agency for se...before they make a...in the securities of c...on the Indian stoc...
- Nominee comp...and subsidiary com...to be treated as se...registration and the...separate registration...
- In view of fo...control in force, F...SEBI another ag...dressed to RBI fo...permissions under...
- SEBI's initial re...valid for five year...general permission...the FII also to be...years, with both m...similar five years a...
- RBI's general pe...FERA to enable the...to buy, sell and real...on investment ma...

ROUTINE STEP, SAYS MANMOHAN

Rupee devalued by 8.5 p.c.

By Business Times Staff
BOMBAY, July 1.

THE Reserve Bank of India announced a drastic adjustment of rupee against all four major currencies (dollar, pound, yen and mark) today, in relation to pound sterling, the rupee touched Rs 37.37 to a pound as against Rs 34.36 on Friday. The rupee exchange rate was last fixed on June 28 when the rupee was upvalued by 0.26 per cent.

The move is widely interpreted as a signal to the World Bank and International Monetary Fund that India is willing to follow their prescription, a standard item of which is a devaluation.

According to sources, the Reserve Bank had finalised three rounds had finalised the...mitted it to the...

currencies in the basket. So the RBI and the finance ministry can legitimately claim (as indeed they have done when queried by news agencies) that this is no devaluation but more of this is no devaluation but more the RBI makes about every day.

However, observers of international money are gratified that the rupee should be marked down so sharply.

Officials are trying to pretend that it is all routine. It is not and is designed to send signals to them we are open to their conditions says a leading banker.

"It is a devaluation" is widely accepted as a first of the kind of confidence boosting steps that India needs to display to the world financial community.

New Delhi (PTI): Asked to comment on the latest revision the finance minister, Dr Manmohan Singh, described it as a "routine" action undertaken by the RBI which "takes various factors into consideration". He denied that it was devaluation, as it was pressure to the...months.

government," however, he said the adjustment of currency is a continuous process. The value of the rupee is linked to the basket of currencies and raises.

Accordingly, the RBI takes a decision on the value of the rupee and petent authority to take such decisions, he said.

The noted economist, Prof S. L. Rao, said the downward revision of the rupee could be of real help to the economy if it was considered as removing or reducing import curbs. If it was part of the IMF package, he expected that there would be customs duty reduction.

Notwithstanding the denial by the government, financial and industry circles see the move as a "first step" towards securing the IMF loan. The revision may be seen as a executive of the foreign exchange.

▶ **BJP reiterates call, Page 12**
Half a step, but welcome, Page 12

cent to 9.7 per cent. The price of standard gold in the Madras bullion market quoting at Rs 3,840 per ten gms at 1 p.m. today, quickly added 60 points and reached Rs 3,900 by 3 p.m. today.

RBI's decision, he said, might be a fall-out of the definitively attributed to it. Mr C. V. Pandurangan, secretary of the Madras diamond merchants' association, the market is awaiting more information on this score from Bombay. While there has been no reaction in the price index fell by 8.62 points today to 788.35.

However, stockbrokers feel that the casing of values was more due to the usual pre-budget fall. They said it could not be directly linked with RBI's decision. In the...

PM to seek trust vote on July 12

NEW DELHI, July 3.

THE Prime Minister, Mr P. V. Narasimha Rao, will seek a vote of confidence on July 12, the parliamentary affairs minister, Mr Ghulam Nabi Azad, said today, according to UNI.

Talking to the press, Mr Azad said that this would be the first official business the government would take up in the tenth Lok Sabha.

Mr Azad also announced that the Prime Minister had appointed the home minister, Mr S. B. Chavan, as the leader of the house in the Rajya Sabha and the human resources development minister, Mr Arjun Singh, as the leader in the Lok Sabha.

Mr Azad said that since the PM belonged to neither of the two houses, he had nominated Mr Singh to act on his behalf.

As his first press conference, Mr Azad was accompanied by the two ministers of state — Mr M. M. Jacob and Mr P. R. Kumaramangalam.

Asked about the resignation of Mr P. Shiv Shanker as the leader of the Rajya Sabha, Mr Azad said that now that the party had a minister from the upper house, Mr Shiv Shanker automatically ceased to be the leader.

Mr Azad said that the election of the new speaker of the Lok Sabha would be held on July 10 and next day the president, Mr R. Venkataraman, would address the joint session of both the houses of parliament.

Mr Azad said that the first session of tenth parliament, to begin on July 8, would continue up to September 10.

"During this period, the railway budget would be presented on July 18. The general budget on July 24 and a vote-on-account for two months on July 30, Mr Azad said.

Earlier, the group of min...

FURTHER DEVALUATION RULED OUT

Rupee down by 10.96 p.c. against dollar

By A Staff Reporter
BOMBAY, July 3.

THE Reserve Bank of India today devalued the rupee by 10.58 to 10.96 per cent against the four major currencies for the second time in three days.

The rupee was depreciated by 10.58 per cent against the pound sterling, 10.96 against the dollar, 10.66 against the deutsche mark and 10.6 against the yen.

This brings the overall devaluation against the major currencies to about 18 per cent.

On Monday, the rupee had dropped by 8.5 to 9.7 per cent against these currencies.

"With this adjustment, the rupee is now at an appropriate level, consistent with the need to maintain our competitiveness in exports," Mr S. Venkitaraman, the RBI governor said at a press meet today — his first since he took over in 1990.

In response to a query, the governor clarified that "there will not be another bout of depreciation now. There has been a lot of speculation about further devaluation — this is not today and Rs 648 in the last three days. Similarly, 22-carat gold rose by Rs 420 and Rs 595.

Stockists were apprehensive that the "havala" rate (unofficial rate for the U.S. dollar) would go up to around Rs 30 per dollar which in turn would push up banded costs of contraband gold.

Traders said the prices of precious metals would rise further and were likely to touch Rs 5,000 mark.

According to the governor, to improve efficiency in exports, moderation of imports was necessary. Ad-

justing the exchange rate was one instrument of doing this and correcting the balance of payments deficit.

Assuming that the country does not go in for commercial borrowings and assuming growth in exports, the total finance gap is estimated at $3 to $4 billion. Part of this has been met through compression of imports [about $1 billion] and the balance had to be accessed as interim assistance of a medium or long-term basis, Mr Venkitaraman said.

"I am optimistic and see a bright possibility of assistance to see us through our immediate crisis and to

medium term problem," he added.

"However, there is no way that we can keep depending money from the rest of the world. We have to learn to be competitive," he said.

The basic motive of the change in exchange rate policy is to promote competitiveness of Indian exports.

According to the RBI the recent adjustment in India's exchange rate is a response to the relative price movements of world currencies. Since October 1990 there has actually been some appreciation of about 2 per cent in India's effective real exchange rate due to both, a much slower rate of depreciation of the nominal exchange rate and the widening inflation differentials in domestic price inflation accelerated after October).

In the five month period between February and June this year, the notional effective exchange rate decreased by only 2.5 per cent. To prevent the erosion of international competitiveness, the exchange rate had to be adjusted, the RBI said.

Agencies add: Ruling out any further change in the value of the

send the right signals to the international community and added he had been assured by donor countries that they would not fail India if it followed the right policies.

He also had assurances from non-resident Indians in the United States that they would do everything possible to see that US $1 billion was remitted to India.

Dr Singh said as a result of what had been done on the exchange rate, India's trading system would get an impetus unknown so far.

Replying to a question, he said devaluation was a dirty word, but for

a realistic appreciation of the value of the rupee one had to look at the exchange rate of the currencies of some of India's competitors on the export front, particularly South

▶ **Debt servicing goes up,**
Forex market active, Page 13

Korea, Pakistan and China.

Asked whether the move would have an adverse impact on petroleum prices, the minister said it was a hypothetical question as the country did not have enough foreign exchange to buy petroleum goods.

He said there had been a savage import squeeze and it was his government's intention to gradually reverse it.

He said the step had demonstrated to the world that the new government was capable of taking "quick, hard and sensible decisions."

Stressing that the devaluation would give an impetus to the country's trading system, he said the consequential changes in trade policy had been worked out and would be announced by the minister of state for commerce, Mr P. Chidambaram, later in the day.

Gold crosses Rs 4,000 mark

BOMBAY, July 3: The sharp downward revision of the Indian rupee had its impact on the bullion market with prices of the yellow metal crossing the Rs 4,000 mark, report PTI & UNI. Standard gold mint was today quoted at an all time high of Rs 4,380 per ten grams at the close, while prices of the 22-carat variety hit a new high of Rs 4,015. The standard gold mint price registered a whopping Rs 232 increase...

rupee, the finance minister, Dr Manmohan Singh, said he was confident that at its current value, the rupee would emerge stronger.

He was of the view that the exchange rate adjustment would lead to export promotion and import substitution. There was a lot of things with high import content, which the country could not afford, he added.

Owning full responsibility for the measure, Dr Singh asserted that it was not prompted by the IMF or the World Bank.

Dr Singh said the action would

▶ **See Edit: Two-Step**
Devaluation, Page 10

Cabinet okays industrial policy

NEW DELHI, July 23.

THE Union council of ministers tonight approved the new industrial policy which is likely to be placed in Parliament tomorrow, reports PTI.

The meeting was preceded by the Union cabinet, which gave final shape to the far-reaching industrial policy reforms.

According to an official spokesman, the government proposes to take certain initiatives in the industrial policy, the underline principle of which would be the "continuity with changes."

"This would be the spirit of the new policy," the spokesman said.

The new policy is expected to cover industrial licensing, foreign investment, public sector and MRTP and other crucial areas to give a thrust in the industrial growth...

constituted by the Prime Minister, Mr P. V. Narasimha Rao...icy and...for its...

IMF to rush $ 2.5 b. worth of credit

By SUBHASH CHAKRAVARTI
The Times of India News Service

NEW DELHI, July 3.

IN a firm and quick response to the Prime Minister, Mr P. V. Narasimha Rao's bold new economic initiative, the International Monetary Fund (IMF) has decided to rush the initial disbursement of credit worth $ 2.5 billion in the next fortnight.

In a message received early today, the IMF said it was impressed by Mr Rao's determination to remedy the distortions which have bedevilled the economy over the years.

A succession of policy changes in wide variety of areas covering industry, trade and investment are being announced in the next few days.

According to highly-placed sources, the IMF has accepted Mr Rao's suggestions that India is quite required immediately. In India is not a more reduction of fiscal deficit but structural and policy reforms.

The Prime Minister, in his directive to the finance ministry, is understood to have spelt out...the element of...market...

(cartoon: "ECONOMIC POLICY" / "I LIKE TO GET A BRAND NEW ONE...")

Automatic okay likely for investment abroad

NEW DELHI, Sept. 13 (PTI).

THE government is working on a scheme to grant automatic clearance to Indians investing overseas and evolve guidelines for setting up joint ventures abroad.

"We are trying to bring some kind of automaticity in the case of money being invested inside the country," according to the deputy commerce minister, Mr Salman Khurshid.

In an interview to PTI, Mr Khurshid said, there had to be two-way flow of invest... country want... Whi...

for setting up joint ventures. Most African countries were looking for joint ventures in ... and small scale indu... ly, the probl...

New incentives hinted at

The Times of India News Service

AHMEDABAD, Sept. 13.

THE Union deputy minister for commerce, Mr Salman Khurshid, has hinted at new export incentives for the industries located in free trade zones in the... country.

Talki...

Prospects of IMF releasing $ 2.2 b. brighten

NEW DELHI, September 13 (PTI).

THE bright spots in the econ... the past few months...

ce ministers and prime ...rs from over 40 countries ...cted to attend the meeting ...ill have before it the special of 'enhancing private invest-...ws for development'.

...finance minister, Dr M... Singh, is leaving for Lo... orrow evening en route ...o attend the crucial meet... a lecture engagement i...

...ingh is expected... to be ac-...ied by... econ-...ntekh... Mr ...tary,

review the world economic situation and deliberate on issues to be the focus of attention at the IMF-Fund Bank parleys.

Fund Bank, Mr N. K. Singh.

Of the $ 2.2 billion assistance committed by the IMF in October last year, $ 680 million has been disbursed and the rest is to be released in tranches uptil June next year after undertaking quarterly reviews of the reform pr...

IMF sou...

ments for resources without weakening support for the traditional borrowers. The formation of the Commonwealth of Independent States (CIS) and their aid... ments will...

estment guidelines

...to time.
...itial regis-...nodal regu-...es markets ...nvestment ...anies listed ...changes.
...s, affiliates ...es of a FII ...te FIIs in ...ve to seek ...h SEBI.

...exchange ...o file with ...tion ad-...ng various ...A.

...tion to be ...while RBI's ...r FERA to ...d for five ...able f...on.

...sion un...stered F...pital gain ...rough in-...to India, ...s offerings ...stock ex-

changes and to appoint a domestic custodian for custody of investment held.
■ The RBI's general permission to enable the FII to open foreign currency denominated accounts in a designated bank, open a special non-resident rupee account, transfer sums from the foreign currency accounts to the rupee account and vice-versa at the market rates of exchange and make investments in the securities of India out of the balance in the rupee account.
■ It also allows the FII to transfer repatriable (after tax) proceeds from the rupee account for foreign currency ... patriate the c... dividend ...

■ No restriction on the volume of investment for the purpose of entry of FIIs in the primary/secondary market. No lock-in period for the purpose of such investments made by FIIs prescribed.
■ Portfolio investments in primary or secondary markets to be subject to a ceiling of 24 per cent of issued share capital for the total holdings of all registered FIIs in an... company.
■ The holding of... compan... of...

Bank deposits growth accelerates: RBI

BOMBAY, September 13 (PTI).

SCHEDULED commercial banks saw a phenomenal growth in aggregate deposits which accelerated to Rs 38,216 crores during 1991-92 from the previous year's Rs 25,583 crores, but the pace of their credit expansion was markedly slower, according to the Reserve Bank of India (RBI).

The RBI in its 1991-92 annual report, said the expansion in aggregate deposits outstripped substantially the revised working estimate of Rs 28,500 crores announced in the credit policy for the second half of 1991-92.

Apart from the sizable foreign exchange accruals, restoration of attractiveness in banks' competitiveness by means of periodical enhancements in bank deposits and special factors like large amounts of additional imports margins imposed against borrowers helped in and kept the rapid rise of deposits, the report said.

The margin money deposits kept by the canalising agencies, and the float money associated with buoyancy observed in the capital market were the other contributory factors, the report said, noting that the tempo of deposit growth had

continued during the first quarter of 1992-93.

Notwithstanding the accelerated expansion in aggregate deposits, no total bank credit witnessed a slowdown, with food credit expansion being modest at Rs 164 crores, against Rs 2,500 crores during 1990-91, it added.

This, the report... account of a fall in... foodgrains in the... higher offtake lead... in their stock lev...

About the tr... quarter of 1992-...the accretion to ...was higher at R...per cent), aga...(3.4 per cen...quarter of 1...

The exp...was even m...crores (6.5...Rs 960 cr...previous

EXPO...
India's 9...1991-9...1.7 per...after s...export...years,...Ho...per...

exchange rate changes. The report said citing both domestic and external factors for the sluggish export performance. Internal factors included the imposition of import compression measures and tight monetary policy.

External factors related to recessionary conditions in major developed countries, particularly the US and UK.

TAX CONCESSIONS FOR INVESTORS
Foreign institutions gain entry

The Times of India News Service

NEW DELHI, September 14.

REPUTED foreign institutional investors (FIIs) will be allowed to enter Indian capital markets under a concessional tax regime announced by the government today.

The scheme will permit mutual funds, pension funds, investment trusts and asset management companies to make investments in Indian markets, though subject to certain restrictions.

There will not be any restrictions on the volume of investment for an FII to enter the primary and secondary markets. The scheme is also free from a minimum lock-in period.

However, portfolio investments in FIIs will be subject to a ceiling of 24 per cent of the issued share capital in any one company. The holding of a single FII in any company will also be subject to a ceiling of 5 per cent of the total issued capital.

For this purpose, the holdings of an FII group will be counted as holdings of a single FII, after taking into account the conversion out of the fully and partly convertible debentures issued by the company.

The investment guidelines released to the press today have obviously incorporated these limitations... take-over bids by...

will make available to designated bank branches a list of companies in which no investment will be allowed on the basis of the prescribed ceiling of 24 per cent having been reached under the portfolio investment scheme.

FIIs investing under the scheme will enjoy a concessional tax regime of a flat rate tax of 20 per cent on dividend and interest income, and a tax rate of ten per cent on

▶ **Highlights on Page 13**

long-term (one year or more) capital gains.

The legislative amendment necessary to give effect to the scheme will be moved with the 1993-94 budget but investments made in 1992-93 will also be covered.

According to the guidelines, the 24 per cent limit for all non-resident portfolio investment will also include NRI corporate and non-corporate investments. But it will not include direct foreign investments, which are permitted up to 51 per cent in priority areas. FII investments through alternative routes, such as offshore single and regional funds, global depository receipts and Euroconvertibles, have also been excluded from the scheme.

The guidelines are in pursuance of the policy announcement made

by the finance minister, Dr Manmohan Singh, in the 1992-93 budget.

FIIs will be permitted to invest in all the securities, including the equity and other instruments of companies, listed on the stock exchanges such as shares, debentures, warrants and schemes floated by domestic mutual funds.

The government has also held out the assurance that it will add further categories of securities later.

To investing under the scheme, FIIs will have to follow certain procedures. First, before making the investment, FIIs will have to register themselves with the securities and exchange board of India (SEBI). Nominee companies, affiliates and subsidiary companies of the FII will also have to register with the SEBI separately.

Second, FIIs shall have to file with SEBI another application addressed to the RBI, seeking various permissions under FERA. However, the RBI's general permission will be obtained by the SEBI before granting initial registration. This will be issued along with the RBI's FERA permission under a single window approach.

The RBI permission will enable the FII to buy, sell and realise capital gains on investments made through the initial corpus remitted **(Continued on Page 11)**

Indian GDP growth may recover: UNCTAD

NEW DELHI, September 14 (PTI).

THE gross domestic product (GDP) growth in India is expected to recover from the low of 2 per cent in 1991 despite its tight fiscal policies and balance of payments (BoP) constraints.

The United Nations Conference on Trade and Development (UNCTAD) in its trade and development report, 1992, however, forecasts that India's tight fiscal policies and BoP constraints are likely to continue until new financial flows resume substantially and barriers to foreign investments are lowered.

In its chapter on regional performance and short-term prospects in South Asia, the UNCTAD report says "India's industrial production should nevertheless accelerate as import restraints on raw materials and essential goods are eased."

Volume of Trade
UNCTAD predicts a modest growth in volume of trade in 1992 and '93; phenomenal growth of trade in East Asia will be curbed

% change in the volume of trade — World; Developed Nations; Developing Nations; Asia; China; C&E Europe, CIS*

Import — Export — Central and Eastern Europe and former USSR
Note: Figures for 1992 and 1993 are Forecasts
Source: Trade and Development Annual Report, 1992, UNCTAD
UNI

imposed by a severe shortage of foreign exchange and the burden of external indebtedness.

To cope with these difficulties, the Indian government took wideranging deregulation measures, including the reform of public sector enterprises, 23 per cent devaluation of the currency and the grant of greater autonomy to commercial banks, the UNCTAD report says. The current account deficit in 1991 is estimated to be considerably lower than in the previous year.

Referring to the economic prospects in South Asia which includes India, the report says that the economic outlook in many countries of South Asia depends not only on the foreign environment, but also on domestic factors, such as political instability, weather con-

ditions, domestic demand and more particularly, the impact and spot of various policy reforms to restructure the economy.

Though the new situations may require a period of adaptation and unforeseen constraints may cause some delay, sustained favourable results are expected over the medium term, the report says.

For the immediate future the outlook is brighter as the subregion adjusts to earlier shocks, being adding, since much industrial input is derived from agriculture, foreign direct investment in agriculture-related industries would help expand exports and thereby contribute to a higher GDP growth.

World economy: "The world economy is in a danger zone," the report has warned. The question to be considered is whether the

financial fragility that has been brought about by a combination of financial liberalisation, tight monetary policies and bank regulation in the 1980s will be self-correcting or whether it will "continue to be a drag on the economic activity" and obstruct economic recovery, the report said.

The private sector in the developed economies is too indebted to be able to provide the impetus to growth. No single country could act as the locomotive.

The UNCTAD secretary-general, Mr Kenneth Dadezi, has cautioned that without urgent policy measures the global economic would continue to be at risk from strong undercurrent of debt, deflation and continued stagnation.

Since no country could become the current problems own, closer coordination is needed to bring about global growth, he said and the 1980s thinking, which allowed to stand and producing another lost decade.

The report, advocating a package of measures to stimulate the world economy, suggested there should be a boost in imports of carefully managed and gradual increases in government spending, especially in Japan, the United States and the United Kingdom in areas such as infrastructure. However, any increase in public expenditure should be linked and should be conducive to new investment.

"This will build up capacity and ensure a foundation for sustained expansion of output, employment and incomes without igniting excessive inflation."

The UNCTAD report suggested that the developed nations should enlarge the debt relief by strengthening the debt strategy to develop more countries in transforming and renewing SDR all...

245

CONSTITUTIONAL REFORM FOR RURAL TRANSFORMATION

Rajiv Gandhi, who had a vision of empowering the bodies of local self-government, laid the foundations of *panchayati raj* (village self-rule). While introducing the 73rd Constitutional Amendment Bill in the Lok Sabha on 15 May 1989, Rajiv Gandhi said:

We learnt that a grass-roots administration without political authority was like a meal without salt. We learnt that however well-intentioned our district bureaucracy might be, without effective elected authority, the gap between the people and the bureaucracy could not be closed. We learnt that the vacuum created by the absence of local-level political authority had spawned the power brokers who occupy the gap between the people and their representatives to distant Vidhan Sabhas and the ever more remote Parliament. We learnt that corruption could only be ended by giving power to the panchayats and making panchayats responsible to the people. We learnt that inefficiency could only be ended by entrusting the people at the grass-roots level with the responsibility for their own development. We learnt that callousness could only be ended by empowering the people to send their own representatives to institutions of local self-government.

The bill, unfortunately, could not pass as it did not muster the requisite majority in the Rajya Sabha. It was re-introduced and passed as the 73rd Constitutional Amendment Act on 22 December 1992. A significant feature was that no less than one-third of the total number of seats, as well as the office of the chairperson at each tier of the village, intermediate, and district levels, were reserved for women. This led to a radical empowerment of women in rural areas and to a transformational change in rural society.

This was followed by the 74th Constitutional Amendment Act aimed at establishing local self-government bodies in towns and cities. Similar provisions reserving one-third of the total number of seats for women were incorporated in this amendment.

This was perhaps the largest experiment in the decentralisation of government in the history of the world, which saw the creation of nearly 240,000 elected institutions, comprising 2.8 million elected representatives with over a million elected women. The dreams of Rajiv Gandhi were finally realised and his efforts bore fruit.

MANDAL COMMISSION AND AFFIRMATIVE ACTION

The Mandal Commission recommendations, which had led to a sharp polarisation in society during the tenure of the previous government, were implemented as per the Supreme Court judgment by the Congress government. Twenty-seven per cent of jobs in the central government and in public sector enterprises were reserved for Other Backward Classes. Institutional structures were created to ensure the welfare of the backward castes and classes. While maintaining the imperative of affirmative action for the weaker sections of society, the Congress Party disassociated itself from the divisive caste agenda.

CHALLENGE OF COMMUNALISM: DEMOLITION OF BABRI MOSQUE

The VHP and the RSS pursued a sinister agenda to exploit the religious sentiments of the people and to polarise Indian society along communal lines. In the mid-1980s, they launched an agitation for the construction of a temple dedicated to Lord Rama on the site of the Babri Masjid (mosque) in Ayodhya (in Uttar Pradesh), erected by a governor of the Mughal emperor Babar in the early sixteenth century. The VHP organised massive rallies to liberate the birth-place of Lord Rama, claiming that this was the exact site of his birth, and agitating for the demolition of the mosque to rebuild the Hindu temple. This issue led to sharp political polarisation and flamed communal passions.

In 1989, when the V.P. Singh government was in power with the outside support of the BJP, the CPI, and the CPM, the Ram Janma-bhoomi issue was adopted by the BJP to further its political agenda. In 1990, a *rath yatra* led by the BJP leader L.K. Advani exacerbated communal tensions across the country. On 6 December 1992, the VHP organised a massive rally of volunteers in Ayodhya and in a moment surcharged with communal frenzy, the Babri Masjid was demolished even as senior BJP leaders looked on as mute spectators. Kalyan Singh, the BJP chief minister of Uttar Pradesh, and other BJP leaders at the centre had given repeated assurances to the Supreme Court and Parliament that the structure would be protected, but the destruction of the mosque took place with the tacit collusion of the state government.

The demolition of the Babri Masjid sent shock waves across the country and remains a shameful blot on the nation's history. It unleashed large-scale communal violence, the most extensive since the partition of the country, leading to massive rioting and particularly affecting cities like Delhi, Mumbai, Kolkata, Ahmedabad, Hyderabad, and Bhopal. A red alert was sounded in most parts of the country and the army staged flag marches in sensitive areas, and curfew was clamped in several towns. The choice before the government was firing on the crowd, which would have created a Hindu backlash, or non-intervention, which would also have left the

Hindutva our mission: BJP

By ANIL SAXENA
The Times of India News Service
Baroda, June 10.

APART from mounting an attack on the three-year performance of the Rao government, making loud announce... "Hindutva"...

trying. Mr Rao got just under 90 per cent of the votes cast in Nandyal. The managers stopped ... below 90, obviously ... any candidate...

the opponents of ... movement...

State government falls as Hindu zealots raze mosque for temple

Holy rage puts India in crisis

Fateful madness at a mosque

Derek Brown on the political cynicism and manipulation sending ripples of blood across a nation steeped in a tradition of non-violence

O NCE AGAIN, India...

Ayodhya events stun world Muslims

By G. H. JANSEN
NICOSIA, December 7.

THE reaction of Middle East Muslims to events in Ayodhya has been somewhat muted because of shock and disbelief that in an orderly, organised country like India, with a very large Muslim population, a mosque could be torn down by zealots of another religion under the nose of the security forces, not far from the capital city.

It was late at night that the first reaction came from statements by the secretary general of the Organisation of the Islamic Conference, Mr Hamid Al-Ghabid. In one, he strongly denounced "this odious crime" and expressed regret" that the Indian government allowed fundamentalist Hindus to cause damage to this great symbol

of Islam in India. Light must be shed on this barbarous act and those responsible must be punished".

The OIC noted that it had on several occasions called the attention of the government to the gravity of the situation. In a second statement the secretary general said that "the entire Muslim world was shocked by this heinous and premeditated crime and expressed regret that the government had "succumbed to the fundamentalists".

The Jordan government denounced the action and called on the government to end "this sedition". The Islamic movement in the Palestinian occupied territories said that the event was "dangerous" because it could lead to a religious war. In typically vigorous terms, the Iranian government referred to the event as "a catastrophe" and condemned the "disgraceful move" and urged the Indian government to reconstruct the mosque. The ... described the event as "a...

blatant violation of the Indian constitution".

The most direct reaction in the area has been a scuffle in the Gold Souk in Dubai this morning between the police and Muslims who wished to demonstrate against the destruction of the mosque. Such verbal reaction has been slow in coming because the Muslim world, particularly the Arab countries, respect India as the country of Gandhi and Nehru. But that will not long endure unless Delhi acts very quickly and strongly to the Ayodhya events.

It should be noted that some months ago, when the OIC was considering the Babri Masjid crisis, the secretary general then spoke of imposing "an embargo" on India, which would presumably be applied to the supply of oil. Such action is not all that likely, though the strong words about direct Muslim intervention in Bosnia at the recent OIC conference in Jeddah is being taken seriously.

The hurt to Muslim feel... much more acute in the A... event than in Bosnia be... Ayodhya, insult has been ... injury by the rebuilding ... temple on the site of ...

If the OIC appli... bargo, India would ... alternative supplie... would add greatl... transportation.

The reactio... Muslims is g... that there a... situation that ... prehensible. One ... the other political. The... for monotheistic Muslims ... Hindu reference to "the birthplace of lord Ram" cannot be anything but a mere myth and fantasy for a god cannot have a terrestrial birth place. So they do not understand or accept the validity of the Hindu motivation. The Hindu action appears to Muslims to be simply an attempt by a majority to bully and humiliate a Muslim minority.

WIDE...
Army c...
out in ...

BOMBAY, Dec. 7.
THE Maharashtra gov... ernment today called upon the army to restore law and order in Bombay where at least 40 people died in widespread viol... in just six hours of the several other parts of the state reeled under backlash in the aftermath of yesterday's incidents at Ayodhya...

communal forces unchecked. The union cabinet sacked the state government of Uttar Pradesh on the night of 6 December and announced a blanket ban on all communal organisations on 7 December. Later the Indian National Congress reaffirmed its commitment to secularism. Recalling this incident, it resolved on 10 June 1994:

December 6, 1992 is a permanent blot on the nation's history and came about because [the] BJP showed utter contempt for the rule of law and indulged in treachery of the worst kind . . . AICC calls upon every Congressman and woman to work even more devotedly to foil the designs of communal forces and to isolate from public life the brand of politics that all communal parties like the BJP preach, propagate and practise.

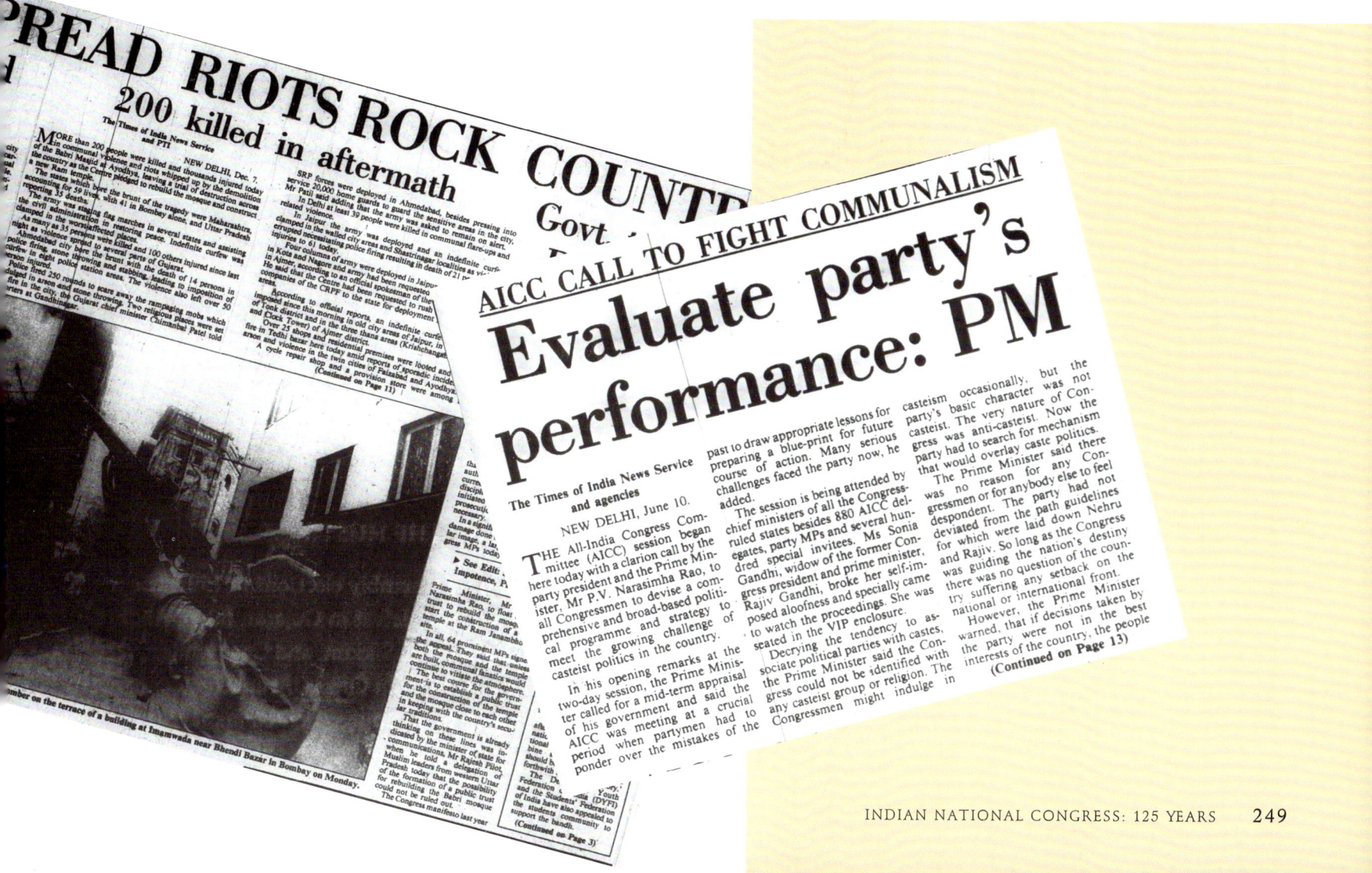

PUNJAB AND J&K: RETURN TO DEMOCRACY

The northern state of Jammu & Kashmir had suffered from organised terror and violence, actively aided and abetted by forces from across the border, leading to much turbulence. In 1996, elections were held in the state, restoring democratic processes and bringing a Congress-PDP (People's Democratic Party) coalition to power.

The state of Punjab had seen much instability over the last decade. Democratic elections were held for the first time in four years following the imposition of President's rule in February 1992, bringing the Congress to power in the state. The secular stance of the Congress, working with like-minded political activists who played an exemplary role in fighting terrorism in Punjab, ensured the return of normalcy. The experience of Punjab underscored that a firm political resolve and a commitment to secular ideology are crucial in the fight against communal forces, which threatened to rupture the secular fabric of the country.

INDIA'S EXTERNAL OUTLOOK

During these five years, India continued with its policy of supporting the non-proliferation of weapons of mass destruction with the eventual aim of eliminating nuclear weapons. President Clinton of the USA strongly endorsed this effort. At the same time, India sought to improve its security requirements, continuing with its indigeneous nuclear and ballistic missile programmes and enhancing its defence spending to effectively meet any threat on its external borders.

The role of Pakistan in providing support to cross-border terrorism against India was effectively highlighted in international fora.

India firmly upheld the demands of the Palestinians for the creation of an independent state of Palestine, but called for a peaceful resolution to the vexed problem through dialogue.

Relations with Iran were developed which enabled India to gain the support of China and Iran in the United Nations Human Rights Commission when Pakistan proposed a resolution in 1994 condemning the human rights violations in Kashmir.

India launched its 'Look East policy' to reach out to the extended neighbourhood in the East Asian region and to establish closer links with ASEAN.

It also continued to support political changes in South Africa.

SETBACK AT THE HUSTINGS

In the state assembly elections in 1994, the Congress suffered defeat in Gujarat, Bihar, Andhra Pradesh, Karnataka, Sikkim, and Goa, while emerging victorious in Orissa, Arunachal Pradesh, and Manipur. In an unprecedented session of the

Congress Working Committee in April 1995, it was brought out that these reversals were largely attributable to internal indiscipline, to losing touch with grassroots workers, and a failure to effectively reach out to minorities and backward classes. A strong demand emerged for the revamp of the party and for a sharper focus on a pro-poor economic reform agenda.

The general elections of 1996 brought a shocking defeat for the Congress and it clearly emerged that the influence of the Congress had waned considerably in the Hindi-speaking hinterland of the country. Efforts to stitch together alliances with regional political parties were unsuccessful. This period saw the emergence of caste-based political parties such as the Bahujan Samaj Party (BSP), which successfully followed the caste agenda, weaning the backward castes away from the Congress. The Muslims, who had traditionally been strong supporters of the Congress, also felt disillusioned and were more attracted to the regional parties. In Bihar, the emergence of a caste-based coalition led by Lalu Prasad Yadav and Mulayam Singh Yadav also resulted in a diminished base of the Congress Party. On the other hand, the BJP with its strident communal agenda appealed to the upper castes.

The 1990s witnessed the emergence of a new political reality, with a growing fragmentation of the polity manifested in the rise of coalition governments at the centre. No single party was able to form the government on its own and had to depend on outside support. In May 1996, the BJP-led government lasted only 13 days in office. The Congress, now the single largest party after the 1996 elections with 140 seats, provided outside support to the two United Front governments led by H.D. Deve Gowda and I.K. Gujral in order to avert fresh elections and to save the country from the communal agenda of the BJP and like-minded parties.

P.V. Narasimha Rao had retained the leadership of the Congress Party until late 1996 after which Sitaram Kesri took over and remained as Congress president until 1998. The Congress continued to criticise the policies of the United Front government when they deviated from the Congress agenda, and was particularly attacked for the country's continued economic decline.

Sitaram Kesri (1919-2000)

President, 80th (Plenary) Session, Calcutta (1997-98).

Sitaram Kesri, a social and political worker, took active part in the Quit India movement. Associated with the Congress for over six decades, he was treasurer of the party for many years and served as union cabinet minister in charge of many portfolios.

The report of the Jain Commission on Rajiv Gandhi's assassination was a point of sharp difference with the government. Following the report, the Congress sought the removal of the DMK from the ministry. But the government refused to comply.

On 28 November 1997, the I.K. Gujral government resigned as the Congress withdrew its support because the government was unable to fulfil its own stated Common Minimum Programme and continued its efforts to undermine the Congress politically. The Congress witnessed a period of drift, and a general feeling of despondency prevailed. Many leaders left the party, further weakening the organisation.

REJUVENATING THE PARTY: EMERGENCE OF SONIA GANDHI

Sonia Gandhi, who had so far refused to take charge of the Congress, was finally persuaded to do so at this moment of crisis. On 6 April 1998, she was ratified as the Congress president at the AICC session in New Delhi. On this occasion, recalling the legacy of the party, she said:

I have come to this office at a critical point in the history of the party. Our numbers in Parliament have dwindled. Our support base among the electorate has been seriously eroded. Some segments, including Dalits and minorities, have drifted from us. We are in danger of losing our central place in the polity of our country as a central party of governance.

SONIA GANDHI (b. 1946)
President since New Delhi session-1998.

Sonia Gandhi entered public life in 1998, in response to widespread demands from the Congress Party rank and file. She was first elected Member of Parliament (Amethi, 1999), and became Leader of the Opposition in the Lok Sabha. In the 2004 general elections, she led the election campaign of her party, which secured the largest number of seats, enabling the Congress Party to form a coalition government (UPA). Resigning from the leadership of the Congress Parliamentary Party, she named Dr Manmohan Singh as her choice for the prime minister. She is chairperson, UPA; leader of the Congress Party in Parliament; and chairperson, National Advisory Council (NAC), a forum that makes periodic recommendations to the government in areas of socioeconomic importance. Sonia Gandhi was named the third most powerful woman in the world by Forbes magazine in 2004.

She outlined her plans for revitalising the party by reinforcing the role of ordinary workers and creating a representative and responsible organisational structure of the party. She set in place an implementation process by appointing appropriate committees to visit states where the electoral performance had been particularly bad and to draw up a strategy of revitalisation. She outlined her commitment to social inclusiveness and said:

> *While it is true to say in the '90s economy, finance and trade occupy a central place, it must, at the same time, be remembered that the economy exists to serve the people and to meet their basic needs. We cannot lose sight of wider ethical issues and concerns such as equity and the environment.*

The Pachmarhi Conclave

The Congress held a conclave at Pachmarhi in September 1998 to reassess the party position and organisation and to consider the new programme outlined by Sonia Gandhi. A whole range of issues were debated and discussed, such as the growth of communalism and caste politics,

the challenge of empowering the Dalits and other backward groups, and the imperative of revitali-sing the party in the Hindi-speaking hinterland. On the economic front, keeping in view the agenda of social equity, an efficient public distribution system, land reforms, and the role of the village *panchayat* were given special attention. At this historic session, Sonia Gandhi exhorted Congressmen and women to respond to the challenges faced by the party and said:

> *We must take up the ideological crusade against the communal virus from whatever source it arises and spreads. Religious fundamentalism is alien to our culture but let us not be smug about this . . . We must acknowledge that we have not successfully accommodated the aspirations of a whole new generation of dalits, adivasis and backward people, particularly in the northern parts of the country . . . Our party must dedicate itself to cleansing public life. We must be a more responsive political force, an effective instrument of social justice.*

Congress president Sonia Gandhi at the flag-hoisting ceremony, Pachmarhi Conclave, September 1998.

In the same session, outlining her economic vision, she said:

Our economic policy will have to be multi-dimensional to meet the needs of our people at various levels. No one dogma, no one formula will cater to the diverse needs of the economy and of our society. The abolition of poverty within the next 10-15 years must remain our fundamental objective. The assurance of a better quality of life and an improved standard of living to all citizens must remain our primary preoccupation.

The Congress deliberated on the changed political realities of the 1990s in which coalition governments were the order of the day. The party became deeply conscious that the combination of diverse political parties without a common national approach or programme would be unable to meet the challenges posed by local or linguistic considerations. In order to have a sound coalition, a common vision was imperative. As the Congress president said:

The fact that we are going through a coalitional phase at national-level politics reflects in many ways the decline of the Congress. This is a passing phase and we will come back again with full force and on our own steam. But in the interim, coalitions may well be needed.

Later in the year, at a special one-day session of the AICC in New Delhi on 18 November 1998, the party reserved one-third of seats in all party committees for women or a minimum of 20 per cent seats for the SCs/STs, OBCs, and minorities.

Within a short span of nine months of assuming office as Congress president, Sonia Gandhi had galvanised the Congress rank and file to rejuvenate the party.

BJP-LED NDA GOVERNMENT IN POWER, 1998-2004

Fresh elections were announced. In March 1998, a coalition led by the BJP was sworn in. This government lasted for barely 13 months. In the next general elections, the Congress won 140 seats, emerging as the second largest party and staked its claim to form the government. Most of the non-BJP parties backed the Congress, while some parties like the BSP, SP, RSP, and the Forward Bloc did not. The Congress could not muster the necessary numbers to form the government, and the BJP-led NDA assumed power at the centre.

Soon after assuming office, the BJP government endeavoured to pursue an extreme right-wing ideological agenda. It embarked on a policy of altering school curricula using education as a tool to further its political agenda. History books were altered and distorted. Sonia Gandhi took a stand against the move to abuse such power aimed at communalising the education system. She wrote to Prime Minister Vajpayee on 21 October 1988 asking why the curricula were sought to be:

Indianised, nationalised, spiritualised. What does this mean? Is it implied that curricula hitherto have been un-Indian or anti-Indian? That curricula have been colonial or foreign, not related to the past and present realities of India? That curricula have been soulless and devoid of ethical values?

NUCLEAR TESTS: POKHARAN, 1998

The BJP carried out a round of nuclear tests at Pokharan, in Rajasthan, on 14 May 1998. The Congress lauded this as a matter of national importance. Addressing the CWC meeting, Sonia Gandhi stated:

I would like to place on record in this formal meeting of the Congress Working Committee the pride we feel in the achievement of our nuclear scientists and engineers for putting India's nuclear capability in the front rank . . . The nuclear question is a national matter, not a partisan one. On this, every Indian stands united.

However, she affirmed the commitment of the Congress to a nuclear weapon-free, non-violent world and India's commitment to peace in the region for fostering economic growth. The BJP government was cornered for inventing a security threat to justify its nuclear tests, and the exercise was rejected as being an act of self-defence.

CHALLENGES WITHIN THE CONGRESS

Sonia Gandhi's projection as prime minister in the 1999 election campaign led to fierce opposition from within the party on account of her 'foreign origin'. On 15 May 1999, Sharad Pawar, P.A. Sangma, and Tariq Anwar in a letter to the party president demanded that the Constitution be amended to ensure that only 'natural born' citizens could become the president, the vice-president, and the prime minister of the republic. Sonia Gandhi, in response to this letter, resigned from the post of party president. The CWC disapproved of the claims made by these three leaders and reiterated its faith in her leadership. Following this, she sought to reverse the legacy of personal bitterness and political animosity towards her. The UPA could not have come to power without her efforts in forging alliances and building relationships with those very parties that had been at the core of anti-Congressism.

THREAT ON THE BORDERS

India's security at the border was severely threatened during the Kargil war in the summer of 1999. Pakistan had infiltrated across the border for several months, and in the absence of timely and decisive action, the situation deteriorated, leading to war with Pakistan in the Kargil sector of Jammu & Kashmir. The Indian army rose to the challenge and bravely pushed back the enemy, but several young men lost their lives on the battlefield.

The Congress Party condemned the incursion by the Pakistan army and criticised the BJP government for gross negligence and for allowing such a situation to develop. The party organised relief work for the refugees in the Kargil sector.

Addressing the CWC on 20-21 July 1999, the Congress president pointed out that the infiltration sponsored by the Pakistan military had been carried out for many months and reports had been reaching the government.

9/11 AND THE SCOURGE OF TERRORISM

The world was shocked by the major terrorist attacks on the United States on 11 September 2001. The CWC in its meeting stated:

India has experienced a very persistent terrorist movement against its sovereignty and its people . . . The scars of terrorism sponsored, aided and abetted from across the border are still writ large in several cities of India . . . The Congress Working Committee expects that in combating global terrorism, the world community will fully take into account India's concerns and predicament in the face of sustained cross-border terrorism.

GODHRA RIOTS:
A SHAMEFUL BLOT ON INDIA

After the BJP-led NDA came to power in 1999, its right-wing organisations such as the VHP, the Bajrang Dal, and the RSS strengthened their commitment to establishing a Hindu nation. Their strident demands for building the Ram temple became increasingly aggressive, and the VHP organised tours of volunteers (*kar sevaks*) from all over the country to keep up the momentum of this movement. This had a direct impact on the communal situation in Gujarat, which saw a sharp polarisation along communal lines.

The VHP held a *yagna* (prayer ceremony) in February 2002, which was attended by thousands of *kar sevaks* from Gujarat. As the volunteers were returning from Ayodhya on the train, the Sabarmati Express, an altercation broke out on the railway station at Godhra, a small town in Gujarat. Fire erupted in a compartment of the train in which the volunteers were travelling. A rumour spread that this was the work of Muslims and a wave of violence spread across the state, targeting Muslims, especially in Ahmedabad and Baroda, leaving more than 2,000 dead and 200,000 homeless.

The report of the National Human Rights Commission concluded that the BJP-led Narendra Modi government in Gujarat had failed to protect the rights of the people through its inaction against non-state elements. Many allies of the NDA like the Lok Jan Shakti, the Telugu Desam Party (TDP), and the Trinamool Congress withdrew support and demanded the removal of the Gujarat chief minister. Sonia Gandhi demanded the setting up of a commission of enquiry headed by a sitting judge of the Supreme Court, action against the guilty, and a rehabilitation programme for all victims. In a charged speech at Porbandar, she expressed

dismay that '*Gandhi's Gujarat was being converted into Godse's Gujarat.*'

Modi's government decided to call for early elections to the state legislature. In this environment, the BJP returned to power in Gujarat and Narendra Modi was re-elected as chief minister.

However, the Gujarat riots left an indelible blot on the nation's conscience and two years later, in 2004, during the Lok Sabha elections, Indians came out strongly against efforts aimed at redefining the nation. The BJP lost, and this was in many senses a reaffirmation of the people's faith in the Congress and its secular ideology.

2004

The Congress in Coalition

2009

The Congress in Coalition 8

2004 - 2009

RETURN TO POWER: GENERAL ELECTIONS, 2004

A party conclave was convened in Shimla in July 2003 to draw up a strategy for the general elections in 2004. This period saw a growing unity amongst the secular parties and the left groups. The Rashtriya Janata Dal (RJD) expressed its willingness to support the Congress and the Samajwadi Party (SP) in Uttar Pradesh also indicated its readiness for a seat-sharing arrangement with the Congress.

The Shimla Sankalp (resolve) adopted at the close of the conclave on 9 July 2003 exhorted party members to defeat religious fundamentalism of all kinds as personified by the communal forces led by the BJP. Sonia Gandhi in her speech indicated that the Congress would work with secular and progressive political parties to check the rise of communal forces. for the first time, Congress had indicated an openness toward leading a coalition government with secular parties. The Congress also articulated its vision of governance in the run-up to the elections, including its commitment to rural development,

empowerment of backward and weaker sections, economic reforms, increased transparency in government institutions, and combating the criminalisation of politics.

At the CWC meeting on 28 August 2003, it was decided that the election campaign would highlight the corruption and failure of governance of the BJP regime. In the forthcoming assembly elections, the Congress emerged victorious in Delhi, but lost in Madhya Pradesh, Rajasthan, Chhattisgarh, and Mizoram.

In the-run up to the elections, the commitment of the Congress to the welfare of the weak and marginalised sections of society was

At the Shimla conclave, 7 July 2003.

clearly articulated. Strengthening the secular fabric of the country was the key plank, drawing upon the values cherished by the leaders of the Congress over the last 50 years.

An overconfident BJP went to the polls with its 'India Shining' slogan, but was rejected because the electorate was clearly disillusioned, especially the rural masses. In the parliamentary elections of 2004, the Congress-led United Progressive Alliance (UPA) emerged successful.

AN ACT OF LEADERSHIP

The Congress had arrived at a pre-election seat-sharing arrangement in the shape of the UPA and a post-election understanding with like-minded secular parties. The UPA, a coalition of 19 parties, secured 218 of the 540 seats and an assurance of outside support from the Left Front. Sonia Gandhi was the principal architect of the party's resurgence and was unanimously elected the leader of the Congress Parliamentary Party on 15 May 2004. The next day, the UPA and its supporters unanimously elected her as the prime ministerial candidate. On 18 May, she, however, declined to take over as prime minister, proposing the name of Dr Manmohan Singh for the post. She resisted the pleas of senior party leaders and Members of Parliament to reconsider her decision and

remained firm in the candidature of Dr Manmohan Singh. Reaffirming her decision at the Congress Parliamentary Party meeting on 18 May 2005, she said:

Throughout these past six years that I have been in politics, one thing has been clear to me. And that is, as I have often stated, that the post of prime minister is not my aim . . . Power in itself has never attracted me, nor has position been my goal. My aim has always been to defend the secular foundations of our country and the poor of our country—the creed sacred to Indiraji and Rajivji.

Sonia Gandhi's act of sacrifice showed maturity and leadership and was widely appreciated, raising her stature tremendously amongst the people of the country. Her renunciation of power mirrored the ideals espoused by Mahatma Gandhi.

On assuming the office of prime minister, Dr Manmohan Singh outlined his vision of change:

This is a mandate for change, for strengthening the secular foundations of our republic, to carry forward the process of social and economic change which benefits the poorer sections of our community, particularly our farmers and workers. We will ensure that we have a development strategy to empower our people to realise their vast latent potential.

AMAZING GRACE

'The post of Prime Minister is not my aim. My inner voice tells me that I must decline this post'

HT Political Bureau
New Delhi, May 18

VERDICT 2004

More on the Web
www.hindustantimes.com

Cong home, BJP makes a quiet exit

It's a victory for secularism: Sibal

CHANDNI CHOWK

Shruti Maheshwari
New Delhi, May 13

WHEN SMRITI Irani congratulated Kapil Sibal for his victory in Chandni Chowk immediately after the returning officer announced the final figures, she said this was "only the beginning" for her. But what a tough beginning it was.

Sibal gave TV's favourite *bahu* a lesson or two in electoral politics, cornering a whopping 71 per cent of total votes polled as he won the seat for the Congress.

Sibal polled 33,575 votes from the dominant Muslim constituency of Matia Mahal. Irani scored only 4,375 there. In the Ballimaran area, Sibal garnered 33,956 votes while Irani polled 12,567. In Chandni Chowk the margin was 12,943 with Sibal bagging 26,186 and Irani polling 15,243 votes. At every round, the BJP tally did not go beyond four digits and Sibal kept touching five digit figures.

A win for secularism is how Sibal described his victory, soon after humbling BJP's Smriti Irani by a margin of 79,417 votes. "This kind of a victory is an additional burden because it shows the kind of expectations the people have from me," Sibal said.

Promises: Development Board for Walled City, modern transport system and parking facility, allowing staging of Ram Lila at the designated Ram Lila grounds.

Kapil Sibal with his sons after he was declared winner on Thursday.

SUNIL SAXENA/HT

'Prime Minister's post is not my aim'

Continued from page 1

on Monday evening, reconsider. She told them to work out a strategy to tackle the Congress's allies and ensure government formation.

Soon afterward, M.L. Fotedar and Natwar Singh met Laloo Prasad Yadav and Ram Vilas Paswan. They gave the Bihar leaders Sonia's reasons.

First, that her children, Rahul and Priyanka, did not want their mother to take up a prime ministership that she did not want.

Second, that she was extremely hurt and upset with the BJP's tasteless campaign against her ethnicity and was unwilling to precipitate a situation that had the potential to split the nation.

And third, that given the ... being whipped up, her at the ...

Manmohan Singh, Arjun Singh and Ghulam Nabi Azad met the CPI-M's Harkishen Singh Surjeet. At one point, Paswan got in touch with Priyanka and requested her to intercede. When she told him Sonia's mind was made up, Paswan reportedly insisted: "*Tum bahadur bachche ho, tum unko mana logey.*"

By late afternoon, there was panic, and a truly dramatic outpouring of support for Sonia outside 10 Janpath. Congress workers and leaders descended in thousands outside the barricaded entrance, waving flags and shouting slogans into TV microphones.

Those protesting outside Sonia's residence eventually sounded like the MPs who spoke later in Central ... They were in denial. The ... pressed shock. And ... them seemed to unde... by their leader ha... They wo...

NATIONAL COMMON MINIMUM PROGRAMME

The Congress had released a manifesto for 2004 elections and when the UPA Government was formed, the constituents of the UPA Government agreed upon a National Common Minimum Programme (NCMP) which would set the agenda for governance. The UPA Govern-ment supported by left parties drew up six basic principles which would guide the Government over the next five years. The NCMP hinged on maintaining social harmony and keeping at bay obscurantist and fundamentalist elements. Economic growth of at least 7-8 per cent was envisioned in a manner that it generates employment so that each family will be assured of source of income. The welfare and well being of farmers, labour and those engaged in the organised sector was given primacy. Political education, economic and legal empowerment of women was given high priority. It was also resolved that an environment would be created which would allow equality of opportunity specially in education and employment for the Scheduled Castes, Scheduled Tribes, OBCs and religious minorities. Policies which will unleash the creative knowledge of scientists, engineers and entrepreneurs would be formulated.

NATIONAL ADVISORY COUNCIL AND SOCIAL LEGISLATION

A National Advisory Council was established as an apex advisory body with representatives of civil society groups to address key policy challenges, especially in the social sector, and to carry out the commitments outlined in the Common Minimum Programme declared on the eve of the elections. A unique model of inclusive governance was established by involving civil society in drafting social legislations.

Moving Towards Transparent Governance: The Right to Information Act, 2005

The Congress had articulated its firm commitment to bringing about transparency in governance and creating greater public accountability. The National Advisory Council placed the agenda of the right to information at the centre stage, and the Right to Information Act came into effect in October 2005. This historic act empowered Indian citizens to hold the government to account and to seek information from designated public authorities within a stipulated period of 30 days. Refusal to provide information within the stipulated time attracts penal provisions. It forces government institutions to take a fresh look at their systems of maintenance of records and removes public decision making from the shroud of secrecy. After the right to vote, the Right to Information

Act is perhaps the most empowering legislation, strengthening the institutions of democracy and ensuring public accountability. The Central Information Commission was established as an apex body to enforce this act.

An Inclusive Growth Agenda: Creating Rural Employment

The Congress leadership had been concerned about the challenges of rural unemployment, especially in the lean agricultural season, and the Common Minimum Programme of the UPA had stated that the government would immediately enact a National Rural Employment Guarantee Act (NREGA) to provide a legal guarantee for at least 100 days of employment.

The National Advisory Council prepared the draft of the National Rural Employment Guarantee Bill, which was deliberated within the government and resulted in the passage of the path-breaking National Rural Employment Guarantee Act in 2005. This act created the largest social security net in the world, based on a paradigm of inclusive growth, making ordinary citizens partners in India's growth story. It drew inspiration from the right to work outlined in the Directive Principles of State Policy, but for the first time gave legislative backing to the assurance of 100 days of legally guaranteed employment to each rural household in public works programmes, such as water conservation and harvesting, afforestation, rural connectivity, and flood control and protection.

NREGA has generated employment for 90 million beneficiaries, providing gainful employment of 3.7 billion man days, more than half of which has gone to women. This scheme has provided unprecedented public expenditure of over Rs 410 billion for the construction of durable assets in rural areas.

UPA chairperson, Sonia Gandhi, felicitating one of the officials at the NREGA Sammelan, New Delhi.

Leading the march,
Rahul Gandhi (left) and
Sonia Gandhi (right), to
commemorate 75th Anni-
versary of Dandi March,
2005.

Bharat Nirman: A Story of Rural Transformation

As part of its commitment to ensuring inclusive growth, a key policy priority for the UPA government was the creation of rural infrastructure to unlock the potential of rural India. This ambitious programme was aimed at ushering in transformational change in rural India. It would ensure rural connectivity to far-flung and remote rural and tribal areas, provide affordable housing to the rural masses, ensure safe drinking water supply to rural households, provide reliable rural electrification to unconnected villages, assure irrigation facilities for all agricultural land, and enhance tele-density and broadband connectivity for rural people. As a result of massive public investment in rural areas, in a five-year period, nearly 55,000 villages were electrified, covering over 52,000 households. Over two million households were provided safe drinking water supply and over 19 million new houses were constructed.

While the whole world was facing acute food shortages, India witnessed a record production of wheat and rice. The UPA government secured the interests of farmers through a historic loan waiver to the tune of Rs 720 billion. Investments in agriculture were encouraged. Rural credit was increased threefold and interest rates on crop loans were drastically reduced.

Prime Minister Dr Manmohan Singh releasing the mission document at the launch of the National Rural Health Mission, April 2005.

Throughout the five years of the UPA government, rural transformation through the creation of physical infrastructure and the provision of gainful employment received priority attention.

Affordable Health Care for All

Recognising the importance of health care in economic and social development and in improving the quality of life of Indians, the government launched the National Rural Health Mission for making institutional changes in the basic health care delivery system. The Mission has adopted a synergistic approach by relating the key determinants of good health, proper sanitation and hygiene, and safe drinking water supply, along with enhanced public spending on health, with a focused approach in reducing regional imbalances in the health infrastructure. The Mission, launched in 2005, has improved the quality and accessibility of primary health care in villages through the training of Accredited Social Health Activists (ASHAs). Over 650,000 ASHA workers were trained in the five-year period 2005–2010 and over 13 million health sub-centres were made fully functional. Over Rs 312 billion has been spent on this programme in the five years of the UPA government.

Prime Minister Dr Manmohan Singh and UPA Chairperson Sonia Gandhi releasing the UPA government's *Report to the People* to mark the completion of two years of its tenure, New Delhi, 22 May 2006.

. . . We have restored the secular foundations of governance. No longer are external tensions being exploited for the polarisation of our society.

We have fought terrorism with determination without targeting any particular section of society.

We have replaced a prejudiced, bellicose nationalism with an all-inclusive nationalism in keeping with our pluralistic ethos.

We have transformed the agenda of public debate that was obsessed with rewriting our past to a focus on the day-to-day concerns of our people. We have called a halt to the distortion of our education syllabus . . .

We have given India a new stature in the world community . . .

—**Sonia Gandhi**
at the 82nd Plenary Session of INC,
Hyderabad, January 2006.

Empowering the Powerless

Recognising the imperative of providing timely justice in rural areas, the Gram Nyayalaya Act was passed in 2008. This act envisages the establishment of rural courts at the headquarters of the intermediate *panchayat* and the setting up of mobile courts in rural areas to ensure the dispensation of speedy, efficient, and substantial justice.

The weaker sections of society were considerably empowered through various measures. The Forest Rights Act of 2006 gave the Scheduled Tribes (STs) and traditional forest dwellers rights over the land they cultivated in forest areas. Reservations for students of Other Backward Classes (OBCs) were ensured by law in all professional institutions in 2007, and scholarships for Scheduled Castes (SCs), STs, OBCs, and minorities for pursuing college and university education were enhanced.

A new act protecting women from domestic violence was passed in 2006, which for the first time also recognised a married woman's legal right to reside in her marital home.

A separate Ministry of Minority Affairs was established in May 2004 to pay focused attention to the welfare of minority communities. The Rajinder Sachar Committee examined the social, economic, and educational status of Muslims in India, and its recommendations are being implemented. An Equal Opportunity Commission is now being established. The Prime Minister's 15 Point Programme, launched in June 2006, sets physical and financial targets for minorities in all welfare programmes of the central government.

The government instituted various social security schemes for underprivileged sections, such as the Aam Aadmi Bima Yojana (life insurance cover for the common man), covering 150 million landless households; the Rashtriya Swasthya Bima Yojana (medical insurance cover) for 600 million non-organised-sector workers living below the poverty line; and the Indira Gandhi National Old Age Pension Scheme for people over 65 years of age living below the poverty line.

The Jawaharlal Nehru National Urban Renewal Mission was launched in 2005 for a period of seven years with an outlay of Rs 1 trillion, covering 63 cities, for upgrading infrastructure and providing basic services to the urban poor.

The National Commission for Protection of Child Rights was set up in March 2007 with the mandate of ensuring that all laws, policies, programmes, and administrative mechanisms are in consonance with the child rights as

enshrined in the Constitution of India and the UN Convention on the Rights of the Child. New laws have been passed to prohibit child labour and child marriage, and schemes to improve the nutritional and educational status of children, especially girls, have been launched. A national mid-day meal scheme providing hot cooked meals was launched in 2004, covering 150 million children in primary and upper primary schools. This scheme is aimed at improving school enrolment and retention rates by providing an incentive in the form of nutritious midday meals for the children of the poor.

Congress ka haath aam aadmi ke saath—The Congress hand in hand with the common man.

FOREIGN AFFAIRS

The UPA government has earned India a new respect and stature internationally and India was called upon to play a much larger role in global affairs. The foreign policy agenda of this period was marked by enhanced engagement with all major and emerging countries of the world, while consolidating relations with India's traditional allies in the developing world. India's growing economic profile was manifested in the emergence of BRIC (Brazil, Russia, India, and China) as a group of newly emerging economies with rapid economic growth rates.

India's relations with the EU were enhanced further through annual India–EU summits and bilateral engagements with member states.

Civilian Nuclear Energy Cooperation

A significant milestone of the Congress-led UPA government was the civilian nuclear energy cooperation agreement with the global community, breaking three decades of isolation. India's impeccable credentials as a nuclear power and its principled position on nuclear non-proliferation were acknowledged in the India-specific waiver by the Nuclear Suppliers Group, paving the way for India's integration into the global mainstream.

For the first time, Parliament saw an intense debate on an issue involving an international agreement, with sharp polarisation along political lines. The Indo–US civilian nuclear agreement having envisaged sustained civil nuclear cooperation between the USA and India aimed at ensuring energy security for India's rapidly growing economy. The Indo–US joint statement of 18 July 2005 provided the framework for this agreement, under which India agreed to separate its civil and military nuclear facilities, placing all its civil nuclear facilities under the scrutiny of the International Atomic Energy Agency. In return,

India's External Affairs Minister, Pranab Mukherjee, and US Secretary of State, Condoleezza Rice, shake hands after signing the US-India agreement for cooperation concerning the peaceful use of nuclear energy, Washington, 11 October 2008.

the USA offered India civil nuclear cooperation.

Apart from the Congress, the agreement was supported by many political parties like the RJD and the DMK, former military chiefs, bureau-crats, and scientists, but came under sharp criticism from the Left Front. The Congress pursued the agreement, acting in India's supreme national interests, and won the vote on the floor of the Lok Sabha by 275 to 256 votes, despite the withdrawal of support by the Left Front.

In pursuance of the India-specific waiver, similar agreements were signed with France, Russia, Canada, and Kazakhstan.

South–South Cooperation

The Congress-led UPA government also fostered South–South cooperation, ensuring India's leadership of the developing world. The first IBSA (India, Brazil, South Africa) summit, an important forum for South–South cooperation, held in 2006, brought together three vibrant democracies—India, Brazil, and South Africa—from three continents—Asia, South America, and Africa. IBSA has since emerged as a significant political grouping that articulates the position of the developing world at all international fora.

This period saw India's greater engagement with the neighbouring countries of Bangladesh, Nepal, Sri Lanka, and Myanmar. A robust

Prime Minister Dr Manmohan Singh, UPA Chairperson Sonia Gandhi, and AICC General Secretary Rahul Gandhi at a function to celebrate the UPA government's winning of the confidence vote in Parliament, New Delhi, 23 July 2008.

economic partnership constituted the basis for an enhanced political dialogue with these nations. Afghanistan was admitted into SAARC, which under India's chairmanship moved from a declaratory to an implementation phase. An agreement was reached to establish the South Asian University in India and to operationalise the SAARC Development Fund.

The Congress-led UPA government reinvigorated India's traditional ties with the continent of Africa. For the first time, the India–Africa Forum Summit was convened in New Delhi in April 2008, in partnership with the Africa Union. India extended substantial development assistance to the countries of sub-Saharan Africa, building on the historic bonds nurtured during the period of Jawaharlal Nehru, Indira Gandhi, and Rajiv Gandhi. The Indian National Congress reinforced its historic ties with the African National Congress through a memorandum of understanding for regular party to party exchange, signed by the Congress President, Sonia Gandhi, and the President of the African National Congress, Jacob Zuma. Sonia Gandhi travelled to South Africa and delivered an address to the South African Parliament.

Sonia Gandhi, Anand Sharma with Nelson Mandela, Johannesburg, 2007.

ENGAGING WITH ASIA: THE LOOK EAST POLICY

During this period, the countries of East Asia, which had witnessed dramatic economic and social transformation, became integral to India's Look East Policy. India became a full partner in the East Asia Summit, which has laid the foundations for the larger integration of the East Asian community, with the eventual objec-tive of establishing a Comprehensive Economic and Partnership Agreement with East Asia.

With Japan, India entered into a strategic global partnership. A dialogue was initiated to conclude the Comprehensive Economic Partnership Agreement with Japan. Similarly, economic ties with the Republic of Korea were given a greater thrust.

Engagement with China

India and China established a strategic and cooperative partnership for peace and prosperity, outlining a shared vision for the twenty-first century. In the words of Prime Minister Manmohan Singh:

The world is large enough to accommodate the growing ambitions of both India and China.

At the political level, ties between the Congress and the Communist Party of China were given a renewed thrust, and the two parties signed a memorandum of understanding for sustained engagement of leadership from both sides, signed by the Chinese Minister of International Department, Wang Jia Rui, and Congress general secretary Rahul Gandhi. The Congress president visited China on two occasions, and the Congress received several party delegations from China.

SATYAGRAHA CENTENARY COMMEMORATION

The Indian National Congress commemo-rated the centenary of the Satyagraha move-ment on 29–30 January 2007 by convening an international conference, 'Peace, Non-violence and Empowerment: Gandhian Philosophy in the 21st Century'. The conference brought together representative leadership delegations from 91 countries and 122 organisations, including Nobel laureates, heads of state/government, economists, philosophers, and Gandhian thinkers. The conference participants under-scored the enduring relevance of Gandhian philosophy, which was summed up in the conference declaration presented by Ahmad Kathrada, freedom fighter and prisoner of conscience. The declaration articulated the collective desire of the conference participants to declare 2 October as the International Day of Non-violence.

To commemorate 100 years of Satyagraha, over 300 delegates from 91 countries, comprising world leaders, Nobel laureates, leading peace and human rights activists, and Gandhian scholars gathered at a two-day international conference *Peace, Nonviolence and Empowerment: Gandhian Philosophy in the 21st Century,* organised by the Indian National Congress at Vigyan Bhavan, New Delhi, January 2007.

ति, अहिंसा एवम् सशक्तीकरण"

कीसवीं सदी में गांधी दर्शन

दिल्ली सम्मेलन, जनवरी 29 - 30, 2007

ace, Nonviolence and Empowerment"

ndhian Philosophy in the 21st Century

Delhi Conference, January 29 - 30, 2007

1 HINDI
2 ENGLISH
3 FRENCH
4 SPANISH
RUSS
ARAB

In pursuance of this declaration, the chairperson of the conference, Sonia Gandhi, wrote to eminent world leaders, including UN Secretary General, Nelson Mandela, Archbishop Desmond Tutu, Brazilian President Luiz Inácio Lula da Silva, President of Ghana and the African Union John Kufour, Spanish Prime Minister José Luis Rodríguez Zapatero, and British Prime Minister Tony Blair. The concerted efforts of the Congress were supported by the government, and Prime Minister Manmohan Singh initiated the process for seeking a UN resolution. The initiative culminated in the unanimous adoption of India's resolution co-sponsored by 154 nations, moved by Anand Sharma, Minister of State for External Affairs, in the United Nations General Assembly on 15 June 2007, seeking to adopt 2 October 2007 as the International Day of Non-violence. Sonia Gandhi addressed the special session of the United Nations General Assembly in the General Assembly Hall on the occasion of the first International Day of Non-violence on 2 October 2007.

Left: Sonia Gandhi addressing the special session of the United Nations General Assembly on the occasion of the first International Day of Non-violence, New York, 2 October 2007.

THREAT OF GLOBAL TERRORISM

On 26 November 2008, armed terrorists from across the border outraged the entire nation by mounting attacks in Mumbai. The brutal attacks across the city killed nearly 200 people and wounded another 300. They brought into sharp focus the syndicate of terror that operates from the soil of Pakistan. Under intense diplomatic pressure from India, Pakistan was isolated in the international community and was forced to admit that Pakistani citizens were engaged in these vicious attacks. The Lashkar-e-Taiba was identified as the principal terrorist organisation that had orchestrated these attacks. The inaction of the Pakistani government despite clear evidence against the master perpetrators continues to hamper the agenda of peace being pursued by India.

INDIA'S RISING ECONOMIC PROFILE

The Congress-led UPA government proceeded along the path of economic liberalisation whose principal architect was Dr Manmohan Singh, now the prime minister. The first four years of the government's term in office saw an impressive growth rate of over 9 per cent, which was nearly two to three times higher than the rates of the developed economies, including the USA, Japan, and the European countries. India emerged as the second fastest growing major economy in the world, next only to China. Per capita income grew at over 7 per cent per annum and 300 million people escaped the clutches of extreme poverty.

The rapid economic growth of this period was powered primarily by domestic savings and investment. India's external debt situation was reaching manageable levels, with the country's capacity to service debts improving rapidly. The inclusive growth agenda followed by the Congress-led UPA government was acknowledged worldwide. This achievement was particularly significant at a time when the world was entering a deep economic recession. The social security net created by the government in rural areas buffered the impact of the global recession on the Indian economy.

A REAFFIRMATION BY THE PEOPLE: GENERAL ELECTIONS, 2009

Having completed a successful five-year term in office, the Congress went to the electorate on the strength of its record and performance, emphasising that it was the only party with a truly pan-India presence, perspective, and vision. For the first time, the Congress named a prime ministerial candidate in Dr Manmohan Singh whose integrity, intellect, and maturity were acknowledged by all.

While outlining its vision for the next five years, the Congress built upon the achievements

Congress President Sonia Gandhi releasing the party manifesto for the upcoming Lok Sabha polls, New Delhi, 24 March 2009.

of the previous five years, promising a National Food Security Act, health security for all, schemes for the well-being of farmers and their families, universalisation of the Integrated Child Development Services (ICDS) schemes by March 2012, and providing every village a broadband network within three years.

The Lok Sabha elections of 2009 saw the Congress-led UPA returning to power for a second time, with a stronger mandate. The performance of the Congress defied the anti-incumbency factor, which had challenged previous governments in recent times. The performance of the party was particularly encouraging in Delhi, Haryana, Rajasthan, Andhra Pradesh, and Maharashtra. The resurgence of the Congress in the Hindi-speaking heartland of Uttar Pradesh was a significant feature of this election.

Dr Manmohan Singh's leadership imparted stability to the government. The Congress projected itself as a party of responsible governance. Sonia Gandhi was seen as the architect of one of the sharpest recoveries in the electoral fortunes of the Congress. From 114 seats in 1999, when she had just taken over as party president, the Congress now had 206 seats and the UPA, 262. Sonia Gandhi also has the unique distinction of having presided over the Congress Party for the longest period in its 125-year chequered history, that is, over 12 years since 1998.

THE ASIAN AGE

● I wish Rahul Gandhi join Cabinet, says Manmohan

● Senior BJP leaders lament absence of Atal Behari Vajpayee

D-DAY PL

** AL ELECTIONS 2009**

ASSEMBLY POLLS
Incumbents YSR in Andhra Pradesh and Naveen Patnaik in Orissa re-elected by large margins. Pawan Kumar Chamling returns to power in Sikkim.

UPA	NDA	LEFT 24 Big Mamata gains in Bengal
258	**160**	**OTHERS 100** Major defeat for Mayawati's BSP
206	116	

http://www.asianage.com 40 PA

NEW DELHI • SUNDAY • 17 MAY 2009

PM REACHES OUT TO SECULAR OPPOSITION, WANTS RAHUL TO JOIN HIS CABINET

KING CONG

CORRESPONDENTS
NEW DELHI

16: Led by Mrs Sonia hi and Prime Minister nohan Singh, the ress-led United

threw up a far more decisive mandate than five years ago, with the UPA poised to secure 260 Lok Sabha seats. Of this, the Congress Party itself was set to get 201 seats.

The UPA's triumph is

SUNDAY TIMES

OF INDIA

Bennett, Coleman & Co., Ltd.

PRICE RS. 4.50 OR RS. 7.80 WITH SUNDAY NAVBHA

CONG GETS FREE HAND

Scores A Double, Sweeps Left, Right & Centre

TEAM TOI

ndia has yet again been surprised by Indians...

Cong's 201-seat tally is the **best for any party since** 1991. BJP's 121 is its **worst since** 1991. CPM's 16 is its **worst ever**

UPA sweeps most big city seats; Cong makes a comeback in UP after 25 years

Advani Steps Into Sunset Of Discontent

New Delhi: The L K Advani era has set. With results derailing BJP's power, bl...

UPA:	261 (145 in 2004)
NDA:	**159**
BJP: 121 (138 in 2004)	
Others: 24 (59 in 2004)	Left: 123

Rise And Surprise Of

Verdict 2009 has also been a decisive judgement the 38-year-ol...

TIMES EDIT

With great power comes great responsibility. The people of India have reposed their faith in the Congress, the Gandhis and Manmohan Singh. The party and its leaders can do one of two things: become complacent, even arrogant and abusive...

ear mandate

offers to quit as leader

Lok Sabha Poll Outcome 2009
UPA (258)   Others (46)   Third Front (79)

COMIC TIMES
ON SUNDAY

SUNDAY 17 MAY 2009 | NEW DELHI | 20 PAGES | Rs 10 ONLY

economictimes.com

THE WORLD'S LARGEST DEMOCRACY

confusion, voting in clarity; voting out schism, r ability. 2009 may just be the beginning of India's oks to the future with humility, unity and hope

FREE HAND

DELHI WITH ASTOUNDING VICTORY

'09

HINDU
ER SINCE I

Vijayawada, Mangalor and Tiruchirapalli

HAYDEN DO IT AGAIN
MAIN SPORTS PAGE

NVEY TO THE WORLD...WE STAND ONE AS A NATION

MANMOHAN SINGH

EMAN & CO LTD

A GENERATIONAL SHIFT: EMPOWERING THE YOUTH

A significant feature of the elections of 2009 was the role played by the emerging youth leadership of the Congress. Demographically, India is a young country where young people are going to play an increasingly important role, and this is clearly reflected in the policy of the Congress leadership to engage them in greater measure in governance and nation building.

Rahul Gandhi entered active politics during the election campaign of 2004 and was appointed the general secretary of the Congress in 2007. In 2009, he played a major role in revitalising the Indian Youth Congress and the National Students Union of India by mobilising young people from all sections of society and bringing them into the political mainstream. For the first time in any political party, there are hundreds of elected youth leaders in Punjab and Uttarakhand. This demonstrates the Congress's commitment to opening up new political spaces for the youth of the country in a democratic manner. In mobilising the youth and democratising the party structure, Rahul Gandhi is only continuing the mission that had first been taken up by Rajiv Gandhi. Rajiv Gandhi had championed the right to vote for 18-year-olds and his government had declared Swami Vivekananda's birthday on 12 January as National Youth Day.

Freedom from poverty is not a matter of charity or luck; it is a right.
— *Rahul Gandhi*

AICC General Secretary Rahul Gandhi takes part in a 'Shram Dan' (voluntary labour activity) at Pinjra village in Baran district, Rajasthan, 2 October 2008.

Rahul Gandhi is working tirelessly to strengthen the party institutions and to build a mass base for the Youth Congress. He refused a ministerial position despite persistent demands from senior party leaders, including the prime minister. He has traversed the length and breadth of the country, reaching out to the underprivileged masses, the poor, and the backward communities with the message of development and progress.

The leadership of Rahul Gandhi in reaching out to the youth, marginalised sections, and minorities had an electrifying effect in Uttar Pradesh where the Congress had been marginalised for the last several years. The Congress made a special appeal to the minorities, reaffirming its long traditions as a party with a secular pan-India presence. The youth identified themselves with the message of Rahul Gandhi, and the resurgence of the Congress in the Hindi-speaking heartland was a significant development in these elections.

Setting the Agenda

for the Future

Setting the Agenda for the Future

RECONNECTING WITH THE MASSES

During the first term of the Congress-led UPA government, the message of inclusive growth resonated with the masses. Core development issues were placed at the centre stage, moving away from the caste-based agenda of previous governments. Historic legislation giving the right to gainful employment and the right to information along with programmes with a social orientation played a significant role.

At the same time, the Congress made a serious attempt to reconnect with the masses. A unique arrangement emerged, with the party agenda being clearly set by the party president, Sonia Gandhi, while governance issues were handled by the prime minister and his team. At the same time, the National Advisory Council played a significant role in drawing the policy contours, especially in the social sector, giving shape to the commitments made in the party manifesto and the Common Minimum Programme of the UPA government.

Rahul Gandhi has been seriously engaged in revitalising the youth wing of the party through a massive enrolment drive and a democratic process of election at different levels. His fresh approach to Indian politics has infused a new energy in the state units of the Congress Party. He has succeeded in engaging the attention of the youth in socio-political issues facing the country through a new campaign called 'Aam Aadmi ka Sipahi' (Soldier of the Common Man), aimed at ensuring the effective implementation of pro-people policies.

Meanwhile, the post-Godhra period has seen considerable political ferment and volatility. The BJP came to be identified with the communal agenda articulated by right-wing extremist groups such as the Bajrang Dal, the Shiv Sena, and the RSS. Communal events in BJP-ruled states such as Gujarat and Karnataka have further isolated these organisations.

Above: AICC General Secretary Rahul Gandhi interacts with local people during his roadshow in Badami, Karnataka, March 2008.

Left: Supporters celebrating the Congress victory in General Elections, May 2009.

President Pratibha Devi Singh Patil administers the oath of
office and secrecy to Prime Minister Manmohan Singh during
the swearing-in ceremony, Rashtrapati Bhavan, New Delhi,
22 May 2009.

A FRESH AGENDA FOR GOVERNANCE

The Congress-led UPA government in its second term is pursuing the agenda of inclusive growth, the foundations of which were laid in the first term, while maintaining its commitment to a liberal and open economy.

Spreading the Light of Knowledge

Recognising that knowledge is the prime mover of growth in the twenty-first century and that India's ability to emerge as a knowledge-led economy will depend substantially on the quality of its human resources, the prime minister constituted the National Knowledge Commission in June 2005, under the chairmanship of Sam Pitroda, to prepare a blueprint for higher education reform.

For the first time since the 1950s, India is working to build institutions of excellence. The UPA government has announced the launch of 18 new Indian Institutes of Technology (IITs), seven new Indian Institutes of Management (IIMs), five new Indian Institutes of Science, Education and Research, 30 new central universities, 20 new Indian Institutes of Information Technology (IIITs), and 374 new colleges in educationally deprived districts. An ambitious nationwide skill development programme has also been announced to prepare India to meet the challenge of the huge skill shortage that will present itself in the coming decades.

The UPA government is equally committed to strengthening primary education institutions. The Right to Education Act, 2010 has made education a fundamental right for every child between the age of 6-14 years. This act will have a hugely empowering impact on millions of children in rural areas and will be a transformational step in the years to come.

Communal Violence Bill

One of the foremost challenges facing the country is the issue of communal violence, which had conflagrated the country in the period following the demolition of the Babri Masjid, the Godhra riots, and the violence in Kandhamal. These instances had clearly brought home the fact that while law and order remains a state subject, the assurances regarding the maintenance of peace have often not been translated into effective action on the ground. The Communal Violence Bill seeks to enhance the powers of the central government to deal with such emerging situations, to declare an area as communally disturbed, and to effectively intervene in such situations. The Congress leadership has been deeply concerned about maintaining the secular fabric of the country and restoring the faith of the minorities in the idea of India as a secular nation.

Prime Minister Manmohan Singh, Pranab Mukerjee, and other Congress leaders raise their hands to unanimously re-elect Sonia Gandhi as the Party President at an AICC meeting, New Delhi, 2 November 2010.

Food Security

Poverty and hunger have been issues of primary concern to the UPA government, and the National Advisory Council has provided a framework for a Food Security Bill that would legally assure the provision of a stipulated quantity of rations every month for the vulnerable sections of society in urban and rural India. The Congress remains committed to ensuring food security for the poor. The bill is likely to be piloted in Parliament in the near future.

Women's Empowerment

Sonia Gandhi has personally led the initiative to create a political consensus for the political empowerment of women through the Women's Reservation Bill aimed at bringing women into the mainstream of decision making and governance.

Rajiv Gandhi had brought about a historic change for women's empowerment in rural areas by introducing mandatory reservation at all levels of village and town *panchayats*. Through a special constitutional amendment, the Congress enhanced the participation of women in bodies of local self-governance from 33 per cent to 50 per cent. The Women's Reservation Bill was recently passed in the Rajya Sabha, but the building of a broad-based political consensus necessary for carrying it through Parliament still eludes the government.

Sonia Gandhi and Rahul Gandhi
at the AICC meeting, New Delhi,
2 November 2010.

INDIA ON THE GLOBAL STAGE

The Congress-led UPA government ensured that India's position was established at the global high table and its voice was effectively heard in international fora. The G-20, which emerged as the apex global body in the wake of the global economic crisis, saw India's position finding support amongst the leaders of the developed world. In multilateral fora dealing with climate change and world trade, India demonstrated leadership and played a conciliatory role in bringing together the divergent perspectives of the developing and the developed worlds on a common page.

India's economic integration with the world was completed as the country signed a Free Trade Agreement with ASEAN and a Comprehensive Economic Partnership Agreement with Korea, Japan, and Malaysia, while engaging equally in negotiations with the European Union, Canada, Australia, and Indonesia. India emerged as the second most attractive investment destination in the world even at a time when the world was grappling with a grim economic crisis. The manner in which India's regulatory bodies managed the financial system in insulating it from the shocks of the global crisis were appreciated across the world, and India emerged as the fulcrum of stability in the continent of Asia. In the wake of economic contraction in the developed world, capital flows froze and millions of people lost their jobs worldwide. The Indian economy demonstrated resilience and rebounded on the high growth path because the fundamentals of the Indian economy were robust, being led largely by strong domestic demand. The Rural Employment Guarantee Act had created employment opportunities for millions in rural areas, giving them disposable incomes and enhancing their purchasing power, which infused buoyancy in the economy.

On completing one year in office, the Congress-led UPA government demonstrated its commitment to safeguarding the interests of the poor and marginalised sections of society, the backward classes, and the minorities. This commitment has permeated the entire thematic approach to governance, and rural empowerment received focused attention. The social agenda is being given a new dimension and thrust through a reconstituted National Advisory Council with Sonia Gandhi as its chairperson. The crucial issues affecting livelihood concerns, food security, and access to quality primary education continue to engage the attention of the government.

Across: US President Barack Obama and UPA Chairperson Sonia Gandhi at a meeting in New Delhi, 8 November 2010.

A global vision is integral to Congress philosophy to work collectively for the welfare of humankind. Remaining connected with the leaders of the major political movements of the world...

Sonia Gandhi with Vladimir Putin (Prime Minister, Russian Federation)

Sonia Gandhi with Hu Jintao
(President, People's Republic of China)

Sonia Gandhi with Luiz Inácio Lula da Silva (President, Brazil)

Sonia Gandhi with Jacob Zuma (President, South Africa)

Sonia Gandhi with Sheikh Hasina Wazed
(Prime Minister, Bangaldesh)

Sonia Gandhi with Mohd. Najib bin Tun Abdul Razak (Prime Minister, Malaysia)

CHALLENGES THAT REMAIN

The government continues to face several serious challenges even as inflation and high food grain prices affect the masses. The Congress continues to advocate that the development of backward and neglected areas is the primary force for bringing back alienated people into the national mainstream.

The threat of terror is real and the forces of violence that operate from across the border still loom large. In the backdrop of the dastardly terrorist attacks in Mumbai in November 2008, the government has put in place institutional mechanisms to prevent the recurrence of such events and has strengthened the internal security network. Naxalism and left-wing extremism pose serious threats to India's internal security and need to be addressed with all seriousness. The situation in Jammu & Kashmir remains fragile.

Probity in public life remains a huge challenge for any government that is determined to provide transparency in decision making and accountability to its citizens. The UPA government has demonstrated its firmness by acting against those in public life against whom there is a shadow of suspicion, displaying no tolerance for corruption.

While much has been achieved in empowering the people and in creating livelihood opportunities in the rural hinterland, millions of people still remain trapped in the cycle of poverty. India remains a land of paradoxes, with one of the largest middle classes in the world and also home to one of the largest poor populations. It remains a monumental challenge for the government to deal with the burden of poverty effectively by creating gainful employment opportunities.

LOOKING TO THE FUTURE

Outlining her vision of a new social order in India, Sonia Gandhi, at the 10th Indira Gandhi Memorial Lecture, said:

We are right to celebrate our high rate of economic growth. We must do all that we can to sustain it. However, let us not forget that growth is not an end in itself. Much more important to my mind is what kind of society we aspire to be and the values on which it should be built.

On 28 December 2010, the Congress completes 125 years of its existence both as a political movement and a national party. It can rightfully be proud of the fact that its leaders were instrumental in laying the foundations of the political, social, and economic structure of the country and in nurturing a secular democracy through this period.

As it prepares to rededicate itself to the task of guiding the destiny of a new India in the twenty-first century, the Congress will need to continue on a path that strikes a balance between growth and equity, between the demands of economic liberalism in a globalised world and the imperatives of social inclusiveness, in ensuring that as India develops and finds its rightful place in the world, all parts of the country grow equally and all Indian citizens feel that they are equal partners in progress.

And, the journey continues to fulfill the aspirations of a billion plus people of India...

PHOTO CREDIT

Gandhi Smriti, New Delhi
34-35, 52-53, 90, 105(t), 128.

Getty Images
111, 120.

Indian National Congress
87, 192, 225(b), 230(b/r), 238, 243, 251-252, 268-269, 278, 280-283, 286-287.

Nehru Memorial Museum and Library, New Delhi
2-3 (main title page), 15, 17-21, 24, 26-29, 31, 37, 41, 42, 44-46, 48, 51, 54, 57, 58, 61, 63-79, 81-83, 85, 88-89, 91, 93-95, 97, 101, 103, 106, 109-110, 112, 114-117, 119, 121-125, 129, 133-138, 140, 145(l) 146(l), 149, 151-153, 155-161, 163, 165-166, 169-175, 176(t), 178, 181(b), 182-183, 185, 187-188, 194, 197, 199, 205-207, 217, 235, 239, 242, 244-245, 248-249, 253, 259, 264-265, 271.

Press Information Bureau (PIB), New Delhi
32, 105(b), 113, 126, 139, 143, 145(r) 146(r), 181(t), 184, 196, 200, 210, 214(t), 215, 225(t), 240.

Press Trust of India (PTI), New Delhi
237, 254-256, 262, 267, 270, 272-273, 275, 276-277, 285, 288-290, 292-294, 296-299, 301-303, 305.

Raghu Rai
176(b), 195, 202-203.

Rajiv Gandhi Foundation
209, 211-213, 214(c,b), 216, 218-219, 221, 223, 226-227, 229, 230(t/l, t/r, b/l), 232-233, 236.

Numerals denote page / range of pages featuring photographs from the indicated source. (b: bottom; c: centre; l: left; r: right; t: top)